Riley Books
A member of **Avery Press**
New York • London

Thank you Clare —

ANGELS THREE:
THE KAREN PERRY STORY

One woman finds her way back from the ultimate loss

Karen Perry

LANDON J. NAPOLEON

"I read *Angels Three: The Karen Perry Story* with a heavy heart. The Aircraft Owners and Pilots Association (AOPA) had concerns with the Federal Aviation Administration (FAA) airspace changes before this tragedy occurred. I applaud Karen for her bravery in writing this book and sharing the lessons to be learned. By telling her story I am hopeful the memory of the six victims—including her three children and their father—will make a difference by educating pilots and policymakers so this kind of tragedy never happens again."

—Mark Baker, President and CEO, Aircraft Owners and Pilots Association

"Amid Karen Perry's terrible tragedy is the inspiring story of the deep and passionate support she received from her colleagues at Delta Air Lines. Her journey is a remarkable one, and we are proud to have her as a member of the Delta family."

—Richard H. Anderson, CEO, Delta Air Lines

"Karen Perry's story is one of heartbreaking sorrow and transcendent strength. Her experience speaks to the resiliency of the human spirit, inspiring each of us to find that light within ourselves."

—Ashley Davis Bush, author of *Transcending Loss*

"A life-changing story from a remarkable woman of courage, strength, and wisdom. The book has inspired me to dig deeper into my own spiritual search. Karen Perry's breakthrough is a constant reminder of God's plan and love for all of us."

—Jonas Elrod, writer/director of *In Deep Shift* (Oprah Winfrey Network)

"*Angels Three: The Karen Perry Story* is a story of finding purpose out of chaos and the courage and determination required to rebuild one's soul after it has been shattered by the unfathomable. In sharing her journey she shows us that we can all overcome and continue to heal, and grow, one day at a time.

—Captain Suzanne Skeeters, Delta Air Lines

Burning Shield: The Jason Schechterle Story

"This enthralling biography injects the intimacy of fiction into a true story of human endurance. Readers are continuously reminded that Jason Schechterle is flesh, bones, and blood, not a fictional character, and they are invited to experience his terror, frustration, and ultimate triumph."

—*Publishers Weekly*

"A maimed cop fights to regain his life in this inspiring true story. ... Landon J. Napoleon, the author of several crime novels, is skilled at painting a scene in slangy strokes while balancing plotlines. ... This true story reads like a novel."

—*Kirkus Reviews*

"Landon J. Napoleon displays a flair for detail in this fast-moving book....The third-person account is an inspiring read, even for those with a passing familiarity with the story from the news."

—*Arizona Republic*

"Sad, exciting, life-changing, and emotional, *Burning Shield: The Jason Schechterle Story* is an amazing story of one man's triumph over tragedy with the support of an entire community."

—Jack Ballentine, former homicide detective and author of *Murder for Hire*

"*Burning Shield: The Jason Schechterle Story* is a powerful, inspiring story of one man's will to survive and to thrive in the face of horrific injuries. It is also a keen look into the workings of our police men and women and the close bonds that knit them together. We admire them, and we especially admire Jason Schechterle."

—Janet Napolitano, former Arizona governor (2002–2009) and Arizona attorney general (1998–2002)

Praise for Landon J. Napoleon's debut novel *ZigZag*

"*ZigZag* is one of the boldest and most original first novels to appear in a long time. It's also very funny, in a way that only the raw street-song of truth can be funny. Landon J. Napoleon has written a gem."

—Carl Hiaasen

"A remarkable debut portraying the inner life of a disturbed ghetto teenager as he attempts to grow up in the frightening world he's inherited. ... An unaffected, moving, astonishing insight into the heart of a troubled, silent genius."

—*Kirkus Reviews*
(starred review)

"This mixture of comic adventure and paean to the values of volunteerism is a vivid read and impressive debut novel."

—*Library Journal*
(starred review)

"[An] affecting first novel that explores the survival of the human spirit in an atmosphere of deprivation and cruelty."

—*Publisher's Weekly*

"Landon J. Napoleon's first novel is an affecting work."

—*Dallas Morning News*

"Landon J. Napoleon conveys the strength of the human spirit through his wonderful creation, and in the process tells an engaging and enriching story."

—Barnes and Noble Discover Great New Writers
1999 Finalist

The Rules of Action

"Briskly told and well-drawn,... this legal thriller *(The Rules of Action)* does what many courtroom-based novels and television shows do not: it stays true to the actual practice of trial law. ... A fast-paced tale of justice in action and a remarkably accurate portrait of a trial lawyer's daily grind. ... Prospective law students are frequently encouraged to read law-student memoirs or legal hornbooks, but for a realistic view of litigation and a great deal more action, they'd do well to add this legal thriller to their reading list."

—*Kirkus Reviews*

"*The Rules of Action* is one of the most compelling and entertaining books I have ever read on the strategy and gamesmanship of the legal process."

—Grant Woods, former Arizona Attorney General

ISBN 978-0-9886519-8-2

Cover design: Brandon Stout
Cover photograph: Eva Morgan ©2015
Other images printed with permission
Editors: Susan Campbell, Lisa Fontes, LeeAnn Kriegh, and Jim Moore
Author photograph: Troy Aossey

Manufactured in the United States of America by
Riley Books, an imprint of **Avery Press**.

Books by Landon J. Napoleon

Nonfiction

Angels Three: The Karen Perry Story
Burning Shield: The Jason Schechterle Story

Fiction

ZigZag
Deep Wicked Freaky
The Flatirons
The Rules of Action

For Morgan, Logan, and Luke

Author's Note

ON THE NIGHT of November 23, 2011, six human beings lost their lives in an airplane that crashed into Superstition Mountain east of Phoenix, Arizona. This book focuses on the life journey of Karen Perry and the three children she lost that night: Morgan, 9; Logan, 8; and Luke, 6.

Because of this focus, the background and stories of the other three victims, while equally important, are necessarily limited. This in no way diminishes the pain, suffering, and loss felt by their respective family members and friends, and we hereby recognize them individually. May they all rest in peace.

Shawn Perry
Joseph Hardwick
Russel Hardy

Foreword

THEY WERE ONLY AIRBORNE FOR SIX MINUTES, and then they were gone.

A backyard camera caught the violent flash on the night my life changed forever. Years later, it still does not seem real: my three young children and their father all died upon impact, along with the pilot and another passenger who had just gone along for the ride.

This most unimaginable pain and horror occurred on November 23, the Wednesday night before Thanksgiving 2011. The day had begun like any other for me, a busy mother of three. But by nine o'clock that night, Pinal County Sheriff Paul Babeu was in my living room delivering the news, and ushering me into the worst nightmare of every parent. We all hope and pray that it will never happen to us.

As a pilot, losing my own children in a plane crash seemed a cruel twist. I had to know every detail. The aircraft had been cleared for takeoff and, two minutes later, the air traffic controller said, "690 sierra mike, right turn approved." That was the last communication with anyone aboard the ill-fated flight. The three men who died in this crash were doing exactly what they, too, loved and had chosen as aviation careers. But my children never had a choice; they were simply innocent passengers.

So what happened on that airplane? Was it pilot error, mechanical malfunction, or something even more tragic that investigators would uncover only later? What happened in the critical moments before impact? How does a sophisticated aircraft, with two pilots and an avionics technician aboard, simply fly directly into a mountain at full speed? Would clues be found hidden in the maintenance logs, the aircraft's history, or elsewhere in narrow crevices near the top of the mountain? I would not rest, would leave no stone unturned, until I had every answer I needed. I have spent my entire life studying aircraft accidents, and had never considered that my lens would be focused so personally. How does a mother comprehend, let alone process, such a loss? The details haunt me still. The cruel irony: my lifelong love of aviation started as a child with my dream of becoming an airline pilot.

Pursuing that path was central to my life and dominated the following decades.

When I wasn't working, I spent all my spare time and money in flight school. I had my private pilot license at 22 and my commercial pilot certificate at 26, and was a flight instructor at 27. I achieved additional ratings: instrument, multiengine, and seaplane. I began with small propeller aircraft and gradually moved up to flying full-fledged corporate jets. During my pilot training, I moonlighted as a flight attendant. This included working for a cultural icon as he and his wife traveled on private charter flights. By the early 1990s, I was one step from my ultimate dream: piloting the largest commercial passenger jets.

I was a pilot two decades before becoming a mother at the advanced maternal age of 39. My daughter Morgan Leigh Perry was born in 2002. Her birth was especially poignant because previously I had been nearly counted out by two separate and major health scares. The beauty is that I went from being at death's door, twice, to creating life. I had never experienced a greater joy than looking at my tiny infant Morgan for the first time.

I was 40 when I had my son Logan Jay Perry, and 42 when Luke Devon Perry was born. Without really planning it, I guess I was "having it all": a career I loved in my twenties and thirties, and then motherhood in my forties. In comparison, as much as I loved aviation and being a pilot, I embraced motherhood as an even more important job, which was exhausting, rewarding—and heartbreaking, as I would soon learn. After my kids were gone I began to understand why I had survived so many emotional and physical challenges in my life.

My beautiful baby girl made my dreams come true, but those dreams soon turned dark when Morgan began having daily epileptic seizures when she was six weeks old. Some lasted more than thirty minutes. Thus began a grueling routine—doctors and hospitals, conventional and unconventional epilepsy treatments, hundreds of tearful days and nights—and, ultimately, giving up my pilot position and taking a two-year leave of absence from aviation altogether to care for Morgan full time. That was 2002, and while I would later return to aviation as a flight attendant, I would never return to the pilot's seat. I'd given up my ultimate professional dream. My final step had been right there for the taking: the front seat of a Boeing or Airbus commercial jet with hundreds of passengers in my care. As dedicated parents know, the arrival of children changes everything. We give them their life, and then we give them ours. God had entrusted me as the mother to these three beautiful babies.

In 2006, life added another challenge. When Luke was eighteen months old he was diagnosed with autism. Already overwhelmed as I was with Morgan's care and difficulties, having another special needs child seemed so unfair. Even my "typical" middle son Logan, innocently sandwiched between two special needs children, became a challenge, as he rightfully demanded the attention he needed and deserved.

In November 2006, I returned to my flight attendant position with Delta Air Lines. I accepted that my lifelong dream of becoming a pilot for a major airline was indefinitely on hold, because I wanted to be there for my children. At least as a flight attendant I was airborne again, as I had been since 1984, with much greater control over my schedule. And then more devastating news: a breast cancer diagnosis in 1998, and a recurrence.

In early 2010, the years of health challenges and demanding parenting responsibilities finally took the ultimate toll on my marriage to Shawn Perry. Such challenges can bond couples or drive them apart. For us it was the latter, and our marriage ended in an unpleasant divorce. Now I was even further daunted by the reality of being a single mother, struggling financially, raising three very challenging toddlers, and fighting my own health battles. I was completely overwhelmed.

My divorce was final in February 2010. One week later, I had a double mastectomy and major reconstructive surgery. Meanwhile, I was sometimes so broke I could not put gas in my car or buy food. But I was more determined than ever to make the best of all the difficulties. My children were the most important part of my life and the only family I had.

The night of November 23, 2011, is the line after which everything changed. I can barely remember the months that followed. The trauma blurred everything into an indistinguishable void. I had friends watching me around the clock. I was a dazed, confused shell of a person; I could barely move because it felt as though cement had been poured around my body. I began seeing a psychiatrist, who prescribed medications for depression and anxiety. I sought additional help in the form of grief counseling. I prayed continually, including the frequent wish to join my children on the other side.

Three months after their deaths, I lost my house to foreclosure, along with the comfort and cherished memories of our time there together. I was completely adrift in an abyss without end. The two worlds that I loved, flying and motherhood, had collided head-on at more than 200 miles per hour and then exploded into indistinguishable fiery pieces of bodies, scorched machinery, and shattered dreams.

About a week before the crash I had been in the car with all three kids. Stopped at a red light, my son Logan reached over to hold my hand and asked, "Mother, if I die next week, does that mean you will still be my mother?"

"Of course, Logan," I said, thinking, *Why on earth would my 8-year-old boy ask such a question?* "I will always be your mother."

Ever since, I have wondered if my little guy, and his brother and sister, had access to some form of precognition, an invisible source foretelling their tragedy. That is the first part of my mission in writing this book: to preserve their memory, our special bond, and to understand their part and purpose in all that has happened. In sharing their stories with you, I preserve our special bond for myself, too, because I never had the chance to say good-bye. This book is my bedtime story to them, a thoughtful good-bye where I can share everything.

People ask how I cope and whether I have lost faith. With all that has happened, my faith and trust in God are stronger than ever. When you sign up to be a pilot, as I did at 19, you watch helplessly over the years as people you love and admire perish in plane crashes. Unfortunately that's part of the agreement; we don't dwell on it, but we accept the risk of going airborne. Odd as it may sound, many pilots I have met over the years have expressed their desire to die in an airplane. That's the last place I would ever want to die. But entering that professional pursuit does give way to acknowledging the fragility of life and sorting out one's beliefs just in case something does happen. Pilots find comfort in saying peers died doing what they loved. But my kids never made that choice, and they didn't die doing what they loved. They died doing what I love and what their father loved.

I am thankful to God for my life. I am thankful to have had these three amazing little people, even if for a short time, who taught me so much. I am thankful for the outpouring of love, compassion, and human kindness that has touched me very deeply in the aftermath of the crash. Beyond that, I try to be thankful for fresh air and sunshine, for the people in my life, for the things I love, for being able to see, to hear, to feel. All things that God has made possible.

In this very personal journey called life, we are all subject to the vagaries of our human condition. Challenges beset us; how will we respond? It seems I've had my share, but so, too, have other people. Regardless, we must each find the will and strength to move forward. We don't have to summit Mount Everest or cure cancer, but we each need some small daily purpose to push us forward. Life is movement and, without movement, we die. Ultimately, how we respond to what life drops in our path is one of the few things over which we have control.

That brings me to the second part of my purpose in writing this book—along with infusing life into the memory of my children—which is to, hopefully, inspire you to know that you can overcome whatever challenges, obstacles, and difficulties arise in your life. Yours might be big things or small things, from the mundane daily annoyances to the challenges of catastrophic health, financial, and relationship issues that can slam us without warning. I will never "get over" the death of my children; I can only continue to embrace where I am and find purpose in each day.

For all of us, no matter how bad things might seem today, everything can change for the better. The sun will rise tomorrow. We get to choose how we react to what life puts before us. Joy, laughter, and a sense of well-being can and will return. If there's one thing I've learned, it's that beauty surrounds us. Nothing is insurmountable when you have trust, love, and calm. That which we give returns to us. It is my fervent wish that this book inspires you, in big or small ways, on your own journey to wholeness.

—Karen Perry
Autumn 2015

"What the caterpillar calls the end of the world the master calls a butterfly."
—Richard Bach

An•gels [noun]—1. One of a class of spiritual
beings; a celestial attendant of God
2. A person having admirable qualities such as beauty, purity, and kindliness
3. Military aviation term for altitude, measured in thousands of feet.

Prologue

AT 6:25 P.M. LOCAL TIME, the Rockwell Commander 690 aircraft took an eastbound departure from runway 4R, out of Falcon Field Airport (FFZ) in Mesa, Arizona, and raced skyward into the blackness of the November desert chill. As the tabled cityscape of metropolitan Phoenix tilted and twinkled below, none aboard could have known the countdown to impact had begun.

Six minutes.

It was Thanksgiving eve, November 23, 2011, and two Honeywell TPE-331 turboshaft engines thrust the aircraft through complete darkness, each power plant driving a three-blade, constant-speed, reversible-pitch propeller. The air traffic controller had told the pilot to maintain the runway heading until advised, due to inbound traffic. About ninety seconds later, when the plane was 1.1 miles from departure, the controller issued a "right turn approved," clearing the flight on course. The pilot acknowledged the advisory and, 1.5 miles east of Falcon Field, initiated the right turn toward the destination airport, Safford Regional (SAD), as the aircraft ascended to 2,600 feet. At the back of the plane, three kids wriggled and squirmed under the cabin light and asked their father endless questions about their Thanksgiving plans. The children were infinitely more interested in the promise of pumpkin pie piled with whipped cream than the physics of aviation.

Ponderosa Aviation, Inc., which owned the plane, was based in Safford, a high-desert town of 9,500 people, 150 miles southeast of Phoenix near the Pinaleño Mountains. Ponderosa also had operations in Twin Falls, Idaho, under the company name Spur Aviation. The company had government contracts to supply aerial command posts for the US Forest Service during wildfire season. Even in those less-than-ideal flying conditions, up to that day in November 2011 the small aviation company had a pristine safety record: thirty-seven years of operations without a single crash or major safety incident.

The company founder, J. Leon Perry, incorporated Ponderosa in 1974 and sold it to Mikel Hardy in 2002. Eventually the ownership was split into equal thirds, including Mikel, Mikel's brother Russel Hardy, and Shawn Perry, son of the founder, who became co-owner and director of operations for Ponderosa Aviation. By that crisp November night in 2011, the younger Perry was divorced from his ex-wife Karen and a single father of three, taking their kids back to his home in Safford for the four-day Thanksgiving weekend: Morgan, 9; Logan, 8; and Luke, 6.

After a rough custody battle, which he had lost, Karen's ex-husband had relocated to Safford in 2010. Whether by air or land, he picked up the kids on most alternating weekends. Shawn Perry was a loving father and hands-on dad with each of his kids from the beginning. He dived right into the parenting trenches with his wife, changing diapers and soothing babies back to sleep in the middle of the night. He loved his kids and spending time with them, and he openly showed his affection. He was especially good with his daughter, with her difficult challenges and many hospital stays requiring 24/7 parental care. Even when it was his turn to exit the hospital for a well-deserved break and quick shower, he often would not leave his only daughter's side.

After the split and his move east, Shawn either drove to Phoenix or made the quick flight when there was other business in metropolitan Phoenix. Up to the last days before departure for this trip, Shawn had planned to drive, until Russel Hardy provided an alternative. Hardy suggested that they take the newest aircraft in Ponderosa's small fleet to Mesa for a quick round-trip test flight; Shawn agreed that was a great idea.

Purchased just one week earlier, the Rockwell 690A airframe had accumulated a total time in service of almost 8,200 hours, which was low for a plane manufactured in 1976. The port-side engine had accumulated 545 service hours since its last overhaul, and the starboard engine 1,482 hours. All those service hours had accumulated in 2009 and before; the aircraft had since been sitting unused for two years at a small airfield in Indiana. Because of that inactivity, without the required Federal Aviation Administration (FAA) inspections under 14 CFR 91.409(f)(3), the plane was not airworthy.

After the team from Ponderosa purchased the airplane, they had to apply to the FAA for a special ferry permit to fly the plane back to their base in Safford, Arizona. The FAA granted the one-time flight permit, and Perry made the initial flight from Indiana to Arizona without incident. Once on the ground in Safford, the plane was not officially authorized for flight again until undergoing the required inspections, which included a 150-hour inspection and an annual inspection by an FAA-designated airframe representative. Perry was trained and authorized to conduct the inspections, as an IA (inspector airframe), and perform any required maintenance.

Oddly, in an industry governed by careful documentation, there would be no written record of any such inspections. This would be just one of the oddities revealed in late 2013 by National Transportation Safety Board (NTSB) investigators in their final report on the crash. There would be other disturbing investigatory revelations of malfeasance, including the most egregious by the US government itself. All of it would raise a cloud of serious and troubling questions for a grieving mother: How does an airplane owned by an aviation company, with two pilots aboard, fly straight into a mountain on a familiar route? Did her three children die unnecessarily? Even more ominously, had personnel at the FAA enacted policy that actually made such a crash a dark inevitability?

ONE

Goodbye, Sweet Loves

ON NOVEMBER 22, TWO DAYS BEFORE THANKSGIVING 2011, Karen Perry worked the red-eye flight 1298 from Kona (KOA) to Los Angeles (LAX), as she had countless times before as a Delta Air Lines flight attendant. After commuting home to Phoenix that Tuesday afternoon, she surprised Logan, 8, by picking him up from school, while the nanny, Jaleesa Shelton, picked up Morgan, 9, and Luke, 6. Hours later, after dinner, baths, pajamas, and bedtime stories, Logan was using the computer for an online video call with a pilot friend of Karen's. The friend asked Logan about going on an airplane the next day and whether he was excited, and Logan said he was. Meanwhile, Luke fell asleep in Karen's bed, and Morgan was asleep in her own bed. It was an end-of-day refrain familiar to any parent: *Two down, one to go.* Then there would be those blissful few moments of household silence during which she could pick up toys, maybe read a book or watch a television show without interruption, or just sit without being summoned.

Other than an afternoon nap while Jaleesa Shelton watched the kids, Karen had not enjoyed substantive sleep since waking up early the day before in Hawai'i. At 8:30 p.m., Logan wanted to take a whirlpool bath in the tub in the master bathroom. Karen had little strength to object, but she tried anyway.

"Honey, it's time for bed."

"Please!"

That was all it took. "OK, but not too long."

After the bath, Logan was in his pajamas and wanted to get online again. Karen told him he could do another videoconference the next day. Logan considered it and then said, "OK, will you come rub my back?"

Karen nodded and smiled. "Of course. Go get in bed, and I'll be right there."

Logan disappeared down the hall. By the time Karen walked into his room minutes later, her middle child was already sound asleep and clutching Eeyore, a stuffed animal Karen's close friend Eva Morgan had given him days before. Logan's dad Shawn had painted the room blue with an airplane theme, and Logan shared the space with his younger brother Luke. There was a six-inch wallpaper border with planes, and a ceiling fan that looked like a P-51 propeller. Logan's bed was perched high, with a slide for quick exits; his little brother Luke had a toddler bed at a ninety-degree angle to Logan's. The area rug had a print of a big dog. Logan had a portable CD player, too: he loved to fall asleep to soft music. His other favorite was downloaded versions of local station KYOT's Sunday morning show *Quiet Music*.

Karen kissed Logan good-night and whispered *I love you* before walking to her room, crawling into her own bed carefully—leaving her little guy Luke undisturbed—and falling into deep oblivion within minutes. During the night, Morgan climbed out of her canopy bed, with its sheer pink drape and pink satin bedspread, which was beaded, sequined, and piled with pillows. She had her own girl-theme room, which her dad had painted bright pink and decorated with many of the Walt Disney princesses. She crept quietly across the hall and slipped into her mother's bed without disturbing either occupant, leaving only

Logan asleep in his own bed.

In the darkness of Wednesday morning, the day before Thanksgiving, Karen felt multiple children stirring in her bed and wondered who else had joined during the night. Without opening her eyes, Karen knew it was Morgan. She held Morgan and Luke tight and felt their heartbeats against her own chest. She cherished this quietude, thinking how lucky she was to have these beautiful babies in bed with her. She also prayed for a few more sacred moments of continued silence. But giggles turned to pokes, kicks, and then someone jumping on the bed, which immediately doomed any possibility of further rest. Still exhausted and far from awake, Karen stretched and resigned herself, eyes still closed. *Lord, give me strength to make it through another day.* In the inky blackness the enormous effort and logistics of the morning routine were under way, rivaling stacking three hundred passengers onto a Boeing 777.

First there was sweet Morgan, who had finally achieved potty training when she was 6, which at least had meant no more diaper changes before school. But every morning, each step in getting her ready for the day could become a pitched battle of wills. The severe seizures that had begun at just six weeks old were caused by a physical brain abnormality. Since birth, many days of her life had been heartbreaking and exhausting. Nine-year-old Morgan took a complicated assortment of seizure medications her mother had to measure, mix, and dispense. But the medications were only one part of the daily challenges.

Dressing headstrong little Morgan Leigh Perry was like getting a first-class passenger to give up a prime spot for a coach seat in the middle between a four-hundred-pounder and a mother holding a colicky newborn—good luck! Depending on the day, as a working mother Karen tried every tactic and strategy, from hard-line militant approaches to sweet promises slathered with ice cream and sprinkles, none of which were reliably effective. Karen's own energy level usually dictated the chosen battle strategy; today, still exhausted, she was deploying frozen confectionaries and rainbows.

"Look, honey, here's a cute outfit."

"I don't like that."

Karen picked out another. "Look how cute——"

"No!"

"How about this pretty dress with the ladybugs?"

"Want fish red shirt. Fish red shirt."

"Morgan, it's dirty."

"Fish red shirt! FISH RED SHIRT!"

Morgan's brain abnormality and subsequent epilepsy had caused other developmental challenges, too, including to her cognitive abilities. At 9, Morgan's speech and articulation were closer to that of a 2-year-old. So, too, were her wild mood swings and tantrums. For a moment, Morgan held still in the silent fulcrum between white-hot defiance and nonchalant compliance. Her exhausted mother could only watch and wonder, *Which way will she go here?* Then, for reasons hidden from all except Morgan, she no longer hated the Coccinellidae family of brightly colored spotted beetles; ladybugs were now authorized to adorn her clothing. In fact, Morgan was now completely onboard with the idea.

"That's a pretty ladybug. Hi, ladybug."

For the moment, Karen was lost in a mother's silent focus of seizing the first victory, because she knew Morgan's state of willful compliance would be as fickle and fleeting as weather patterns at lower altitudes. Karen worked with the steady efficiency of flying an instrument approach near a thunderstorm, deftly interweaving Morgan's momentarily willing limbs into clothing, pushing buttons through tight slots, pulling on socks. *Done: daughter dressed!* Karen moved on to the next task: get up Logan—who, for unknown reasons, lay in bed sobbing. On her way to his room, Karen caught a blurred glimpse of a naked Morgan running the halls.

"Morgan, where are your clothes?" Morgan ran wild through the house, in her awkward gait, not answering. Karen followed the trail—dress, sock, underpants, another sock—scattered in a telltale evidentiary pattern leading to her naked daughter in the kitchen.

"Morgan, I don't want to play this game with you today."

The articulate language of diplomatic negotiations and adult logic processed in Morgan's innocent brain as the honking guffaws of a clown car, a sound that made her giggle and *run* with all the speed her small legs could generate. Morgan was a lot of things, but fast she was not. Stubborn: *yes*. Difficult: *yes*. Loving: *yes*. Disarmingly sweet: *yes*. Cooperative: *not so much*.

"Mommy, I want budday." That would be "butter," and Karen had long ago given up asking the obvious: *Butter for breakfast?* The naked child ran from view. Then Karen heard: "Uh oh, Mommy."

Karen had a good idea, but asked anyway: "What is it now, Morgan?"

"I go poot."

No translation needed. *Hopefully she hit the tile* was Karen's only thought as she grabbed paper towels and a bottle of bleach cleanser. She exhaled. Not yet fully conscious, she felt the beginnings of a virus spreading its pain throughout her head, throat, and stomach. Outside, the golden glow had yet to scatter the darkness. To get everyone delivered on time, all three children and their gear had to be stowed and secured for pushback at 6:30 a.m. The normal school-drop order: Logan, Morgan, Luke. Karen sighed; she had not yet checked a single box on the departure checklist.

Every day there were homework assignments to be collected and organized, lunches to be made and nestled in backpacks, and three children to be clothed just enough to conform with Arizona Revised Statutes regarding indecent exposure: that is, holed knees, tattered pant cuffs, food stains, and gross mismatching of socks, shirt, and pants were of absolutely no consequence. Breakfast had to be made and at least partially consumed. Brushing teeth was officially mandatory but often skipped in the blur to rush out the door. Combing and/or styling hair was like a surprise free upgrade to first class on a twelve-hour transoceanic flight: *Ha! Probably not going to happen.*

First there was the little accident to clean up. Then, after she dressed her daughter for a second time (and sometimes there was a third and fourth), Morgan also had to put on her orthotic devices, the contraptions she hated that compensated for her severely pronated arches. Designed to remold her small feet and assist with walking, they were also effective weapons. With shins as primary targets, the heavy devices had landed numerous direct hits on Karen's lower legs.

Finally there was the medication routine. Getting her daughter to actually ingest said substances was slightly easier than getting Morgan to let her mother comb her hair, which is to say it was nearly impossible. Karen deployed every tactic to win the corrective orthotics and medications skirmishes. That's why the aesthetic hair battle mostly went to Morgan, and she arrived at school many mornings looking like a mini Haile Selassie disciple, eschewing materialism and oppression, a free spirit and independent thinker. *Irie, mon!*

Karen took another deep breath and ventured back into the fray. With the long task list, the sands of time were tumbling fast. At least there was no Montessori School for Luke today; an early start to the long Thanksgiving weekend meant one less child to immediately dress, feed, and prep for the outside world. The only task there: Karen had said she would take Luke to the Thanksgiving party later that morning at his school. Of the three, Luke helped balance the mornings with his amazing optimism. Every morning Luke would look outside the window and proclaim, "Today is a beautiful day, Mommy!" He had a way of instantly turning the crazed morning chaos into a thing of beauty.

Logan, meanwhile, was channeling his sister and begging Karen not to take him to school. For whatever reason, he was still in bed sobbing. Karen had to call her ex-husband for help. Their own adult differences aside, Shawn had a way of talking to their children, the boys especially, that defused defiance. Except on this morning, the phone conversation did not move his son out of bed. Next Karen called a pilot friend who promised he'd take Logan on a trip if he got out of bed. The strategy worked, and the pilot asked where Logan wanted to go.

Without hesitation, Logan said, "Mall of America in Minneapolis," as though he had long considered and carefully prepared a list of his priority destinations for just such a question.

Karen laughed—she had not heard this one, but she did recall Logan asking if she would take him to see Justin Bieber in concert, which she might have considered except the tour stop in question was in Spain. *No, honey, we're not going to Spain to see Justin Bieber.* Other destinations on Logan's list included Rio de Janeiro, San Francisco, and Las Vegas. Logan would fully research each possible outing online and then hand his mother a printout dossier of the information.

The pilot agreed, Mall of America it would be, and Logan climbed out of bed. Luke, at least, wasn't adding to the melee as he settled in for some cartoons.

"It was a really weird morning," Karen recalled.

Years later, in the stark sadness of a quiet house, Karen would wonder if the children could have possibly been sensing their own looming finality, the yet-unseen inevitability toward which they were being marched. Perhaps children were still attuned and sensitive to energy transmissions adults could no longer access. That is, the ever-increasing burdens of adulthood scrambled the innate intuitive radar. The burden of the divorce, for example, which had only been official for nine months. Karen and Shawn were both exhausted and saddened by a union that had unraveled. As a divided couple, they dedicated themselves to co-parenting and took out their frustrations on each other like many couples in distress. As G. K. Chesterton said, "The true soldier fights not because he hates what is in front of him, but because he loves what is behind him."

In the run-up to the Thanksgiving holiday, Karen and Shawn had been back and forth on how and when Shawn would arrive to pick up the kids for the weekend. Was he driving? Flying? He finally called and said they would fly to Phoenix to pick up the kids and then he would make the two-and-a-half-hour drive back on Sunday afternoon.

Karen made breakfast for Morgan and Logan and gave them hugs before they left with Jaleesa Shelton, who took the children to their respective charter schools: Logan to Edu-Prize and Morgan to Leading Edge Academy, where she was enrolled in the special needs program.

As the morning progressed, Karen's physical state worsened. She called an administrator at Luke's school to say they were going to skip the Thanksgiving party as she did not feel up to it. By early afternoon, Morgan and Logan were back from school. Karen was expecting company, an out-of-town friend for the weekend, and trying to get the house in some semblance of order. For some reason, Karen felt inspired to clean her closet. She also reminded herself to make Thanksgiving dinner reservations at the Hyatt in downtown Phoenix, for a table in the rotating restaurant on the top floor.

"Let's go swimming," Logan said.

Karen looked up and smiled. "Logan, summer's over. It's too cold to swim."

"But I'm not even cold. Feel my arm."

Yes, but when you immerse yourself in 50-degree pool water you'll be hypothermic in minutes. Karen checked the arm and smiled. "Wow, you're right. Feels like ninety-eight point six."

"What the heck are you talking about, mother?"

"No swimming today, honey. You need to get ready for your trip. Why don't you go start packing, OK?"

"Can I take my Nintendo Wii?"

"Of course, honey. Remind me to make sure it's charged before you go."

At 3:30 that afternoon, the nanny gathered the children and their luggage and repeated a somewhat diluted edition of the morning routine. Morgan had a pink Brookstone rolling suitcase and looked the part of a seasoned traveler, just like her pilot mommy and daddy. Logan and Luke, too, each had their own Walt Disney duffel bags.

"Get back in here, Logan," Karen said, smiling, "and say good-bye."

Morgan and Luke had already properly hugged their mother, given her a kiss and a distracted *I love you, too,* and bounded off for the car and greater adventures aloft. *A real airplane our dad flies all by himself! He has lots of planes, all different colors. I get the window. No, I do!*

Logan ran back, and Karen scooped him up in her arms. She would be taking them to the airport herself except she was feeling utterly dreadful now with the virus knocking her back. Once they were gone, she would immediately seek refuge in bed.

"You be good for your father," Karen said. "I love you."

Logan nodded and smiled his amazing little-boy grin. She squeezed him up and closed her eyes. She was making a mental note to remind Shawn later about Morgan's different medications, times, and dosages, which they always reviewed together to keep everything straight.

"Love you, too," Logan said, wriggling out of her arms and running to the car. The car door slammed, and Shelton slowly backed her pearl-white Plymouth PT Cruiser out of the driveway. Karen stood, smiled, and waved. She watched and waved until she could no longer see the car. She felt the odd mixture of emotions departing children always evoked: relief and longing, with the ever-present fear and concern. From the moment their babies emerge into the world, loving parents will never know a life without that immutable bond that changes everything. Now she would expectantly await the phone call to let her know everyone was safe on the ground in Safford, just a thirty-minute flight east. Only later would Karen return to this moment and fully comprehend its enormity.

Like a seasoned National Transportation Safety Board (NTSB) investigator sorting twisted wreckage, hindsight would time-stamp the inconsequential exchange as pertinent and push it to the apex of reverential value. Then, give it a solemn name: *The Final Good-bye, the last time I saw my children alive.* For now, bound to time and linear trajectory, there was little more for Karen than the steady inner voice of boilerplate motherly guilt.

I should do more. I should be with them on holidays. I should take them to the airport myself. I should be home more. I should spend more time with my kids. I should be a better mother.

And then, quiet relief—children successfully away and accounted for, a full four-day break. With that came the further realization that an empty house awaited, with an equally unoccupied bed. Karen barely noticed the motherly mantra repeating as she turned and walked toward the house: *I should do more.* Instead, at that moment the entire universe could not have offered up greater lucre for the exhausted mother of three—stone-cold silence and a long, uninterrupted nap.

Two

Departures

THE INBOUND PONDEROSA TWIN-ENGINE AERO COMMANDER WAS LATE. Landing at approximately 5:46 p.m. at Falcon Field Airport (FFZ) in Mesa on November 23, 2011, the airplane stopped on the jet ramp. The pilot cut power, and the propellers stopped spinning. After emerging from the aircraft, Shawn Perry and Joseph Hardwick hand-spun each propeller approximately fifteen times. Inside the cockpit, a flashlight beam bounced around as Russel Hardy ran some checks. Shawn Perry walked into the hangar to greet his three children, who swarmed him as starstruck fans greet idols.

Almost immediately Morgan had a meltdown and refused to get on the airplane. Admittedly, it was difficult to distinguish between typical bad behavior and seizure symptoms, which Morgan had figured out and started using to her advantage. She would throw herself down and start screaming to get her way.

Right now, for whatever reason, she did not want to get onto the airplane. Inured to Morgan's rage, Luke calmly turned to his nanny and said, "Good-bye, Jaleesa. I'm *really* going to miss you."

She smiled and said, "I'll see you on Sunday."

Luke repeated himself with emphasis: "I'm REALLY going to miss you, Jaleesa." Shawn Perry was preoccupied with trying to calm his daughter, while Luke's odd demeanor sent a chill through Shelton. Eventually, the three walked up the drop stairs onto the plane as the blanket of night enveloped the desert. The flight back to Safford would be under night visual meteorological conditions. The FAA defined night as one hour after sunset. Tonight there would be no natural illumination to mark the mountain peaks standing sentinel to the east.

Now under complete darkness, the aircraft taxied to runway 4R for an eastbound departure, with a red rotating beacon pulsing in the night. Similar standard navigation lights glowed red on port wingtip, green on starboard wingtip, and white at the tail. Every aircraft in US airspace flying in darkness at that moment had the same lighting configuration, as required by the FAA. Joe Coffey worked for Falcon Executive Aviation at Falcon Field Airport (FFZ) and was familiar with the children and their father. Coffey saw Perry get into the back of the aircraft with his three children. Soon after landing in Mesa, the aircraft was airborne again.

Perry was not the pilot on the Mesa-Safford leg on this night. Instead, sitting left-front was his business partner and Ponderosa Aviation President Russel Hardy, 31. Also aboard was avionics technician and mechanic Joseph Hardwick, 22, who was engaged to be married in the coming weeks. The airplane continued its climb.

Five minutes.

If ever there was a definition of a routine flight, the return to Safford should have been ripped straight from *Webster's Dictionary*: perfect flying conditions, little wind, no weather, and just thirty minutes airborne with three experienced career aviation professionals aboard. Winds from 350 degrees at five knots were inconsequential; visibility was forty miles with only a few wisps of clouds well above at 20,000 feet. But while almost everything else had aligned perfectly in the script for ideal flying conditions, the dark, moonless night was now an ominous element in the equation. Under the glowing illumination of a full moon, the crash almost certainly would never have happened. As always, in a pursuit that defies and taunts gravity, nothing was ever automatic.

The moon, which was a waning crescent of 3 percent, had officially set two and a half hours prior, at 4:05 p.m., and local sunset had occurred more than an hour prior, at 5:21 p.m. Ambient light was nonexistent. Under such conditions, the immovable rock fingers of Superstition Mountain were completely invisible—5,057 vertical feet of solidified resurgent dome at the eastern fringe of metropolitan Phoenix.

Four minutes.

This volcano of rhyolite and rhyodacite had anchored its range for forty million years, recording the comings and goings of glacial time, of breathing, two-legged creatures and the lore they carried, the mysteries and myths of a fabled area. Found gold, lost gold. Jacob Waltz exhaling the secret location of his shiny motherlode to Julia Thomas on his deathbed in 1891, the legendary Lost Dutchman's Mine still nestled in a shaded canyon slot for the taking.

Three minutes.

For these tens of millions of years the place had evolved; now the human timeline was being marked in imperceptible fractions of grains. At 6:28 p.m., after momentarily climbing to an altitude of 4,700 feet, the aircraft descended to 4,500 feet, where it tracked eastbound in a straight line. The airplane's transponder was transmitting on a code of 1200.

Two minutes.

Hardy had flown the same round-trip flight from Safford to Mesa several times, including a trip two days prior under very similar night visual meteorological conditions. He knew the route and surrounding terrain. He typically used an iPad with navigation software that displayed aeronautical charts and terrain depictions. No one will ever know whether Hardy was using the iPad in the darkness of November 23, 2011, but the application he normally used would have alerted him that his airplane was speeding directly toward solid rock.

One minute.

Because the initial right turn had been delayed due to inbound air traffic,

Hardy's normal flight course had been altered and put the airplane on a track that intersected the mountain. Imperceptibly, a second lethal variable had been introduced in the form of the delayed right turn. Normally he would have piloted the plane three miles south of the highest peaks; the short delay before turning right put the aircraft five miles north of his normal flight track. Darkness and a brief delay in turning were each a link in a chain that would form to cause tragedy. But there would be other links, too, and darker, unimaginable questions.

Perry was preoccupied at the back of the cabin with his three children. That left either pilot Hardy or Hardwick, the avionics technician and mechanic, to make a last-second visual realization of the impending catastrophe. At more than 200 miles an hour, they were gazing into a black-on-black canvas of mountain and sky with nothing to discern one from the other. Whether anyone aboard realized their collective fate or not in the last seconds of life, there was no time to react.

Zero minutes.

A massive explosion and secondary blast ripped open the night and bled white-hot orange into the crystal sky. The colorless, straight-run petroleum distillate combusted into a second fireball inferno, sucking oxygen and blackening the cliff face sitting almost a mile above sea level.

A small cluster of raptors, Harris's hawks, leapt from a tree in the blast zone and caught flight at the first sound of impact to outrace the ripple-blast of heat. Gecko lizards and scorpions scrambled into deep cracks, away from the deathly surge, a perfect half-arc radius down the mountain. Diamondback rattlers found tight snake holes. People up to thirty miles away, and three stranded hikers near the mountain peak, witnessed or heard the fiery collision just below where the mountain met starry sky: manmade machine at more than 200 miles per hour versus timeless granite. A backyard surveillance camera, far below at a lower elevation, captured a bright silent flash on video.

The force of impact scattered the sleek white skin of the aircraft and wedged twisted aluminum into igneous crevasses never before touched by human technology. Thermal-acoustical insulation evaporated into flame and funneled up to the heavens, the wispy ash of a thousand glasswool fireflies. The floor and sidewall panels and light gray leather interior were immediately rendered perverse blobs of black nothingness; precise avionics born in white clean rooms were now sickening spiderwebs of mangled hot wires. Carbon soot choked land, rock, scrubby vegetation, and twisted wreckage, and fed a furious, thick plume of the blackest smoke, oil ablaze.

Two distinct debris fields pumped obscene light into the night, together covering a steep sloped area at about forty-five degrees downhill to the northwest, abutted by a vertical rock formation. Burning debris and body parts scattered the sloped area 150 feet across one way and 80 feet the other. Much of what was left of the aircraft clustered at the base of the vertical face, with debris wedged right into the timeless rock. The entire scene looked as if it had been napalmed and was fire-damaged, soot-covered, and scorched. The aberration attracted the curious stares of two bone-thin coyotes, heads cocked and then howling at a safe distance from the pulsing flash. Amid the freakish wreckage site, somehow a lone tree stood unscathed in the field of black desolation. The northwest edge of the sloped debris field was about 150 feet southeast of where the mountain became very steep, near vertical, and then fell away to the valley floor thousands of feet below.

There were six mangled human bodies, too, in the inferno, with its menacing lash of oily heat and smoke, mountain and dismantled machine ablaze and voraciously consuming fuel. The darkest nightmare could not conjure an equally gruesome scene. Only later, mostly through dental film comparisons, would investigators be able to identify the individuals. First responders from Arizona Department of Public Safety and Pinal County Sheriff's Office would encounter a macabre scene, including a severed child's hand settled in the dirt, with the same color of fingernail polish Morgan wore.

For now, the mountain alone held the mystery of what happened, and why, and who might be hidden up there in the raging flames, twisted metal, and scorched crevices. The place bore briefly a new scar of soot-blackened rock that would quickly fade, erode, and disappear altogether. In three years, under the ever-efficient drumbeat of desert sun, rain, and the cycle of fragmenting temperatures, the outer blemish would be mostly gone.

Forevermore the events of November 23, 2011, had been time-stamped in the lineage and evolution of the place, a reverent historical marker in the forty-million-year march of plate tectonics, birth and death, and the quiet flutter of leilia hackberry butterfly wings. The rock face marked new sacred space the mountain would guard until the sands of time ran out.

PART I

THE AVIATOR

THREE

California Girl

THE CRATE LABELS TIME-STAMPED an earlier era and belied the promise of succulent golden sunshine in citrus bites. Balboa Barony and Blue Vase. Man O'War, Red Breast, and Siren. Colonial Mother.

For all anybody knew, these might have been 190-proof rectified spirits in clear bottles stacked in pickups, under canvas, awaiting transport at nightfall. But there were at least three growers and manufacturers with overt nods to both product and place: Anaheim Orchid, Anaheim Supreme, and Nightcap Pride of Anaheim. Although the latter name still sounded like knockback moonshine, it was indeed the orange being offered in the town Germans had pioneered and staked using "Ana," from the nearby Santa Ana River, combined with *heim* for home.

Karen Sommerstedt was born February 5, 1963, in Anaheim, California, population circa one hundred thousand at the time, a fragrant hub of citrus blossoms, crystal air, and hearty soil, where churned farmland was quickly turning to shiny suburbs. The smog from the north had not yet arrived, but it would be pushing in heavily by decade's end. Walt Disney had already set up shop here almost a decade prior, in 1955, when officials from the city of Burbank, later red-faced, famously declined a theme park proposal by Mickey Mouse's creator. Meanwhile the singing cowboy, Gene Autry, secured a Major League Baseball franchise in 1960 at the American League winter meetings. On April 9, 1964, team officials announced the Angels would move to Anaheim for the start of the 1966 season in a brand-new stadium.

This was a transformative time in Southern California, the 1960s, an era of back-combed bubble haircuts and wash-and-wear geometrics, when gas guzzlers ruled America's fresh asphalt boulevards and milk still clinked in thick glass jugs delivered right to the front door.

Karen's father, Reinhold Vern Sommerstedt, and mother Marsaline (Baio), were in their twenties when they married and began a tumultuous relationship that never quite found its footing. Reinhold served in the US Army and had been stationed in Germany; Marsaline was a housewife. There, in sun-drenched Anaheim, with its celestially named Angels baseball team, Marsaline brought Karen a baby sister—her own angel—on October 31, 1965, when Karen was almost 3. Baby sister Kathleen was an unbridled joy to her doting big sister, but Karen's notion of her as an angel would soon prove ominously prophetic.

"My vivid memory is that it started as a sty in her eye," Karen recalled.

There was a biopsy and an official diagnosis: leukemia. A man in a white coat explained that leukemia was too much of a good thing, a type of blood cancer that began inside the marrow of Kathleen's little bones, at the soft center where blood cells come to life. Kathleen had too many white blood cells, leukocytes that fight infections and other foreign substances. The cancerous cells spread into her bloodstream and lymph nodes, brain, spinal cord, and throughout her small body.

In an attempt to stem the infectious spread, doctors removed Kathleen's left eye. Big sister Karen remembers being in the examination room watching nurses change Kathleen's bandage after the surgery. She remembers the dark void where the eyeball had been and then riding the hospital elevators to assuage the effects of the scary image. From that time forward, the antiseptic smell and atmosphere of hospitals induced immediate nausea for Karen. It was a cruel foreboding, because she would one day be spending a lot of time in hospitals: first fighting for her own life, and then with her own epileptic daughter. Two years after the initial diagnosis, in 1967, leukemia took Karen's baby sister.

"That was my first experience with hospitals and death," Karen said. Today she doesn't remember most of the fine details of Kathleen's departure, but she does recall a palpable sense of loneliness and vague sadness that settled around her, the family, and the household, and how the feeling lingered throughout childhood. Within the family, the domino effect was immediate, as Karen's mother went into an emotional tailspin and turned to alcohol for comfort. Only 4 years old, Karen shuddered as though a towering dark swell of cumulonimbus doused the California light.

"I felt horrible about my sister, but didn't fully comprehend it," Karen recalled. "I just knew she wasn't there anymore. Then I watched how my mother crumbled. I kept thinking, *'But what about me? I'm still here.'*"

The downward spiral quickened as Karen's mother, who'd been a largely upbeat person, was simply unable to process the loss. Within a year of their baby girl's death, Karen's parents divorced. From the outset, the foundations of the marriage had been wobbly; Kathleen's death toppled the relationship completely. Karen's mother descended into darkness and drink and never quite came back during Karen's childhood. In such a state, she could not care for her eldest daughter; the court awarded Karen's father full custody. It was another early milestone that shaped the little girl.

Karen's well-meaning father vowed to protect his daughter by keeping her separated from her self-destructive mother. While the intention was soundly benevolent, the 5-year-old girl needed her mom, too. From that point forward, any chance of a carefree childhood altogether vanished for Karen. She might have been brought up barefoot and gloriously immersed in innocence washed with golden California hues. Instead, her less-than-traditional childhood was the starting point for assembling the elemental framework for a career aloft.

REINHOLD Vern Sommerstedt worked in aerospace for Hughes Aircraft Company and then Garrett Air Research, in Los Angeles. The building where he worked was near one of the busiest airports in the world, Los Angeles International (LAX). In 1968, Reinhold moved the family of two to a duplex in Redondo Beach, where he already owned several rental properties. The house at 506 South Pacific Coast Highway was just a few blocks from the beach, and Karen spent the next five of her formative years there, living with just her dad, on the bottom floor of the duplex. Karen could not hear or see the ocean from her house, but her time there was saturated with the thick cloak of pungent sea salt and the cosmic repetitive force of oceanic water working its efficient power just minutes away.

Karen's immediate neighbors were the people who rented the top unit from her father. Like Karen, Heather Horton, 15 when Karen was 9, and her brother Jamie, 12, lived with their father Richard, minus a mother. Heather, older and already a teenager, offered Karen some approximation of a mother, and she gave Karen what Karen might have similarly offered her own baby sister Kathleen. With the unconscious bond and transference, Karen idolized everything about Heather—her hair, her makeup, her clothes, her confident walk and quick smile, and the wisdom of her years—and Heather became the female template for the young girl adrift with only her father's hand to guide her.

Karen's father was an intelligent, curious, energetic, and passionate man who carefully researched whatever piqued his boundless inquisitiveness. He never went to college, but worked in the high-tech world and spent long hours huddled over drafting boards. He was a talented sketch artist and painter, too, who also enjoyed spinning fantastic tales for his young daughter. Veracity aside, whatever story he spun was magically entertaining to Karen. He was like an eccentric soothsayer who could opine on any number of subjects. Karen never quite knew what to believe, but she never dismissed anything outright because she knew her dad was smart and, she later realized, he even hit the mark here and there. His tales usually interwove narratives on the price of gold and the roving eyes of the federal government with the history, politics, and intricacies of Federal Reserve notes. At restaurants, Karen watched waitresses become curious-faced when asked by her father, "Do you accept Federal Reserve notes?" As a 5-year-old girl, and for many years thereafter, Karen heard much about the dynamic interplay between money and politics, truth and conspiracy, self-reliance, science and art, and about the hard-earned freedom of motorcycling.

Karen also remembers her father shopping her around to various adoption agencies. Her father was not malicious or uncaring, but rather the opposite: he wondered aloud whether he had what it took to raise his daughter properly on his own. Karen remembers the abject fear of losing, perhaps, both parents. She begged her dad not to give her away to someone else. His fears of being a single father, in his mid-twenties, were profound. As he sorted out what was best for her, the young girl was clinging to the last immediate family member she had. First baby Kathleen. Then her mother. If dad left, too, it might be too steep a tailspin, one from which she would never recover. The painful "Will he or won't he?" game played out over days and weeks and mercifully concluded when her father made the decision to step up and raise Karen himself. Crisis averted!

Determined to do right by his daughter, he enrolled Karen in a private Lutheran school in Torrance. Like a responsible single parent, he drove Karen to school every morning himself. However, unlike any other parent she knew, he did so on his road-worn Ducati motorcycle. The unusual mode of transportation, a rare two-wheeled school bus, produced powerful imprints on the young girl. The first revelation was all the heightened sense impressions while aback the bike. Cool California mornings were downright frigid at 50 miles an hour, and could produce numb fingers and toes by the time she climbed off at school. For refuge, Karen would wrap her arms around her father's midsection and squeeze tight as they sped through wispy trails of morning fog. Balmy afternoons, sun blazing, were unbelievably hot as they sat at stoplights and the heat rippled off the asphalt and rumbling engine in steady waves. The *whoosh* of rushing air was a cacophony compared to the sealed bubble of automobile transport. The tiny splat of insects was mostly imperceptible until a thick bumblebee collided with Karen's cheek and left a red welt. The unique creak and smell of sun-bleached leather, as she leaned into her father's shoulder to buffer the wind, induced odd comfort that might scare the living hell out of most: *I get to go to school on a motorcycle!*

Once at school, Karen often noticed tiny burn marks left on her tights from the white-hot cylindrical muffler. There was usually a smattering of bugs, too, who'd met their demise along Karen's tights and shoe tips, with an occasional live survivor struggling to break free from the web of her tangled hair. Simultaneously, she often noticed mismatched socks because, from an early age, she was up and dressing herself in the dark as she shook off slumber. Karen cooked her own breakfast, too, and did her own laundry.

"I basically raised myself," Karen said. "I had my mother and sister, and then all of a sudden it was just me and my dad."

She was unconsciously mourning two devastating losses: baby Kathleen and her wayward mother. Jumping on the back of a bullet-fast Ducati was pure escape. That two-wheeled machine followed the same route as the wide, lumbering cars but, in some secret way she didn't fully understand, also took the young girl to magical new places along the way.

Some days Reinhold, with his head brimming and spilling over with ideas, theorems, projects, and plausible government conspiracies, simply forgot to drop his daughter at school. Instead, she'd ride with him all the way to where he worked, near LAX. Looking almost surprised that she was still perched on the Ducati—*Who are you? And how in the world did you get there?*—he'd laugh, and they'd each shake a helmeted head of recognition. *Oops, Dad did it again!* Then he'd backtrack with a hard-angle U-turn Karen had learned to lean into rather than away from. Her father grabbed a wrist full of throttle and sped back toward the blown turn, his mind already refocused on that day's top-line tasks.

Karen held a secret then that she never shared. She could have easily tapped her preoccupied father's shoulder to remind him of the correct turn, but she stayed quiet and thought other thoughts in hopes he would forget—again—because his lapse meant one glorious payoff: airplanes.

As they neared LAX, there was the oily fragrance of fuel burn that made her giggle each time. Inbound and outbound: Karen marveled at the vast array of gleaming craft demonstrating Newton's laws of motion in real time and space. She reveled in the metal thunder of air-breathing turbofans at full thrust. She imagined the excitement of passengers who had just crossed nations and oceans and smaller chunks of America on commuter flights. Or outbound planes ferrying people to exotic locales inaccessible before commercial aviation. Almost immediately, Karen imagined stepping from the glorious two-wheeled bullet ride into these even more-evolved machines honed by precise engineering and boasting fixed wings and powerful engines.

Karen could have sat there all day by the side of the road, watching these beautiful and efficient machines cutting the bonds of whatever here-and-now had delivered. She loved watching them speed skyward with untethered freedom. Day after day, week after week, month after month, it was already happening for the young girl, aboard the speeding Ducati under a blitzkrieg canopy of amazing aircraft. Destiny itself reached in and touched off the tumbler gears, which silently meshed inside a girl charting four decades of high-speed motion that would not stop until November 23, 2011.

AFTER school, while her dad worked, Karen stayed for secondary programs until 6 p.m. That's where she made some of her closest friends. Her best friend Tina was almost full-blooded Native American Paiute, adopted by her mother, Caroline Eisle. When Caroline repeatedly saw Karen's mismatched socks and tights with tiny burn holes, she took Karen under her wing. There was an immediate bond, and she became an anchor for Karen. What the upstairs neighbor girl Heather had started, Caroline took to the next level of surrogate mothering. When her dad had to work late, which was often, Karen was at her friend's house with her new surrogate mother. Then her dad would pick her up on the motorcycle long after dinner, and they'd race back to Redondo Beach in the cold darkness, Karen's nose buried in that sweet-smelling shoulder of leather. During this time, Karen did not see her own mother a single time over two full years.

"Caroline was a good role model and mother figure in my life," Karen explained. "I was very lucky to have met her."

Her dad worked a lot and was gone for long stretches. So when she wasn't at Tina's house, Karen often had to find ways to keep herself occupied. To get to the beach, she first had to cross the busy Pacific Coast Highway. She'd walk to Curly's liquor store on the corner and buy Pall Mall cigarettes for her dad. Then she'd wander the few blocks down to the beach, through open spaces and quiet residential streets, and walk on the pier. She liked to watch the fishermen dangle lines, with the unique waft of the ocean and the sodden pier pilings a stabilizing presence. The steady roar of tumbling waves provided solace not unlike another place of solitary comfort, the Redondo Beach library. There, Karen could browse the stacks and find quiet refuge. Some of her favorite books were *Where the Wild Things Are* by Maurice Sendak and *Charlotte's Web* by E. B. White. She also loved the Laura Ingalls Wilder books and read them all. She tried surfing, but was terrified when a wave toppled her and the board whacked her head. She played flute in elementary school, as well as guitar and piano.

One night when her father was still at work, someone tried to break into the lower half of the duplex while she was in the shower. It was a rare rainy night in Southern California, and Karen remembers the steady plink on the old tin roof being interrupted by the thundering foot blows of someone trying to slam through the front door. Paralyzed with fear, she couldn't move or scream. She just waited it out until the pounding stopped. Karen dialed the operator and then a friend to pick her up. Then she wrapped herself in a towel and ran out to Pacific Coast Highway to wait for her friend's parent to arrive. For whatever reason, she felt safer being out of the house wrapped in a towel, still dripping from the shower. She was 8 years old.

When she was 10, Karen's dad decided it was time to teach her about the birds and the bees, and he announced, "If there's anything you want to talk about, I want you to talk to me. My parents never talked to me about this stuff."

Nudge, nudge. Wink, wink.

She did not understand much in this arena, but she definitely knew she was mortified by her dad's suggestion. So instead, she'd hide in the closet with a flashlight and leaf through a set of illustrated sex education books he had given her.

Karen sensed her life was different, but she did not know any other metric for normal. Karen's early "family" vacations were with her father. They took weekend trips down to Ensenada, Mexico, on the sun-soaked Baja Peninsula. The two would kick up the sand dunes on the Ducati, with Karen gleefully clinging to her father's waist. Concurrently, here was a father who had the discernment to enroll his daughter at a private Christian school because that is where, he believed, she would get the best education. This was the only life Karen knew.

After the sad and quick dismantling of her nuclear family, Karen felt unusually alone. But her emotions were just beyond the edge of her consciousness and perception. Without fully grasping it, she was attuned to the same intense emotional devastation her parents were enduring: the loss of a child, with its searing void of permanent midnight. Mother, father, and daughter each privately sorted through the emotional rubble and ruin of what was and what might have been.

Already Karen was confronting the specter of her own death when she should have been running free through the Anaheim orchards, giggling with friends and stealing a sweet treat for the walk home. Instead, a heavy cloak cloistered her. First her baby sister. Then she watched as, one by one, more people in her life passed away: her father's 18-year-old brother died riding his motorcycle, and then she lost her paternal grandfather. Karen did not want to go to her grandfather's funeral but her father insisted, saying, "This will be your only opportunity to say good-bye." The service was open-casket; adult hands pressed Karen forward toward another lifeless body. She looked once at the plastic face caked with powder, and shuddered. By the time she was 10, all Karen's grandparents were gone.

If necessity was the mother of invention, Karen was becoming a resolute and independent young girl. Her strong psyche, intelligence, and instincts were pointing the way to survival. Without realizing it, a sense of place was becoming one of the anchoring tenets in Karen's life, where other such necessities had untethered. Like invisible caissons driven to bedrock, Karen came to trust what was timeless—the steadying force of geology.

Place, the young Karen sensed, imbued the larger realms being touched on at her Christian school. God, she discovered, was everywhere: in the sweet tang of the ocean air and the vibrating wings of bees descending on the endless fragrant orange blossoms. Alone at home after school, when Karen peeled back and bit into a perfect Anaheim orange, it was as if the fine spritz painted the entire universe of possibilities. The timeline and cycle and rhythm of seedling, blossom, and fruit were a poem within a story within a larger narrative. The fragility and entire life cycle of a baby sister had already played out before her young eyes, ephemeral. But place, for Karen, had an immovable and impervious solidity that brought calm. The only place Karen had known was, of course, also changing—weathering, eroding, cleaving, shifting, and moving—and then slowly dying, to give rebirth.

The young girl sensed that geological change, with its time scale imperceptible to human eyes, fastened everything together in a way that made sense. For Karen, the California brightness, crystal air, and endless cerulean sky were forever frozen in perfection. Baby Kathleen was alive there, too, and her mother, interwoven back into the beauty of ease and timelessness.

Anchoring it all, just down the street from the duplex, was the calming churn of waves onto sand, fine particles rounded for millennia, and the cool blast of sweetness when the motorcycle dipped low along roads running past orchards, illuminated by long golden rays fanned wide. Atop a vibrating Ducati every sense impression was keenly amplified and magnified, and the blueprint of Karen's lifelong pursuit was laid down. Place was superseding home, molding a beautiful young girl and her mind into someone and something beyond that immediate sphere.

Karen marveled at the power of flight to warp speed, time, and distance, and to provide unparalleled access to all points. For Karen, eventually her place would include destinations north, west, east, and south of California, new addresses reached in the three dimensions of her beloved aviation. The freedom of flight would unshackle her from the grim reminders of baby Kathleen and a lost mother, and transport her back to a time and place where they still smiled. In the coming years of adulthood, Karen would begin glimpsing the unlikely and important succession of places that lay before her as fresh three-letter symbols from International Air Transport Association tags.

Sheridan, Oregon, via Portland, PDX.

MSY, the Big Easy.

The islands, HNL.

And the frozen mountain west, SLC.

And ultimately, the last stop on a wonderfully glorious path, the rugged outcrop in the Sonoran desert in the state due east, a place Karen had never heard of: Gold Canyon, Arizona (PHX).

For the young girl, two decades of maturation, sunrises and sunsets, life, check rides, thrilling departures and takeoffs, white-knuckle landings, love, marriage, divorce, and career still lay ahead before arriving at the place where she would feel the hot pulse of breath straight from a hole in the earth. Before all that, she was a schoolgirl whose innocence had been temporarily blotted but never completely overwhelmed. There were smiles and whimsy and poetry to be had on the back of a motorcycle and, Karen somehow already knew, in airplanes. There was the imperfect yet anchoring love of a father who, though he might have shopped his daughter to adoption agencies, ultimately brought her home, vowed to raise her right, and protected her with the fierce love only a father can provide.

At the outset of a new decade, the 1970s, Karen's possibilities and eventual imprints all rippled outward in perfect waves of completion. She merely had to find and step into the footholds already carved in her path. In each she would unravel riddles and pin a foundational sense of calm—fine particles rounded for millennia.

Karen Sommerstedt was going to be an aviator.

FOUR

Homemade Butter

IN 1973, WHEN KAREN WAS 10, her father came across Scientology. The discovery occurred largely through happenstance and proximity. Down the street from the duplex where they lived, Karen's father owned a single-story building zoned for business. By 1973, the tenant occupying that building was conducting Scientology courses. On the heels of the freewheeling 1960s, and still in the dark shadow of Vietnam, L. Ron Hubbard's Scientology offered a new slant on the way of things. With his eccentric and naturally curious nature, Karen's father ended up taking the courses himself, and he soon had signed up his daughter for the same study courses.

"My father had raised me in the Lutheran religion, but Scientology was not a typical religion," Karen said. "I was confused because it was not in line with what I grew up learning. I didn't buy into the cultish way of things."

For the girl who had lost her mother and sister—and grown up on the back of a Ducati and at a private Lutheran school—the new methodology was intriguing, if nothing else. She was by the far the youngest person taking courses. Karen found that the study course provided a lot of good information, especially techniques for how to learn and study effectively. She read the books and, as her dad had encouraged, looked up words she did not understand. Paying close attention to the nomenclature helped broaden Karen's vocabulary considerably, and she was making her way through books considered difficult for adults. After each chapter, a mentor would ask Karen questions to see whether she could demonstrate the concepts using modeling clay; no student advanced until mastering each level.

"I would go find out what a word meant before progressing," Karen said. "The concept stuck with me the rest of my life. To this day I'll stop reading to look up a word."

For her age, Karen was very articulate and presented herself differently than most kids. People usually thought she was older. She held eye contact with adults and could converse easily.

"There was a lot of spiritual awakening going on at that time," Karen said. "Things were changing in our society, and thought patterns were evolving." Even at 11, Karen was astute enough to keep what was helpful, but she never bought the whole package.

"I'm generally opposed to things that are all or nothing," Karen said. Instead, her path would take a different direction to a more open spirituality.

Concurrently, Karen's dad began talking loosely about moving to Nevada, where a potential job opportunity awaited. Although that post never came to fruition, the winds of change were kicking up. By 1974, the tenant family living upstairs included Richard, his new girlfriend Linda, and his two kids Heather and Jamie. That foursome, too, began studying at the center. This communal style repeated in the next chapter in Karen's life. The entire clan—Karen and her father, along with Richard, Linda, Heather, and Jamie—moved to Sheridan, Oregon, to help establish and open The Delphian Foundation, a university community based on the principles of L. Ron Hubbard's Scientology. Dr. Alan

Larson joined the school as the founding headmaster, along with several of his colleagues, all of whom wanted to reverse declining standards in education.

For Karen's father, the move was an opportunity for change; his mission was to help oversee the environmental project as director of planning and design. The 1970s energy crisis was in full swing, and he wanted his daughter to get out of the city and experience rural life, where being barefoot and walking in the grass was a daily given. Karen was both excited and tentative about the move north. She had never lived anywhere but Southern California, her place, and she'd be even farther away from her estranged mom.

That latter issue continued to fester: Karen still resented her mother for the divorce, her absence, and what the daughter saw as an inability to move beyond the death of baby Kathleen. Karen didn't know the term then, but survivor's guilt was also doing a number on her young psyche. She said, "I can't say all the problems were entirely my mother's fault, but that same thought kept coming back: *'What about me? I'm still here.'*"

The move, then, was also a chance to make a clean break. And in 1974, that's exactly what the father and daughter did. After loading the moving van—including Karen's tropical fish tank, complete with water and fish—packed tightly with their belongings, Karen's father found Interstate 5 and headed north. Along the way, the tank toppled, and Karen's fish never saw Oregon.

THE city of Sheridan was just off Highway 18 in a green valley, cut through by the South Yamhill River. Other points were only a short drive away: Portland, Salem, and the rocky foam of the Oregon coast. At inception, The Delphian Foundation was a 100 percent self-sufficient operation that provided living quarters, a school, and food sources—including gardens and livestock (cows, pigs, and chickens)—for the initial one hundred residents. The main building was an old Jesuit novitiate on a hill. Although the bathroom facilities were shared, Karen had her own bedroom. In the parlance of the day it was a commune. But if that term was pejorative, to this day The Delphian School is operational and a coveted private institution.

Because the school was not yet up and running upon their arrival, Karen worked the first year at the in-house dairy farm and with the horses. She certainly was not in Kansas—or Anaheim—anymore. Along with apprenticeships in dairy farming, which met twice daily, and learning animal husbandry, the 11-year-old was operating a tractor before she was old enough to drive a car.

Karen's new routine was that of a farm girl. She was up before the chickens, worked twelve to fifteen hours a day until her hands were cracked and blistered, and fell into bed at night exhausted. The children were treated more like adults in little bodies than like kids. Play time was minimal, and Karen never went to the movies, hung out at the mall with friends, or did most of the things girls her age were doing back in Southern California. And yet she never felt like she was missing out.

"I thought I was lucky," Karen said of that time.

This preteen girl had no time for or interest in Jordache bell-bottoms or sterile and fluorescent-lit shopping malls: she already had a larger purpose, which was to continue to mold and solidify her own firebrand independence. One time she and a boy, renowned keyboardist Chick Corea's son Thad, went camping overnight in the nearby forest without telling any of the adults. They put up a tent not far from the building, and Karen kissed her first boy, a brief, tight-lipped peck that made them both laugh. When they returned they both caught hell, even though the entire experiment was only silly childhood innocence.

Karen had traded the ocean mist and orange blossoms of Southern California for a forested playground that was hers for the taking. The earthy rural canvas of the Pacific Northwest made Karen feel safe in a way the concrete and asphalt never had. She was also learning and doing things that conjured Laura Ingalls Wilder herself, including churning fresh butter from cream that was so frothy and succulent her mouth watered at its mere mention. Karen was eventually in charge of the horse stables, too.

At night she took solace in books. She found a cover-worn copy of the paperback *Helter Skelter*, which she read all the way through, with a fascination for its dark weirdness. She read a thick, sweeping gothic novel called *Cashelmara*; not yet even a teenager, Karen navigated the adult themes in the book by Susan Howatch. In the novel, published in 1974, a lonely widower in Ireland meets and marries a bright young American, a relationship that devolves into darkness, murder, and retribution. No doubt, the young Karen identified with the English author's family plight (minus the murder) and the attendant and weighty religious and philosophical themes. Another favorite was *My Wicked, Wicked Ways: The Autobiography of Errol Flynn*.

Once The Delphian School was operational, Karen was one of six students in the inaugural class. They shared one classroom under the tutelage of a tall, thin, young, and patient teacher named Ted, with thick chunks of wild red hair. The kids just called him "Red."

Eventually the school began attracting students from wealthy, progressive-minded, out-of-state families. Karen excelled in English, less so in mathematics. Overall, though, she was very happy there. When they had a spare moment, she and her classmate Debbie played records, with Steppenwolf's "Magic Carpet Ride" one of their favorites. It was a song title prophetic of both her life and eventual career.

"MY Friend Gus B" was his registered name: a Tennessee walking horse with a beautiful gait, called a "running walk," and a light tan coat with a black stripe down the back to match his dark mane and tail.

If every girl had dreams of owning a horse, from the moment Karen saw Gus she knew he was the realization of hers. It was a Wednesday, New Year's Day 1975, and Karen's father had driven her to Jake Price Stables. Elsewhere on this same day, former US Attorney General John Mitchell, former presidential Chief of Staff H. R. Haldeman, and John Ehrlichman would be found guilty by a jury: conspiracy, obstruction of justice, and perjury in the Watergate mess. But for a young girl, those adult machinations could have been playing out on Mars, or not at all, for all they mattered. Staring at a perfect horse she just had to have, there was nothing in the entire universe that could pierce her field of focus: "Gus B" was the sun, the moon, and the stars.

Karen knew it was not any sort of guarantee that her father had taken the time to hook up the horse trailer before they had left. He was just an efficient "What if?" planner. So with every power she could summon, she tried to silently bend her father's will to bringing home that beautiful horse.

"We don't usually have people on a holiday," Jake Price told the duo. And he was right: Karen and her father were the only potential customers around. He gave them the tour and eventually saddled up Gus. Karen climbed on and immediately fell even more in love. The gaited horse, with the ceremonial smooth glide, appealed to her father's eccentricity and appreciation of careful breeding and lineage. He paid cash, and they took Gus home.

Soon Karen was taking Gus to 4-H shows and riding him in parades. She and her father traveled to horse shows throughout Oregon, Washington, and northern California. Her father had sold several properties before they moved north, and so he had the means to finance Karen's expensive new friend and hobby.

But by late 1976, after what seemed like a brief flash to young Karen, the back-to-nature experiment was over for the 13-year-old. Her father announced they would be returning to California. Karen's emotions were mixed, but hinged primarily on the four-legged factor: Would Gus also be moving back to Southern California? *Yes, of course,* Karen's father said, smiling. He would move back alone to get an apartment set up and then send for Karen. He had already arranged to have Karen stay temporarily with Jake Price's parents, who lived on the Jake Price Stables property. Karen loved Oregon, but she had no choice: the materialism, temperate coastal breezes, and chaos of SoCal beckoned. Upon her return, the harsh juxtaposition to her life in the Oregon woods could not have been more stark or shocking.

For starters, Karen's father set them up in Beverly Hills, in a three-bedroom apartment on Robbins Drive. Her father chose the apartment complex, isolated from the hoi polloi, specifically, and only, because across the street was one of the best public schools in Southern California and, therefore, the nation: Beverly Hills High School, 90210. But that was where any potential life benefit ended for the teenage girl.

In every way, Karen was not wired for Beverly Hills. She had left Anaheim as a surprisingly independent 11-year-old girl; she returned as a teenager with a slew of practical new life skills. She could churn her own butter from scratch and shoe a horse, and was comfortable wandering the misty Oregon forest at night, alone. During her time in Oregon, Karen had been free to be herself without the normal outside influences impinging on her carefree self-expression. Now, at Beverly Hills High, she was thrust into a skewed world where previously unimportant issues took center stage. Chief among those: the hard currency of the economic hierarchy.

"I was the poorest kid there," Karen said.

She was also one of the smartest. By seventh grade Karen was reading at a grade twelve level. Meanwhile, she was less enamored with mathematics, saying, "I didn't like math until I became a pilot."

Had she been stronger in mathematics, she would have skipped two grades instead of just one. Nevertheless, at her new high school she skipped ninth grade and entered as a sophomore instead of a freshman. From the outset, Beverly Hills High was a bizarre world for Karen. Her life in Oregon had been wonderfully insulating: no material symbols, no drugs, no peer pressure, and no competition. At her new school, drugs were seemingly everywhere she looked, and usage was equally rampant. Kids wheeled into the school parking lot in brand-new Mercedes-Benz 300Ds and BMW 2002s. Kids of movie stars, and teen idols (Shaun Cassidy), were her classmates. Her sun-bleached brunette Southern-California-girl look met the aesthetic standard of her new high school; Karen had her headshots done and got a few small modeling gigs. But that one trait, being physically attractive, was not sufficient currency to move up the social strata in a microenvironment awash with Farrah Fawcett knockoffs and Leif Garrett look-alikes. Karen's only hope for social relevance was to join the misfit clique, and that was only made possible because she agreed to try smoking pot.

She excelled at singing and drama and pursued both at Beverly Hills High and at the local community theater. Her growing fascination with airplanes had not dimmed, so she took the closest class she could find, which was automotive mechanics. Karen was unknowingly blending the tactile with the academic, the intuitive, and the sensory—all the skills of a good pilot. For fun she took a class to learn how to be a DJ, in the days when shiny black vinyl ruled the music world.

Meanwhile, her father was producing documentaries and a musical called *Alaska*. To do so, he was collaborating with a talented songwriter and piano player, which is why the male songster soon moved in with Karen and her father. As she tried to get a foothold in the strangeness of Beverly Hills life, Karen took refuge in an old friend: Gus.

Her father had found an affordable stable in Burbank, which meant that each time she wanted to see and ride her beloved horse, Karen embarked on a day-long odyssey. Too young to drive, she had to ride three different city buses to reach Gus. Her northern route rolled straight through the epicenter of depravity and seediness at Hollywood and Vine. An hour and a half later, Karen would be walking up to Gus, who'd shake his head up and down each time he saw her approaching. She'd stroke and coo to him and ride him for a bit, but then always had to hurry back to the bus stop for the long return trip. Gradually, as much as she loved him, Karen was going less and less often to see Gus. She did not fully understand or process the unfortunate reality: little girls grew up, and the ponies of their dreams ended up, alone and mostly unattended, at a stable in Burbank. Their friendship was following its natural course. Her dad delicately broached the subject one night: the cost of feeding and boarding a horse she was barely seeing and riding was a big factor in the decision. Then her dad said it flat out: "We need to sell Gus."

What might have been life's greatest trauma was not, because Karen already had the perspective of her experience with baby sister Kathleen. She was strong, purposeful, and independent; there were other, bigger adventures to explore.

"I don't remember the good-bye part," she recalled.

The classic rite of losing one's pet was another passageway for Karen, from adolescence to adulthood, from being a girl to being a woman. It was 1979, and although she was just 16 and a high school junior, the confines of Southern California could no longer contain her free spirit, nor slow the whirling machinery of her humming wanderlust. She had the whole world ahead of her, awaiting her next move.

"I do not want to go to this school anymore," she told her father one evening after a particularly inane and superficial day among the silver-spoon set. She wanted to learn, she told her dad. Her plan was already in play: her boyfriend Bill was graduating and moving away to college. Karen had already borrowed money from a friend, bought a plane ticket, and was dropping out of high school to follow Bill to a new city. (What Karen did not tell her father was that Bill was unaware of this plan at its inception and would learn of it only when Karen arrived, unannounced, at his front door in another state.)

Karen's father did not immediately react as most might. He was an intelligent and open-minded man who produced documentaries, owned a company involved in offshore oil trusts, and once purchased a gold mine in Ecuador. He was multifaceted and would be supportive of what Karen truly wanted. In all the important ways, he was a really good father. Of course he tried to talk her out of moving away, but he knew ranting and raving and belittling her would not produce the effect he desired. He wanted her to stay and graduate high school, and then she could go explore. But he also saw too much of himself in his little girl, some of that same wildfire burning as a deep passion for knowledge and firsthand experience. He would miss her terribly, but he loved her and would let her go. All of which led to the million-dollar question: where, exactly, did his 16-year-old daughter plan to move to, with no money, job, or income?

"New Orleans," she said casually, smiling, saying it as if they were back at the duplex near the beach, and she was popping down to Curly's to buy him a pack of Pall Malls.

FIVE

The Big Easy

NEW ORLEANS WAS A HUMID HOTBED, a subtropical entrepôt and architectural amalgam of funky weirdness, fantastic foods, and crystal beauty from the pages of some wonderful fantasy tome. She was 16, she was bulletproof, and that was a good thing, because this experiment started horribly and then hit its nadir before the voodoo hold of the place spawned actual magic.

Studying the scribbled directions and walking water-reflective streets, Karen Sommerstedt noticed the way the light was different, diffused through rain-scrubbed air that turned to thick humid haze that made her forehead drip. The heft of her suitcase sent a dull throb into her shoulder. The tears from her first lover's flat-out rejection and humiliation intermittently blurred her vision.

What are YOU doing here?

The details didn't matter. She had scrimped together the airfare, made her movie-style surprise appearance, and been summarily sent away from his doorstep. *What a dumb schoolgirl move*, she thought. He had been her first boyfriend and intimate partner, both of which she had misread as something more. He was done with high school, with California, with *her*, and wanted a clean break to start college here at Tulane University. There was no *her* here, only a wide pipeline flowing with beer and smiling Southern-belle coeds. Although Karen had woefully miscalculated the tenor of things, she was equally resolute in her determination to see this through—whatever "this" was to be now—and not go running scared back to her dad. Except she *was* scared, and alone, and slogging past old carriage houses without any sort of plan. A busker blew a tenor saxophone and threw a hardened wink that made Karen want to abandon her determination and *run* all the way to the airport for the next flight to California. Instead she steeled herself in a dark city crevasse, between two cool brick walls rubbed wax-smooth after 230 years of offering refuge and harboring fears such as hers. She stood there and she cried.

"I was devastated by what had happened, but I had way too much pride to go home," she recalled. "I was really sad. But I was already pretty good as a traveler and embraced the change. Even though I was heartbroken, I was enthralled by the city. Of course, moneywise I didn't have a clue as to how I would make it."

Right there in that darkened, humid slot, Karen started to formulate her plan. Wiping away tears, she resolved to stay: going home was not an option. She had too much pride for that. With that stance solidified, next on the list was to find shelter. The now ex-boyfriend had given her a piece of paper with the name and address of a cheap flophouse scribbled in pencil: she'd find the place and stay there tonight.

At least partially steadied, she emerged from the city canyon, plunked down fifteen cents, and took a streetcar. What she saw and smelled and heard was pure N'awlins, a funky, funky town in the 1970s. The streetcar rolled past restaurants wafting baked oysters with garlic and other local specialties. Karen encountered the smells before she knew the names: sizzling hot beignets dusted with powdered sugar and served with café au lait, the hometown blend of coffee and chicory. Po'boy sandwiches and Italian muffulettas; boiled crawfish, étouffée, jambalaya, gumbo, and red beans and rice.

The smells mirrored the architecture, a historic blend of cultures, styles, and rich uniqueness. The streetcar passed Creole cottages and American townhouses, double-gallery houses, and raised center-hall cottages. Sprawling European-style Catholic cemeteries conjured the memory of baby Kathleen. There was ethnicity, too, more African Americans in one city block than Karen had seen, collectively, her entire life. The distinction, too, between white and black was a hard line drawn down streets. Karen found that puzzling; she had been taught by her dad to embrace all people. Segregation seemed an unnecessary oddity. There were no overt Whites Only postings, but the delineation glowed neon-strong in the invisible subtext everywhere she went. From her streetcar seat, Karen was getting it all, a firsthand view of the most important strategic trading hub and distribution center for waterborne commerce along the Gulf of Mexico.

When she eventually disembarked and found her quarters for the night, she collapsed on the sidewalk and cried again because the place looked awful. Once inside her room, she fell to dirty linoleum and cried more. The room was three dollars a night for good reason: she had opened the door with a heavy skeleton key and first saw the thin mattress sitting barely off the floor. The only other furniture was a small table with a hot plate and two mismatched chairs. The one small window sported a tattered "curtain" that was just a torn piece of dirty cloth nailed directly to the wall. Just one floor above the street, the superfly thump, vibe, and sugared swirls poured through the open window, inseparable from the heat and humidity, and reminded Karen how far, far away she had traveled from her familiar home. It was a long, lonely first night in New Orleans, with lunatic flashes playing out in neon across dingy walls.

DAYS later, Karen lied about her age and got a job at a local yogurt shop Humphrey Yogart. She was able to move from the carnival-scary flophouse into a marginally better apartment in an equally bad neighborhood. She intuited, without incident, that she probably should not be walking these streets alone at noon on a bright day, much less after dark. But nothing bad happened as she soaked in the atmosphere.

Two months later she got a pay bump by getting a job at Tape City USA in uptown New Orleans. She rode the streetcar from her apartment to work and, as she had at the yogurt shop, lied about her age to get the job. Because she had applied for a cashier position, the employer informed her that she'd have to take a polygraph test to ensure her trustworthiness. The polygraph test was a nerve-wracking affair for the 16-year-old hiding her big lie. Rick Stanfield was the polygrapher who administered the test. Karen had to admit that, although Rick was older, he was easy on a girl's eyes. Eventually, as she knew it would, the question came up.

"Did you lie about anything on your application?"

Whether it was Rick's dreamy eyes and easy way, or that she feared her secret would immediately doom her chances, she lied again: "No."

Rick studied the machine and then Karen, making marks on the scrolling paper with his pen. Later, he circled back and asked again whether she had lied about anything on the application. Again, Karen said she had not. Rick pressed her; she passed off any electronic aberration he might be reading as something else. Rick passed her, authorized her for the job, and then asked her out on a date.

Rick had a master's degree in psychology and had worked in state hospital wards. He told Karen amazing patient stories. She was able to confide in him, about her own struggles with her mom and her ill-fated trip to this city, chasing a boy across the country and getting dumped. For 1970s New Orleans, Rick was a flat-out square who was not hip to the vibe. He did not partake of drugs in a time and city submerged in mind-altering possibilities.

"From the age of 10 my dad had drilled into me how bad drugs are for mind and body," Karen said. So that was a good fit. What was less of a fit, and unspoken, was the age difference, and the fact that Karen was underage. Rick had no idea of her age when they moved in together, and Karen was 16 going on 25. Eventually she told him, which was scary because he was her only anchor in a new city. Rick was initially shocked because Karen carried herself so well. But in the freewheeling '70s, in the anything-goes port city, the age difference did not torpedo the relationship. Today it might land him on a sex-offender registry; in 1970s New Orleans it was the "Love the One You're With" way of the times. They stayed together for most of the year she would spend in New Orleans.

"New Orleans to me was magic," said Karen. "So different from what I had grown up with. It was my first experience of racial tension. I was brought up that we embrace all races and all people. I'd never been exposed to such segregation. It was a crazy social awakening. There were horse-drawn carriages and Mardi Gras. Men in drag at The Most Beautiful Guys strip club. There was so much diversity. People I worked with and my friends were different than people in California or Oregon. With all the craziness, there was also this conservative Southern mentality. I loved it there: the ambience, architecture, and streetcars. If I hadn't lived it, I wouldn't believe it."

As Karen carved out a new daily routine, her contact with her father and mother was minimal. She saw herself as 25 and fully capable of keeping herself safe. Besides, Karen was having fun working and being on her own with her new social circle that revolved around Tape City USA. The store was a large outfit that sold LPs, cassette tapes, and the latest and greatest stereo equipment at the back of the store. A woman named Patty Ballard was the owner and entrusted Chuck, Karen's boss, to run the store. Chuck had a good sense of humor and was a nice Southern gentleman who invited Karen out with him and his girlfriend. Rod Morris, from Philadelphia, worked there, too, and a guy from New York everyone knew only as Audio because he was into the latest high-fidelity sound equipment. The store's biggest competition was New Attitude, which the Tape City USA faithful dubbed "Bad Attitude." The big sellers of the day: Kool and the Gang, Chaka Khan, Earth, Wind & Fire, the Commodores, and Donna Summer.

"I was just a sponge taking in all the newness," said Karen. "I was completely on my own earning a living." She was discovering music, too: jazz artists Gato Barbieri and Al Jarreau. Audio turned her on to a slew of other groups: ABBA, Bee Gees, Blondie, Crystal Gayle, Genesis, KC and the Sunshine Band, and Emerson, Lake & Palmer. She especially liked Supertramp, with "Take the Long Way Home" resonating in a profound way for her. Place was her home—not the other way around—a revolving set of doors dropping her into new worlds whenever she chose to step out.

If Karen Sommerstedt was heartbroken over her first boyfriend initially, which she was, she quickly moved past the hurt through necessity and resiliency.

New Orleans, at 16 with no job, was brass-knuckles gutsy, the kind of adrenaline dump she would encounter later during midair stalls. Freefall in the silence, unsnapped in every direction, then sparking power and finding skyward thrust. The girl was born to fly, and fly she would.

Eventually she had a falling out with Rick and moved across town to live with a lady named Vi Hayes, whom she had met at Tape City USA. Shortly thereafter Karen got a second job working at a wedding gown preservation business, which would be her last post in the Big Easy.

By then it was March 1980. Like some crazy funhouse-mirror rite of passage, Karen had survived the bad voodoo, endured, and then grabbed special magic to thrive in New Orleans. She had proved to herself and her father that she could, indeed, make it on her own. But her sense of place was shifting again, and the siren call she was hearing, at 17, was emanating from the west, where the vast continent tumbled back into the sea. She had chased a boy halfway across the country; now she was moving forward with a sense of self and adult independence that had deepened even more since her magical time in the Oregon woods.

As the airplane descended toward LAX, Karen saw, in flashback, an almost silly schoolgirl pining for Gus that long-ago New Year's Day, the epicenter of her universe dwelling in those amazing watery-brown eyes. She pondered baby Kathleen for the first time since she'd seen a massive cemetery her first day on the New Orleans streetcar. She thought about her mother and whether she would recognize her grown eldest daughter.

When her father picked her up at the airport, there was an immediate and overwhelming rush of welcome relief. A valve was released she had not realized was closed off, and Karen could finally exhale. She had done her solo year of exploration, but the steadying hand of a loving parent—her smart, crazy, fun, wonderful dad—imbued an immediate warmth and sense of comforting security Karen had missed more than she wanted to admit. Her dad, meanwhile, did not disappoint, immediately regaling her with lightning-fast and fascinating stories about his continued work on the *Alaska* musical production, which came with a growing and immediate urgency to head there himself, to more fully round out the final pages.

Karen smiled: barely back in California, her place was already shifting again. The revolving doors spun and offered new possibilities. This news was serendipitous because she had feared stepping off the airplane and back into the apartment on Robbins Drive, where the drugs and plastic sensibilities of Beverly Hills might choke off her air. The last frontier, indeed, was exactly what she needed after the seedy grittiness and jambalaya kaleidoscope of southern American streets.

Her father laid out the plan as he drove: they would stop in Seattle and then continue north for two weeks in Alaska. After that, he had a love interest awaiting their arrival, he said mysteriously, "in an archipelago created by hot-spot volcanism forty million years ago." The epoch did not register as immediately relevant to the returning girl, but it was in fact the original time spool creating worlds, pushing up solidified rock, and now spinning down to the last strand of the forthcoming thirty-one years. Forty million years to bring everything forth, the place already formed. The young girl's heart was strong, but not yet strong enough to endure what her life and time would one day reveal in a flash atop a mountain.

Karen's father liked to do that—say things in an intriguing way that immediately piqued her interest. Where were they going? He continued: they would be visiting and exploring an area of 132 islands, plus atolls, reefs, shallow banks, shoals, and seamounts spanning 1,500 miles, southeast to northwest, in the middle of an ocean. When the Pacific Plate had shifted over a hot spot below, that plate changed direction and these islands and submerged seamounts pushed up from the depths: the Hawaiian-Emperor chain.

"You mean Hawai'i?" Karen asked.

"That's exactly what I mean," he said, nodding.

But before arriving at this volcanic upthrust, Karen and her father first were to bear witness to another immense example of geologic time and pressure. On May 18, 1980, at 8:32 a.m. local time, they were en route to Karen's new life, flying above the mountain known as Lawetlat'la in the Cascade Volcanic Arc, a segment of the Pacific Ring of Fire teeming with active volcanoes. It was no coincidence that she was there at this historic moment, in an airplane defying gravity, directly above the loaded charge when the massive and historic ash explosion poured from a hole in Mount St. Helens. The pilot even changed course to provide a better view of the once-in-a-lifetime event.

The stratovolcano blast was ninety-six miles south of Seattle, Washington, which they had just departed, and fifty miles northeast of Portland, Oregon, near where Karen had come of age in the misty woods around Sheridan. Now she was witness to the actual formation of place, an extreme rarity in a human lifetime, like watching those submerged seamounts push up from the murky depths to form an island paradise.

From her window seat, with her forehead pressed against icy plastic, the fury below was silent, masked by elevation and the steady precision of jet engines pushing an aircraft. But what was happening down there was the exact opposite of serene calm. The ripple effect of the unleashed energy was catastrophic and deadly destruction: fifty-seven people killed, 250 homes and forty-seven bridges evaporated, fifteen miles of railroad ripped away, and 185 miles of US highway obliterated. The massive eruption blew off the top 1,300 feet of the mountain, leaving a mile-wide horseshoe crater. Better known by its English name, from a British diplomat and lord who was a friend of the explorer who surveyed the area in the late 1700s, Mount St. Helens was evolving as it had for forty million years.

Karen Sommerstedt was, literally, watching the formation of place as her own metamorphosis tracked forward, LAX, PDX, and MSY already in her past, her course now firmly fixed on the next place in her timeline: HNL. Spin the revolving doors and step out to the moment she would move fore, take her position in the left-front seat for the first time, and watch her innate life passion and career come to fruition.

Six

Island Girl

KAREN SOMMERSTEDT FELL IN LOVE with Hawai'i. The land and sea were bathed in watery light, with the fragrance of flowers carried along by steady temperate breezes. Unlike many mainlanders, she immediately bonded with the locals, too, and avoided the notorious cliques accessible only to island natives. Well, for the most part—minus a certain subculture she would soon encounter amid thousands of eggs, stacked high and deep.

She and her father rented a two-bedroom condominium on O'ahu's North Shore in Punaluu. There was a restaurant nearby with a bar that featured live music every night, where Karen struck up friendships with two of the musicians in the band. Soon Karen and her father were staying at his girlfriend Jane Ruhl's house in Hawaii Kai. Ruhl taught fifth grade at Aliiolani Elementary School, and she and Karen got along famously. One month into their stay, Karen's father returned to California. But Karen had found her new place and made long-term arrangements to live at Ruhl's condominium. Just as Heather Horton and Caroline Eisle had been back in Redondo Beach, Ruhl—who didn't have children of her own—was another surrogate mom to Karen.

"She was very motherly toward me and watched out for me," Karen said.

In Hawai'i, Karen attempted a return to high school to get her diploma, but after Beverly Hills, the funkadelic New Orleans voyage, and all the emotional and experiential terrain she had covered, Karen was just too far removed from that narrow social strata. So instead, she went to work at the Rocky Road egg farm in Waimanalo. If the sultry ethnicity of the Gulf Coast port city had been a major cultural shift at 16, Rocky Road egg farm was equally enlightening.

As the only Caucasian, Karen got her first taste of native disdain for mainlanders. She was neither Asian, Hawaiian, nor Samoan, which every other employee was, so from day one she was stuck between those groups on her own lonely island of one. Karen could handle being ostracized; she had grown up on her own in Redondo Beach and navigated the Beverly Hills scene. And although her time and work in Oregon had toughened her up mentally and physically, the backbreaking toil of processing eggs was something that gave her pause: Could she keep up with the *titas*, Hawaiian slang for the local tough chicks? They were all built like Mack trucks, powerful and wide, and had personalities to match. The *moaks* were the male counterparts: hardcore locals with bulging arms, mean smiles, and cut T-shirts. Karen might have been in tropical paradise, but the immediate working environment was a foul-smelling and noisy departure from anything heavenly.

From Karen's first day, the Samoan girls had a betting pool on how long the cute, skinny white girl would last. One day? Two? There was no action on anything beyond one week. The hiring boss, too, had his doubts when he first saw Karen, who looked like she should be striking alluring poses on the beach for a bikini calendar, not doing bottom-rung grunt work with the locals.

"I convinced him," Karen said. "I had worked on a farm, and I assured him I could do that job."

The egg processing line included three different stations, which everyone worked in rotation. The first station was the entry point for thousands of eggs, stacked ridiculously high in dirty wooden crates. The operator at this station unloaded rack after racks of eggs onto the conveyor belt. The challenge here was all physical: the egg crates were heavy, which made it difficult to lift and move them repeatedly for hours without stopping.

The second station was for sorting and removing the unusable eggs: those covered with hardened feces and those with developing embryos. A bright light illuminated any suspect embryonic cargo within the eggs. The challenge at this station was more mental than physical: sitting and watching thousands of eggs roll by was hypnotizing, horrible duty.

The final station at the end of the twenty-five-foot conveyor belt was for stacking and packaging the usable eggs. The physical challenge at the end of the line was compounded by the speed of the conveyor belt—you had to really hustle to keep up. Otherwise, the eggs tumbled off the end of the belt and broke on the floor. Each of the employees worked two hours at a station, then got a short break, and then switched to a new station for the next two hours.

Lather, rinse, repeat.

Her coworkers all laughed and pointed at Karen when they saw her wearing gloves. Karen decided on the gloves the first time she saw cockroaches scrambling among the eggs. In fact, her coworkers laughed and pointed no matter what she did, or how well she did it. After surviving two weeks along the loud, stinky conveyor belt, Karen might have earned some grudging respect from her peers, but no one said anything. Finally, a month into it, the others gave up the betting pool because, for whatever reason, the skinny *haole* girl was still around. No one knew why or how she had hung in there. Nor did they care to ask. They had seen lots of bigger, stronger men and women leave inside of three days. So instead of wagering on Karen, at some point they just completely ignored her. Karen lasted six months, never missing an eight-hour shift.

From the egg farm she went to work at a nearby nursery that shipped orchids and other flowers around the world, a heaven-sent job change where the pleasing waft of fresh-cut flowers replaced the stench of chicken shit. After a year at the nursery, Karen became a secretary, first at a welding company and then at a travel agency owned by a Korean who, for some reason, screamed instead of talking at a normal volume: *Sa jang nim! Sa jang nim!* Karen always assumed she worked for a self-important man named Sa Jang Nim who liked to remind her of his name. It wasn't until years later some Korean friends at the airline told Karen what he was really yelling: *I am the boss!*

Karen was trying her hand at different jobs, looking for something that clicked. She was getting closer when she applied to work on a deep-sea-fishing charter boat, a post listed in the newspaper classifieds with, "Need capable first mate to work on boat. No experience necessary." As Karen approached the small vessel for her interview, a second girl was also walking up. This was Hawai'i, so no one expected interviewees to wear a business suit, pantyhose, and heels. But Karen didn't expect to see her competition in a transparent T-shirt, sans bra, with Bo Derek beads in her hair: the Bo Derek look-alike got the job. However, a week later the helmsman called Karen. The salty sea veteran was stamped from the same captain-cliché mold as Quint in the 1975 blockbuster *Jaws*.

"Guess what?" he asked.

Karen had no earthly idea.

"Well, I'll tell you what: she gets seasick."

Karen laughed: *serves you right, you dumb bastard.* The image was magical: Bo Derek, perky tits stretched against her tight T-shirt, draped port side as she sprayed her breakfast to the sea. Karen knew why the captain was calling another cute girl, and it wasn't because of any vast seafaring experience Karen might have offered. Sleazy boat captain aside, the notion and calling of travel was something she had to explore. She took the job and, well, it didn't take long for the old sleaze to confirm her worst fears. The captain, all-over slippery from sweat and few showers, leered and gawked more inside of a week than the front three rows of teenage girls at a Bay City Rollers concert. Although Karen quit after only a week, at 18 she had found the right field: travel.

THE *Rella Mae* was a large schooner that took happy travelers and made them happier with booze cruises off the coast of O'ahu. Nothing guaranteed well-being better in the early 1980s: the sun-splashed free flow of alcohol through bikini bodies and shirtless male torsos as the ship cut warm seas and churned a beautiful smooth V-trail of foam around paradise. In darkened corners during the booze cruise, giggling new acquaintances shed swimsuits and stamped their Sea Level Club membership cards. In 1981, Karen was a cocktail waitress aboard such a craft, which was owned by Windjammer Cruises. Six months later, when a ship engineer was goofing off and started squirting all his coworkers with a huge fire hose, everyone involved got fired. Karen had done nothing wrong except get drenched. While the job lasted, she had loved being on the ocean, and she began searching for a similar gig elsewhere.

In between jobs she was working part-time as a waterskiing instructor and landed a photo shoot for a French swimsuit magazine (she got to keep the swimsuits, but never saw the photos). Modeling just wasn't that inspiring or intriguing to Karen. She'd much rather be waterskiing behind a speedboat on the Wailua River, which was what she was doing when she corkscrewed her left ankle. She ended up with a big cast on her leg, a lifetime first.

"The crazy part is that it didn't stop me from waterskiing," she said. Her doctor was not happy about having to change the soggy cast several times. Karen worked briefly for the father of Mike Suyderhoud, a 1977 world champion in waterskiing who had been featured on ABC's *Wide World of Sports* and in a Wheaties commercial. His father had a waterskiing shop in Hawaii Kai.

Around this same time, during one of her regular checkups, the gynecologist diagnosed Karen with endometriosis. She would have several laparoscopic procedures, also known as minimally invasive surgery, over the next few years in an attempt to ease the severe pain the condition caused her every month during menstruation. She learned too that, according to the gynecologist, she would likely never have children. This was devastating news for a young woman who eventually wanted a family of her own.

In 1982, Karen noticed a classified advertisement for a larger cruise ship operation, American Hawaii Cruises, that was hiring ten cocktail waitresses. When Karen arrived, she found hundreds of young women vying for the limited slots. With a legal drinking age of 18 in Hawai'i, Karen made the cut. But that, along with her good looks, was about the end of her qualifications. When one of the two men interviewing her asked her to recite the proper call order for drinks, Karen could only hesitate and then guess.

"You don't have any idea, do you?" one of the men asked.

"No."

"How about if I ordered a neat drink?" the other said.

"Well," Karen said, searching for her bluff, "that would be super-duper?" She smiled and offered a thumbs-up. This got a laugh and smile from both interviewers.

"That's no ice or mixer, just a straight pour," he said.

"Of course," Karen said. "Neat: no ice or mixer, just a straight pour. See, I'm a quick learner."

Out of the thousand or so applicants, Karen was one of the ten women hired as a cocktail waitress. Karen was more interested in hands-on sailing and the mechanical aspects of ships, but women were not allowed in any of the deck or steward jobs. But even as a cocktail waitress, she had to attend the Harry Lundeberg School of Seamanship, with her 350 new-hire classmates, for six weeks in Piney Point, Maryland. The group took a flight to Dulles (IAD) in Virginia near Washington, DC, and then a bus north to Maryland.

Seamanship school was like a military school for firefighters that crammed two years of college course work into six weeks. They learned how to survive a ship fire and evacuate people from the ship. They performed extinguishing exercises with live fires burning.

"The first time, I ran into the fire and ran back out," she said. "It was a very intense school."

There were written tests every day and stern-eyed US Coast Guard observers watching the trainees constantly. The final examination included launching lifeboats, with passengers, from the ship into the water. The training seemed a bit excessive for serving gin-and-tonics, but Karen had to be sea- and ship-worthy. When she made the cut, Karen was thrilled with the extensive training she could now list on her résumé. She had her merchant mariner license and lifeboat ticket, with the title of ordinary seaman.

American Hawaii Cruises had two ships sailing opposite routes around the islands: the newer SS *Constitution* and the SS *Independence*. Karen started in June 1982 and worked seven days a week as, officially, a deck lounge stewardess, which is fancy maritime terminology for cocktail waitress.

With Karen's place evolving again, the cruise ship itself became mother to the crew. Most crew worked alternating twelve-hour shifts, seven days a week, which meant no rent or grocery costs. They lived and worked on the ship, and the ship housed and fed them. For the first year Karen worked in the discothèque, with its heavy bass thump and spinning mirrored ball.

"It was a good place for me to be," Karen said.

When Karen moved to a better location in the Starlight Lounge, her shift ran from 6 p.m. to 2 a.m. That meant, after grabbing some sleep after work, Karen had her days free to wander the ship's decks and explore the islands at landfall. She had no car, no housing or food costs, and few other fixed expenses. Her workplace was a beautiful cruise ship, and she was getting paid to explore the islands. During one record stint, she lived and worked on the ship for seven straight months without sleeping on land. In fact, after a time, it was difficult to sleep without the rocking motion of the ship. She was even offered an officer's position, which would have meant moving from her modest bunk room in the ship's darkened bowels to much better living quarters, bathed in natural light, several decks up. But the officer position paid less than she was earning, because tip money flowed easily from the pockets, wallets, and purses of inebriated vacationers on island cruises. Karen pragmatically stayed in her waitressing post and continued counting her nice stacks of cash.

During this same time, Karen had been tagging along for island flights in a small aircraft. One of the ship's officers had his pilot license and offered up stunning views of the islands from a Piper Warrior. Each time Karen went up she relayed her fascination with aircraft and retold the story about the Ducati rides to school, eyes closed in hopes her dad would forget again and take her all the way to LAX. Each time the story took her back … the oily fragrance and vast array of gleaming craft … the metal thunder of air-breathing turbofans at full thrust. Finally, a fellow crew member who had heard Karen's reminiscences one too many times turned, looked at Karen, and said, "Why don't you stop *talking* about it and just go do it?"

Karen shook herself from her reverie: her friend had a point. Then she smiled and nodded. Yes, indeed, it was time to take her first official discovery flight up and around Honolulu. The next day she booked it, for December 11, 1982. She was 19, and her life would never be the same after her first taste of piloting a Cessna 152. Aviation would become her new life and, eventually, would also take the life she knew.

FLEDGLING Ozark Air Lines, founded in September 1943 in Springfield, Missouri, began its earliest flights in January 1945 with short runs between Springfield and St. Louis in Beech 17 Staggerwings and later in Cessna AT-17 Bobcats. The slogan "Go-Getters Go Ozark" was their battle cry of the 1960s. Then "We make it easy for you" in the 1970s, and "Ozark flies your way," into the decade when Karen was signing up for pilot training in Hawai'i.

Routes expanded, including adding St. Louis to Chicago, and by 1955—when Walt Disney was setting up shop in Karen Sommerstedt's hometown of Anaheim—Ozark had a fleet of thirteen Douglas DC-3s flying to thirty-five Midwest cities from its hub at Lambert-St. Louis Airport (STL). By 1980, the fleet had grown to include thirteen Fairchild Hiller FH-227Bs, seven Douglas DC-9-10s, and thirty-three Douglas DC-9-31/32s. Karen first applied to Hawaiian Air in 1984, when she finally turned 21 and was eligible. Then she applied to Ozark Air Lines, crossed her fingers, and waited. Since her discovery flight two years earlier, her lifelong fascination with aviation had blossomed into a full-blown passion.

While she continued working on the cruise ship, she had officially started her pilot training in January 1983. One of her early instructors was Barbara Scimeca, a petite aviator in her early thirties who led by example as a female role model. Her instructions to Karen during those early lessons were always firm, specific, and continually reassuring: "Keep the nose of the airplane on the horizon. Good. Pull back a little more on the yoke. Scan for traffic. Always fly the airplane first. Pitch, power, and airspeed."

Because Karen's days off varied, she worked through flight school depending on which port city her cruise-ship home had landed at the night before. That meant that, rather than a single instructor, she had numerous people showing her how to become a pilot. One of her favorites was Al Merrill, now a captain for Southwest Airlines. He was young and fun and hailed from an aviation family that owned Anuenue Aviation, a flight school in Hilo. Another influential instructor was Art Emery, who signed her off to take her private-pilot check ride. Having multiple instructors gave Karen a unique introduction to aviation, as she was able to absorb varying viewpoints, techniques, and philosophies. During one flight lesson, instructor Dave Osman, out of Maui, asked her how serious she was about becoming a commercial pilot.

"I'm very serious," she said.

"I would like to see you continue because you have a lot of talent," the instructor said. And then he relayed the reality of a woman attempting to enter what is still primarily the domain of males: "It would be easier for you to become a brain surgeon."

Karen nodded and smiled, and the memories tumbled randomly through her mind: baby Kathleen, her wayward mother, and her nose pressed against the cool leather of her dad's shoulder. The cold, dingy linoleum in a neon-washed New Orleans room rented for three dollars a day. Tape City USA, and the shoulder burn of churning butter by hand. The vacant stares and evil slant of mouths at Rocky Road egg farm in Waimanalo. Karen nodded and said, "I'm up for the challenge."

As she studied at flight school, she signed up for a GED course on Kaua'i. A pleasant retired university professor with creeping tangles of ear hair and a PhD taught the course on Thursday and Friday nights. Karen studied hard and passed the test on her first attempt. Meanwhile, because she did not have unlimited funds, her flight training was going to have to stretch out, commensurate with her ability to pay the steep fees. There were other challenges, too.

"Reflecting on my early flight training, as enjoyable as it was, I also had strong feelings of fear that I had to overcome," Karen said. "This is perhaps easier to do in one's youth."

Her fear was reasonable and consistent with the reality of her new chosen passion. On December 20, 1983, Ozark Air Lines Flight 650 struck a snowplow while landing at Sioux Falls Regional Airport (FSD). The McDonnell Douglas DC-9-31 killed the driver of the snowplow, but none of the crew or passengers suffered injury. In plane versus snowplow, plane usually won. But on every machine she was on that left the earth's surface, Karen would be battling an ever-looming heavyweight opponent with a string of knockouts against airplanes: gravity.

"I do remember throughout my flight training one thing that was always fascinating to me was aircraft accidents, and everything about them: when they happened, how they happened, and most important, why they happened," she said.

So serious was her interest in crashes that Karen began considering applying for a job with the National Transportation Safety Board as an aviation accident investigator. Each time a major crash occurred, Karen studied the accident reports, unpeeling them piece by piece. She always wondered how such a terrible fate could bestow itself on the lover of aviation in the cockpit, those aboard, and their families. Like a twisted horror novel, accident reports guaranteed reading that was equally macabre and intriguing to an aviation student who wanted to learn from others' mistakes. Over the years, as Karen's friendships in the aviation community grew, she would experience people she knew dying doing what they all collectively loved. It would happen again and again. But at that moment, those realities had not yet crystallized, and she was anodized against fate—hot-rolled, tempered sheet steel, like the resolute girl slogging alone through clawing southern mist: bulletproof.

To be a successful pilot, Karen was able to compartmentalize thoughts of crashing. Flying, like almost anything in life, was a managed risk, and as safe as the person making the decisions. She quickly learned that good judgment and critical decision-making skills were a big part of returning home safely. Obviously things could happen in and around airborne machines that would be completely out of her control, but those mishaps and crashes were the smallest percentage. She started to see that pilots were, generally, straight-up control freaks, which was a suitable mindset for the cockpit but not always the best in personal relationships. In other words, a little obsessive-compulsive disorder in the cockpit—checking and rechecking the flap position and then checking two more times ... and then once more—was not a bad trait. And while crashing was always at least a possibility in the back of the young pilot's mind, Karen still felt safer flying her airplane than in her car surrounded by distracted drivers with little training in the metal machines that daily produced horrific carnage.

After Karen had accumulated the required flight hours, her instructor one day rolled the airplane to a stop on the tarmac on the Big Island of Hawai'i, turned to Karen, and smiled before saying, "Now you're going to go off by yourself."

Had Karen's heart just skipped a beat with excitement? This was the moment, July 25, 1983, another rite of passage for every pilot, her first solo flight from General Lyman Field in Hilo. Karen shifted in her seat; she was thrilled, but did not think she was ready.

"I was nervous as hell," she would later recall. But as she always had, she pushed through her fear and, literally, took the controls. She reran the preflight checklist inside the cockpit, with a visual flow scan of the myriad dials, knobs, buttons, and switches: left to right, top to bottom. They had already done the formal preflight as well as the same on the exterior. This was a 1980s aircraft, so she was looking at traditional steam gauges, those with needles that moved, in the days before electronic readouts. What had first appeared as a nonsensical blur of gadgetry now had a uniform flow and meaning to Karen. Every aircraft she had flown, and each of the more than 30 makes and models she would one day fly, had some variation of the six basic gauges: indicators for airspeed (the speedometer in nautical miles); attitude (indicates pitch and bank); heading (what direction); vertical speed (the rate of climb or descent in feet per minute); an altimeter (how high); and a turn coordinator (the rate of a turn and amount of centrifugal force). There was also a throttle, with a tachometer to show power, and fuel mixture control knob.

In a deft tactile dance of her feet, the aircraft gently rolled to a stop at the run-up area for a final preflight power check. With her feet firmly holding the aircraft in place, she pushed the throttle control as the roar of wind deepened in a stentorian crescendo that vibrated through Karen's body. Satisfied that the engine was flight-worthy, she pulled the power back down.

She double-checked her seat belt clasp and adjusted her headset. The automated terminal information system (ATIS) was broadcasting into Karen's headset including wind speed, approach, takeoff, and runway updates. She broadcast, "Hilo tower, seven five seven, romeo hotel, with information bravo. Staying in pattern, for touch and go's, first solo."

"Seven romeo hotel, cleared for touch and go's, runway two six."

Karen lifted her feet, and taxied to the thick stripe of paint marking her start point for takeoff. She could already feel her heartbeat quickening. Her throat had gone dry, and her palms glistened with the adrenaline push of what was about to happen. With her heart pumping hard, she stared down the straight shot of bleached runway disappearing into a V-apex.

With the engine already humming and the propeller spinning, Karen's toes were pointed on the top portion of the rudder pedals, which held the plane motionless and also connected back to, and controlled, the rudders. As she released her toes from the brakes and advanced the throttle to full power by pushing in the black lever, the sun-glazed Cessna 152 started rolling along completely under her control. Light touches with her feet moved the control linkage at the nosewheel and kept the airplane on the white centerline on the hot, faded hardscape. Unlike anything she had ever experienced, the moment bathed her in an energized buzz of euphoria and serene calm: the white-noise static in her headset, the light bounce of the aircraft's tires over cracks in the tarmac, the comforting whirl from the blurred propeller.

Sheathed in her riveted aluminum skin two hundred thousand years in the making, using solely her mind, feet, and hands, Karen Sommerstedt controlled a machine capable of flight. Karen scanned each of the large dials and corresponding needles, in the flash of seconds, making sure each indicated what she wanted.

Now any cognitive recognition of her heartbeat gave way to a pervasive calm as she focused and rumbled down the long and wide slab. The ghost mantra, *Here we go*, flashed through her mind as the airspeed indicator needle vibrated toward 60 knots, the magical moment when the immense force of gravity began to lose its grip on the rubber tires. As the anchoring pull of that force splintered and then disintegrated altogether, the dense molecules in the undercarriage of tubular steel legs expanded like a billion tiny balloons being pumped with air. Each takeoff and landing added another such microscopic tear to the stress-fracture timeline of tempered steel under duress in the extremes of aviation: constant heat and rigid cold and descending weight loads that could eventually fracture and snap precision-machined parts.

At that moment the small nosewheel lifted from the runway, followed almost immediately by the main wheels, everything was a speeding blur of land falling away and underneath the rising aircraft in a perfect takeoff roll. Karen checked airspeed and moved the flap lever, which, outside in the wind-whipped atmosphere, raised the single-slotted flaps to the neutral position. Now there was no separation between the warm pocket of island air and Karen Sommerstedt, wrapped in a human marvel as the thrill of the adrenaline boost bolted through her body: she was flying! Alone. First solo.

Flying. *Oh my God!*

It was the moment all pilots knew, and the sensation she enthusiastically chased, discussed, studied, anticipated, and repeated thousands of times.

"I realized I was on my own," she said, recalling that beautiful space of first flight. The instructor had told her to perform three touch-and-go's by herself, which used every skill she had ever learned.

"As you come in, your airplane and flaps are configured for landing," she said. "Then to take off you have to reconfigure everything: air speed, attitude, and heading. I don't think anything in flying came naturally to me."

Karen had to study hard to learn the fine relationships between pitch, power, airspeed, and how to read and mentally compute all that from the instruments. She was learning, too, at the very busy Honolulu International Airport (HNL) and other smaller island airports. She became adept at reading and trusting the altimeter, the airspeed indicator (displayed in knots), and the heading indicator. She studied aerodynamics, weather, regulations, and airplane systems. She performed dozens of standard GUMP checks, in a pursuit full of acronyms: gas, undercarriage, mixture, and prop. She adopted the mantra and ordered template of flying: *aviate, navigate, communicate.* She followed her instructors' early admonishments.

Flaps up.
Gear up.
Sit up, shut up.
And don't touch anything red!

Now she had completed her first solo flight. Karen, prepared, had worn two shirts for the traditional aviation rite of passage. This occurs once parked safely back at the hangar and off the aircraft, when the instructor rips off the pilot's shirt. But because she was female, the instructor instead dumped a bucket of cold water on her head.

Then, after all the anxious waiting, Karen got a call: a job offer to be a flight attendant with Ozark Air Lines. Although the cruise ship company was opening a new route around Tahiti, Karen sensed it was time to go all-in and trade her sea legs for wings. It was 1984, and she quit her deck lounge stewardess position with American Hawaii Cruises and accepted the Ozark Air Lines job. She took a flight to St. Louis, Missouri, for an intense six weeks of training. Once completed, the airline furloughed her entire class. That meant she was qualified and ready, but had to wait for an open slot. Meanwhile, she had put out applications elsewhere, too, including Western Airlines. Just back from St. Louis, she walked into Jane Ruhl's house after six weeks and a long flight back to the islands as the phone was ringing. Karen answered: it was a hiring manager at Western Airlines, who said, "We want you to come to L.A. for an interview." Karen was on a flight back to Los Angeles the next day.

KAREN'S new chosen industry had an old adage, inside joke, and consistent truism about how to make a million dollars in aviation: start with two million. Ever since December 17, 1903, when Wilbur and Orville Wright made those four brief flights in a powered aircraft, men and women of every stripe—aviators, barnstormers, corporate moguls, entrepreneurs, hopeless romantics, and industry tycoons—have been trying to unravel the secret formula to running a profitable airline. Those efforts left a wake of untold carnage, of mergers, acquisitions, spinoffs, brand-name variations, and liquidations unlike any other industry, all of which continues to modern day, with only a handful of major US airlines left standing and operating on razor-thin margins.

By 1984, Karen's prospective new employer had an industry-standard history, which meant rich, zany, and tumultuous, that began in 1926 when goggled aviators, with sun-blistered leather helmets and rippling white scarves, made eight-hour flights in Douglas M-2 biplanes for Western Air Express. Those hearty open-air jaunts, between Salt Lake City and Los Angeles, were under contract with the United States Postal Service to carry airmail. The biplanes buzzed along at 80 miles an hour, which is why it took so long to cover 650 miles. One month after the first mail cargo flight, Western Air Express began offering passenger services on April 17, 1926. In 1928, company leaders reincorporated as Western Air Express Corporation and, by the 1950s, were operating at nearly forty airports as Western Airlines.

The company entered the jet age in 1960 with the introduction of a Boeing 707 and flights between Los Angeles, San Francisco, Portland, and Seattle. It was during this era that an advertising slogan for Western Airlines took hold and became embedded in popular culture. Spoken by the animated Wally bird grabbing a ride aboard a Western fuselage, veteran actor and voice talent Shepard Menken exclaimed, "Western Airlines—the o-o-o-nly way to fly!" Business peaked in the 1970s and early 1980s, just as a new flight attendant arrived from Hawai'i for her job interview in Los Angeles. But the days of Western Airlines were numbered, and by 1987 that brand would not exist, ending a sixty-one-year history aloft.

BACK on that bright California day in 1984, Karen Sommerstedt found herself in a large hotel conference room near the airport (LAX) that had first kindled her passion for flying. Although she could not smell the succulent citrus, she could envision the curled labels on the wooden crates and the way the Balboa Barony paper cracked off in her fingers. Likewise, the foamed churn of Redondo Beach was now only a wistful schoolgirl memory. But neither mattered: she was home. Everywhere she went, the place followed.

She was perched at the back of her dad's Ducati again and racing to her future through air so clean and cool and fresh it made her head buzz. The free-spirited New Orleans girl had become a woman, and the woman walked with steady purpose in a white linen blouse, form-fitting navy skirt, dark pantyhose, and ankle-killer pumps. She had stopped in the airport restroom to smooth her blonde coif, touch up her makeup, and roll on a fresh coat of red lipstick. She paused, assessed her overall effect, and sighed as the resigned reality hit her again. Although she herself was now capable of piloting aircraft, this interview was for a job on the other side of that golden cockpit door, back in the steerage with the huddled masses of humanity and the other eye-candy flight attendants. The 1980s was an agonizingly slow decade of transition, so while the job was no longer officially the all-female, gratuitous T-and-A insult of the 1960s, the airlines still were not verifying SAT scores or requiring Mensa membership for prospective flight attendants. Size still mattered, as in big boobs, small waist, and small number on the scale. Karen sighed again: would there really be a scale involved in the hiring process? She had her answer almost immediately.

In the carpeted conference room with a thirty-foot ceiling, a hundred or so women—and some men—were gathered for the first indignity of becoming a flight attendant in 1984: stepping on the scale. No one outwardly questioned the practice as they all lined up to be measured and weighed. Karen recalled the 4-H contests she'd participated in during her time in Sheridan, Oregon, and suddenly felt oddly like one of those voiceless farm animals being silently judged, solely by shape and girth. Any person who was above the designated number for height/weight ratio—even by one pound—was eliminated before anyone had bothered to ask a meaningful question.

Thank you very much. Next!

As a skinny girl who had done some amateur modeling, Karen suspected she would meet the aesthetic and maximum girth standards. Nonetheless, it angered her that she and the other applicants were being screened in such a ridiculous and demeaning way. To join Western Airlines, flight attendants had to be at least five feet two inches tall but could not be taller than six feet. Along with the weight-maximum figures there was a minimum of one hundred pounds, with a monthly weigh-in to monitor whether the flight attendants were still "qualified" as employees, which included the basic physical prowess and mobility to efficiently evacuate an aircraft under duress.

At just five feet three inches, Karen's battle was meeting the minimum weight of one hundred pounds. On the hiring day, it did occur to her to ask whether they'd weigh her again before she one day became a pilot, because she knew they sure as hell weren't weighing the men in the cockpit. A short walk through any concourse at any airport confirmed as much: numerous plump pilots waddling along.

After being weighed, Karen underwent a series of six interviews. In June 1984, she was hired as a flight attendant with Western Airlines. To meet her minimum weight requirement of one hundred pounds, Karen decided she'd wear ankle weights hidden under each pant leg just to be sure. The next burning question: Where would she be based? The answer was an eye-opener worse than any cattle-call weigh-in.

Karen was born under California sunshine, spent a year in steamy New Orleans, and currently lived in Hawai'i. She had barely seen snow in Oregon, had never driven a car on icy roads, and now the revolving doors were spinning her off into a strange frozen place: Salt Lake City, Utah.

Seven

Aviator

THE GREAT SALT LAKE, a remnant of the Pleistocene Epoch and Lake Bonneville, a nine-hundred-foot-deep inland sea that once immersed much of present-day Utah, gave today's modern Salt Lake City its name. Founded in 1847 by Brigham Young and other Mormon devotees, this place nestled along the Wasatch Range, which unofficially delineated the western edge of the greater Rocky Mountains and the eastern edge of the Great Basin region, had the "Great" dropped from its name nineteen years later by the territorial legislature. From the moment she arrived in 1984, Karen Sommerstedt was in full agreement with the early government's foresight in removing any positive adjective from the moniker: Salt Lake City was no Honolulu, Sheridan, Redondo Beach, or Anaheim. It wasn't even a mattress on a dirty linoleum floor in a cheap New Orleans flophouse. Salt Lake City was no place for a California island girl.

"I just remember I cried a lot," she recalled.

The most brutal new reality was winter weather, which meant the hard slog of scraping car windows, perpetual black ice and snow, and bone-chilling temperatures Karen had heard about but never experienced firsthand. *So that's what nine degrees feels like on your face.*

Socially, as a 21-year-old, single, independent woman, she might as well have been back under the mean glares at Waimanalo for all the cold ostracizing she felt as an outsider to the Mormon faith. But there was one gleaming thing at the center of her new place that aligned it with brighter possibilities: aviation. That is where Karen oriented her social and work life, her career and spare time. A steady mantra anchored her resolve and efforts: *Keep your eye on the prize. You are going to be a pilot.*

"I loved it because I have an incredible passion for airplanes and flying," Karen said. "Starting as a flight attendant, I was determined to network my way up front to a flight deck position."

Her official start date as a flight attendant, day one of training, was June 11, 1984, with Western Airlines. Her first official flight was the next month, on July 17. As a new flight attendant in a new city, Karen began her immersion into the strange and wonderful flying subculture that would be her life for the next three and a half decades.

In the crazy world of aviation, with odd time schedules, Karen's friends were exclusively work peers, a similarly transplanted collection of men and women energized by the excitement of a new career that somehow simultaneously promised glamour and luxury along with almost no money. Therefore, they banded together like first-year college students living on the cheap: Karen joined five other flight attendants who rented a house in the suburbs south of Salt Lake City. Two of her male roommates were gay. Collectively, all six roommates were at an age of self-discovery and first professional jobs.

"We didn't know they were gay, and I don't think they knew, either," Karen said, laughing. "But we were all young and excited and having a lot of fun. And none of us made any money."

Like new police recruits plucked from the academy and banished to the dreary overnight shifts, Karen and her peers were all on reserve, which in the industry meant endless days on call with a pager clipped to a waistband. Being on "ready reserve" meant that for the next three days Karen's beeper might go off at any odd hour. During reserve, she was required to stay within a one-hour drive of the airport. With an ever-packed suitcase at the ready, she might get sent anywhere. She was the modern-day equivalent of the revolutionary-era Minutemen: part of a generally young, highly mobile, rapidly deployable force that allowed the airlines to respond immediately to ever-shifting flight schedules, employee absences, delays, mechanicals, and the general endless chaos of the industry.

"No one wants to do reserve," she said. "But you didn't have a choice, and you would usually be on reserve for years." Only the more tenured flight attendants were eventually able to "hold a line," which meant a regular schedule with days off and no pager.

Like her battle-tested peers, Karen quickly became inured to the rigors of going airborne with hundreds of people. On one flight in 1985, on a Western Airlines DC-10, Karen was strapped into her jump seat facing aft toward the large section of passenger seats dubbed El Segundo. The flight was bumpy, which did not agree with a pregnant passenger who immediately vomited. A phalanx of call bells lit up, but the flight attendants were unable to move from their seats in the steady turbulence. Soon many passengers in El Segundo were similarly vomiting like some ridiculous scene from a Monty Python skit. Karen, meanwhile, reached in her bag and started eating her sandwich, thinking she might not get another break once the air settled. By the time the plane landed in Hawai'i they had to take it out of service to scrub out the foul spray of gastroenterological debris. There were many similar bodily flotsam-and-jetsam events.

On a 1985 Western flight, on a 737-200 somewhere above Montana, an elderly man got out of his seat and walked in a hunched position down the aisle, leaving a trail of brown liquid from one pant leg. When he finally reached the lavatory and closed the door, an explosion audible in the cabin quickly followed. When he opened the lavatory door to return to his seat, a hot, foul stench permeated the cabin, which lingered through the flight.

In another instance on the ground, during a 737-200 mechanical delay, a male passenger complained about the heat in the cabin and took off all his clothes, right down to his underwear. During the 1980s people having sex in dark cabins was so commonplace that flight attendants sometimes just threw a blanket over the couple rather than trying to intercede.

After one emergency landing in Portland, with passengers evacuating the airplane by sliding down the inflatables, one passenger asked: "Am I going to make my connection in Salt Lake City?"

Karen soon discovered that being a flight attendant was almost like being in a sorority. An instant bond and connection was formed with hundreds of new friends—along with, of course, lots of juicy gossip. There were also some powerful connections made during "jump seat therapy," those precious moments during takeoff and landing when the flight attendants exchanged information and shared their joys and woes.

Meanwhile, when she wasn't working or on reserve, Karen was paying her own way through the ongoing rigors of flight training.

"I was very serious about my flying," Karen said. "It's a very expensive pursuit, so I worked a lot of hours at the airline." The only time she wasn't in the air was during layovers on work trips. Then, without warning, Western Airlines furloughed her, which meant a temporary layoff. Her flight attendant union more or less protected her job by stipulating that the airline had to hire her back in order of seniority. However, there was no guarantee when that would happen. Luckily, the furlough was short-lived, and Western recalled her to work just before the holiday season of 1984.

TO become a pilot, Karen and other flight students operated under Federal Air Regulations (FAR) Part 91: Air Traffic and General Operating Rules. Everywhere she went she lugged the two-inch-thick Airman's Information Manual, which documented the laws of aviation. And during her training in Salt Lake City, Karen met one of her all-time favorite flight instructors.

Harold Haring was a throwback of sorts, a surly aviator who walked with a slight hunch and chain-smoked Camel cigarettes. A divorced man in his forties, he was five feet eight inches, with thinning hair. Aged beyond his years, he was not a physically attractive man by most female standards. Haring subsisted on a steady stream of muddy black coffee, sipped day and night, plus candy bars and potato chips. Poor nutrition and craggy looks aside, Haring was a crack pilot with a sharp, dry sense of humor. The general consensus was that Haring, once an aviation mechanic for the US Air Force, was the best flight instructor in Salt Lake City.

Haring was uniformly loved by his students for his odd personality assemblage, traits, and aviation acumen. For his part, Haring liked flying with women, and he had a small cadre of young female students, including Karen. He was always fun to fly with and be around, and he pushed his students to become better aviators in ways that terrified every one of them. During lessons, he routinely scared the hell out of Karen, which he enjoyed immensely.

While airborne, Haring intentionally fiddled with knobs, pushed buttons, and pulled levers to see how Karen would react. Like a child, he'd depress a button and ask, "What does this do?" or, "What happens if I pull this?" Without warning, he'd reach over and pull back the fuel/air mixture knob until it was so lean the engine would quit. With the propeller dead in the air, Haring would just shrug his shoulders and say, "Looks like your engine just quit. What are you going to do?" It was a bold approach to teaching his students to react to the unexpected situations and distractions that were always a part of flying.

The first time this happened Karen wanted to slap him. Then she quickly refocused: she needed to restart the engine. Although the engine was dead, the propeller was still spinning from the rush of air. The first thing Karen noticed was how quiet the inside of the cabin became with no engine running. Karen pushed the yoke forward, which sent the plane into a thirty-degree dive. The rush of air spun the propeller faster. Then she pushed the fuel/air mixture knob back in to deliver fuel to the engine, which restarted. This exercise was not a standard teaching maneuver. Instead, Haring liked to push the limits. In a real engine-out scenario, Karen would also have to manage the glide ratio, which is the greatest distance each particular airplane can travel without power.

Haring loved inducing "unusual attitude" scenarios in airplanes. He would put his student airplanes into a stall and then stomp on one rudder pedal to put the nose toward the ground with the plane spinning around. The first time she experienced it, Karen had mixed emotions. No question, it was a fun sensation. But at the same time, it was a scenario that could be lethal if not resolved correctly.

During lessons with Haring, both he and Karen smoked cigarettes. Karen had first tried cigarettes when she was 12 and living in the Oregon woods. It started as a cool and rebellious activity among teenagers. If they could not get a new pack, Karen and her friends dug through ashtrays and smoked discarded butts. By 13, she had developed a pack-a-day habit. In the 1970s era, when few wore seatbelts and many parents smoked, including Karen's mother and father, it wasn't viewed as a cataclysmic health risk. Eventually, as a student pilot, Karen chose Benson & Hedges menthol, and the regular habit helped combat her constant anxiety. Haring smoked Camel cigarettes to combat his blood pressure medication.

TWO aircraft were considered the gold standard for basic flight training: the Cessna 152 and the Piper Warrior (PA-28-151). Both were single-engine, single-propeller, very forgiving aircraft with straightforward systems. The twenty-four-foot Cessna 152 was an updated version of the proven 150 model. From 1977 to 1985, almost eight thousand of the 152s, a two-seat aircraft with its wings above the fuselage, rolled out of the manufacturing plant in Wichita, Kansas. A Lycoming 0-235 engine gave the airplane 110 horsepower, a top speed of 110 knots (126 miles per hour), and range of almost five hundred miles with a service ceiling of 14,700 feet.

The Piper Warrior came in both two- and four-seat configurations and, in contrast to the Cessna 152, had low-mounted wings that served as a step into the cockpit at the single door on the port side. The PA-28 first received a Federal Aviation Administration type certificate in 1960 and remains in production in various models. The Warrior had a Lycoming O-320-E3D engine producing 150 horsepower.

During her earliest flight training, Karen would depart from sea level before navigating the aircraft over active volcano vents. Her instructors would have her intentionally cut power and just hover over the active Kilauea Volcano, with the thermal waves supporting the craft.

In Utah she was dealing with the opposite end of the aviation spectrum: high altitude and mountains where severe weather was common. Her departure point for each lesson was Professional Flight Services at Salt Lake International (SLC). In Hawai'i, she was ever alert for the possibility of having to ditch into the open sea. In Utah, the backdrops for those emergency scenarios were frost-shattered granite, towering pines, and deep snow.

"I was introduced early to the harsh reality that people die while flying," Karen said.

Back in Hawai'i the previous year, in 1983, a pilot who had become a friend was ferrying a plane for Aloha Airlines. He was young and talented and engaged to be married. During the flight he sent a Mayday distress call over the ocean above the Alenuihaha Channel. Rescuers never found a trace of him or the airplane, as he and any wreckage were likely sucked into the channel and out to the great sea. In Utah, another friend and young flight instructor hit a mountain and died with his student strapped in the copilot seat.

That there was inherent risk in becoming an aviator was a given. As in life itself, all Karen and her nascent peers could do was focus on what they could control. And, from each tragedy and crash, pull something useful they could fold into their own training and knowledge base to avoid a similar fate. In an emergency, they followed the "five C's": confess, climb, conserve, communicate, and comply.

Karen had started her flight training in Honolulu at the age of 19. After study, practice, working as a flight attendant, and paying her own way for flight lessons, she was ready to test for her first rating: private pilot, airplane single-engine land. With it, Karen would be free to fly single-engine aircraft solo. The Federal Aviation Administration minimum for the rating was 20 hours of dual flight time (with an instructor) and 20 hours of solo flight time. Most student pilots, however—Karen included—usually went above the minimum and accumulated around 60 total hours.

To get to this point in her aviation training, she had passed up numerous opportunities to do fun things because, when she was not working, she was studying or taking a flight lesson. Finally, on May 7, 1985, she was ready for her first solo cross-country journey. The series of flights had to include three points, each with a full-stop landing, each more than fifty nautical miles apart.

"That was really a scary feeling, flying off alone into never-land," she said.

Most of the flight was over mountainous desert on a hot, windy day. She had already done more than 20 hours of solo flights in and around airports as part of her training, but this was her first cross-country solo flight to obscure destinations. For a young aviator, it conjured the anxiety and excitement of Charles Lindbergh leaving the mist of St. Louis in the cold dawn. As Salt Lake City grew smaller behind her, Karen was finding her checkpoints on the oversized VFR (visual flight rules) paper charts, but not as she had planned. She had carefully calculated time, distance, speed, and fuel burn, but strong headwinds were bucking her progress.

Overall, landings present more challenges than takeoffs. Topography, wind direction and speed, and different airports are all variable factors. At her first destination in Nevada, Karen made an initial pass perpendicular to Wells Municipal Airport/Harriet Field (LWL) to assess the wind direction and any other traffic. Whenever possible, pilots landed and took off into the wind; the wind sock or wind tee indicated direction. Flying at 1,000 feet, she was above the standard traffic-pattern altitude of 800 feet, which meant a two-hundred-foot cushion between her and any other planes. But there were no other planes anywhere near this dusty strip of nothingness. At 5,679 feet, the airport sat on the barren high-desert floor with outcroppings of mountains well off in the distance. The airport opened in 1947, but four decades later humanity and commerce still hadn't found Wells, Nevada.

Karen ran her GUMP check: gas, undercarriage, mixture, and prop. At airports with no tower, pilots communicated their intentions "in the blind," which was not to any specific person but over the airwaves so that other nearby pilots could monitor. She tuned to 122.8, the common traffic advisory frequency called UNICOM.

"I'm entering a left downwind for runway two six," she said over the radio.

Runways at airports around the world are oriented to the 360-degree compass dial and correspondingly named, so for final approach on runway 26 her plane's heading indicator showed 260 degrees.

She pulled back power to bleed off airspeed and added flaps, which increased the lift without increasing airspeed. Two ninety-degree turns put her westbound, and she aimed for the 1,000-foot marker, a thick strip of white paint across the runway. From there, it was a light tactile dance: a stabilized approach and constant rate of descent and airspeed balancing pitch and power. She used her hands to guide the yoke while her feet lightly tap-danced the rudder pedals.

Once on the ground, she taxied and parked at what constituted the airport, a small building where she used the restroom. There was no one else around, so Karen climbed back in the Cessna 152, took off, and made her way to Elko Regional Airport (EKO). She landed successfully, went inside, and got a weather briefing from the man attending the flight service station. Back in the Cessna, Karen returned to Salt Lake: she was almost ready for her check ride.

First, to boost her flight hours, she made two more solo cross-country flights to two vibrant Utah hotspots: Milford (MLF) and Fillmore (FOM). On the ground in Milford, the only restroom facility was a dried stand of scrubby desert bushes. *Welcome to the glamorous world of aviation!*

To get her private pilot license, on July 10, 1985, Karen first had to pass a written examination with at least a 70-percent score before taking the check ride, which consisted of an oral examination and a practical flight test with an FAA-designated examiner.

"It was nerve-wracking," she recalled. "There are a lot of ways you can fail a check ride."

The ground portion of the testing was two hours, followed by two hours for the flight portion. Karen brought the written test, which she had taken and passed as a precursor. The examiner then reviewed the test with her and asked her to explain her thinking for the questions she had missed. Then for the next two hours Karen had to answer a seemingly never-ending stream of questions that began innocuously: *What limitations apply to a private pilot?* If Karen earned her private pilot certificate, she would not be able to act as a pilot-in-command of an aircraft carrying passengers or property for compensation or hire. She would need to earn other ratings to perform those duties.

What are the required maintenance inspections for aircraft? Easy enough: an annual inspection (within the preceding twelve months) and a 150-hour inspection.

What are "Special Flight Permits," and when are they necessary? Karen was able to answer, but could not have known that, two decades later, this regulation would come into play for the ill-fated flight on November 23, 2011.

After answering numerous other basic questions about flight certificates and documents, the questions about weather became increasingly more technical: *What is a "trough" and a "ridge"? What are the standard temperature and pressure values for sea level? At what altitude above the surface would the pilot expect the bases of cumuliform clouds if the surface temperature is 82°F and the dew point is 62°F? What causes the winds aloft to flow parallel to the isobars?*

To become a pilot, Karen had been required to learn numerous new terms and concepts, which the examiner asked her to define: airfoil, angle of incidence, angle of attack, Bernoulli's principle, density altitude, load factor, and torque effect. Then more questions: *What is the normal climb-out speed? What is the maximum flap extension speed? What is the stall speed in the clean configuration? What engine glide-out speed will give you maximum range? Where are the fuel vents for your aircraft? What is the final gross weight? What is the weight of oil being used? What is the octane rating of the fuel being used by your aircraft? Why are some aircraft not allowed to perform forward slips with flaps extended?* It was a dizzying jumble of physics and intuitive sense, because that is what constitutes flying: lots of science, and intuitive art.

Karen had been studying endlessly, and was able to answer each question. From there, the examiner asked her more detailed questions about airplane systems, cross-country flight planning, night operations, and aeromedical factors such as hypoxia, which is oxygen deficiency in the body. She had to go through an entire flight plan and then a mock flight based on hypothetical parameters given by the examiner.

Then the examiner posed a few scenario-based questions similar to those annoying story problems from algebra: *After an exhausting three-day business meeting, you are loading up the rental airplane for a two-hour flight home when you discover you have lost your reading glasses. You can see in the distance, but can't read instruments or a chart easily. The weather is good, and if you depart in the next twenty minutes you can be home before dark. What will you do?*

Karen took a breath and thought through the scenario before answering: first she would ask anyone available to help search for the glasses. Second, since any vision correction would be required on the medical certificate, takeoff would not be permitted. She would cancel the flight, spend the night, find new glasses, and fly the next morning in the clear light of day. The examiner nodded: Karen had sufficiently demonstrated sound risk management and aeronautical decision-making in her response.

Two hours later, after all that mental grilling, she had to go airborne.

"By the time you're done with that first two hours you're exhausted and ready to throw up," she said. "But then you have to go out, get in a plane, and fly like a pro."

The examiner reviewed all her flight documentation and training hours. Each examiner was licensed and designated by the Federal Aviation Administration. He gave her a hypothetical flight that Karen had to document, including weather and calculating fuel burn with her E6B flight computer, known as the "whiz wheel" but today mostly relegated to the dustbin along with slide rules and eight-track tapes. Eventually, Karen and the instructor walked out onto the tarmac under brilliant sunshine at South Valley Regional Airport (U42), approximately ten miles south of Salt Lake City International Airport (SLC).

They climbed aboard a Cessna 152, that stalwart single-propeller airplane. Once airborne, Karen readied herself mentally for the practical test standards she knew were about to get under way.

"Let's start with a standard stall series," the examiner said. That series included approach-to-landing, departure, and straight-ahead stalls.

"OK," she said.

"Give me a departure stall."

Karen took a deep breath. The procedure was a little creepy until she got used to the sensation. She was not actually stalling the engine, but banking the airplane at full power and establishing a climb. She added back-pressure on the control wheel, which increased the pitch of the nose and the angle of attack until it interrupted airflow over the wings. Pilots had to be prepared for such an eventuality. Once the stall was under way, the yoke shuddered hard in Karen's hands as a loud and annoying warning indicator beeped.

If the recovery was not done correctly, stalls could turn into inadvertent spins. Until 1949, intentionally initiating spins and recovering was required of private pilot applicants. At that time, the FAA removed the requirement, with more focus on stall recognition and recovery because spin training, when done incorrectly, could be dangerous. To this day, all flight instructors must demonstrate proficiency in spin recovery.

Airplanes fly because there is higher pressure under the wing than above. Karen's early instructors explained the motion as similar to water flowing around a rock in a river and lifting it from underneath. Called "stick shakers," stalls on bigger planes really rattle the controls. Karen thought, *Pitch, power, trim.* To recover, she rolled the wings level, released back-pressure on the control wheel and simultaneously adjusted the power to bring the airplane's nose back to the horizon. As she did so, her examiner lit another cigarette and made some notes on his clipboard without saying anything.

So far, so good, Karen thought. His silent smoking and writing meant she had not done anything stupid. Except the air vent was blowing the ash from his cigarette right into her eyes, which was pretty annoying. Then she was surprised to hear him say, "How about demonstrating a spin?"

She knew it was not required, but she said, "OK."

As she went into the spin entry, the air vent caught the ash from his cigarette and blew it into Karen's right eye as she watched the ground spin below. She fought through the pain in her eye and recovered from the spin without incident.

After landing safely and taxiing back to the hangar, they walked back into the building. The examiner, Al Alder, disappeared for a few minutes to fill out paperwork. He came back, tore off a portion of the sheet, and handed it to Karen. Once he submitted the paperwork to the FAA, she would officially be a private pilot.

"I was really excited, on top of the world," she recalled. "My examiner even said I flew better than most of the guys. I was thrilled that I finally completed it."

Karen had achieved her license to learn: pilots spend a lifetime perfecting their skills. To that end, in her job as a flight attendant for Western Airlines, Karen was commuting via standby flights from Honolulu (HNL). A pilot friend, Bobby Norris, worked helicopter traffic watch in the days before ubiquitous freeway cameras, and Karen would ride along and pick his brain about all things aviation.

"At any experience level I wanted to pair myself with pilots who were more knowledgeable and learn everything I could," Karen said.

As ever, aviation was a cruel master. Just thirteen months after getting her private pilot rating, an aircraft very similar to the Piper Warrior Karen had learned to fly disintegrated in the skies near Karen's hometown of Anaheim. On August 31, 1986, an Aeroméxico Douglas DC-9-32 collided midair with the much smaller Piper PA-28-181 Archer above Cerritos, California. The crash killed all sixty-seven people aboard both planes, along with fifteen people on the ground, not far from where Karen had leaned into the cracked leather of her father's jacket atop the speeding Ducati.

One of the worst air disasters in the history of metropolitan Los Angeles, that crash resulted in regulatory changes requiring all airliners to be equipped with a traffic collision avoidance system (TCAS). Additionally, all light aircraft operating in class B airspace had to be equipped with a mode C transponder, which emitted altitude data to air traffic controllers. Although she didn't know it then, "class B airspace" would one day become a haunting term for Karen Perry.

Ten days later, on September 9, 1986, Karen's employer Western Airlines entered into an agreement and plan of merger with Delta Air Lines. The merger agreement needed the approval of the United States Department of Transportation and shareholders, both of which were accomplished before year's end. With that, the sixty-one-year history of Western Airlines ended, as the company became a wholly owned subsidiary of Delta, which discontinued the Western brand altogether and merged the employee workforces fully by April 1, 1987. In her day-to-day world, not much changed for Karen other than the company name stamped on her paycheck, her uniform, and the airplanes.

DURING her instrument training, Karen took her ground lessons in the lobby of Hudson General fixed base operations, with a steady stream of people in and out to the taxiway. One of those people was Dave Harker—tall in his nice-fitting pilot uniform, blond-haired, and blue-eyed—who worked for Rocky Mountain Helicopters as an air ambulance pilot. At some point the student and the pilot struck up a conversation. Throughout Karen's lessons she often saw him, and they'd talk aviation. As she studied for exams, Harker was a reliable sounding board. A casual friendship soon developed between the thirty-something pilot and the younger pilot-in-training. Harker was married with two kids and lived in Salt Lake City.

On October 8, 1987, Karen received her instrument rating, which meant flying with sole reference to instruments. She was 24 and had 125 hours total airtime. She was well-versed, too, in the reality of becoming a pilot: it was an involved, time-consuming, and expensive pursuit. She was expected to know and apply volumes of data, facts, and practices, and to perform well while flying under stressful conditions. Seven months later, on May 19, 1988, she had accumulated 250 hours and received her commercial rating at age 25.

Her friendship with Dave Harker was growing and began to include conversations about Harker's dissatisfaction in his marriage. Karen could not suppress her attraction. She was becoming a pilot herself. She and Dave would be equals, as peers. As pilots, too, they shared some of the same stereotypical personality traits: controlling, impatient, and intelligent. Harker eventually divorced, and he and Karen had their first official date: a picnic lunch at a city park. By the fall of 1988, they were living together in an apartment in the Sun Arbor complex, five minutes from Salt Lake City International (SLC). He was still working as an air ambulance pilot; Karen was on reserve as a flight attendant with Delta Air Lines.

On July 15, 1989, Karen married Dave Harker; one of the best pilots she had ever flown with was now her husband. The first phase of their honeymoon was the annual air show in Oshkosh, Wisconsin. They camped in a tent, which proved challenging to pitch in the falling darkness. Part two of the honeymoon was in Puerto Vallarta. Clearly, aviation was the commonality that bonded them.

"He was an excellent pilot and one of the more knowledgeable people I've ever known in aviation," Karen said. "If I hadn't been flying, I never would have met Dave Harker."

As it turned out, other than aviation the two had little in common. Karen was outgoing and social; her husband was more introverted. They would both discover that relying on the solidifying bond of aviation alone as cement for the relationship would gradually spell trouble.

THREE days before she turned 27, on February 2, 1990, Karen had her next rating: airplane multiengine land. That meant she was authorized to fly airplanes with more than one engine. A few months later she sat for her flight instructor certification on May 30, 1990.

There were two written tests and a two-day oral examination with the FAA inspector. Previously she had not passed her first oral examination and so had to repeat it, which was not uncommon; the process had a fifty/fifty pass/fail rate. On that first attempt, the inspector had asked her about a weight/balance formula, which she did not know. During the second attempt, at the end of May 1990, the inspector told her she was at a stage of training that went well beyond just being able to pilot an aircraft. The important larger question of the day was whether Karen was knowledgeable and skilled enough to teach someone else to fly, and it was within that framework that she was being carefully evaluated. Not too far into the flight check, the inspector said, "Let's go back for a landing."

Oh, crap, Karen thought. She was certain she had already messed something up. But back on the ground, the inspector told her she had passed and was now a certified flight instructor able to teach private and commercial students.

And Karen did just that. She scheduled lessons with new students at the site where she had studied: Professional Flight Services at Salt Lake City International (SLC), on the west side of the airport. She took walk-ins, too, curious people who wandered in and started asking questions about being a pilot. The more serious putative pilots would schedule a discovery flight with Karen wherein she could properly introduce them to aviation. With a linked set of dual controls, once airborne and cruising at a safe maneuvering altitude, Karen would offer the passenger control of the airplane, which almost always clinched the deal. Just as had happened with Karen in Hawaiʻi, most who took a discovery flight and held the controls for the first time were immediately hooked.

Two different FAA-approved tracks were available for Karen to train students to become pilots. The more formal was using a Part 141 program spelled out to the letter by the FAA. In other words, the instructor had to teach from an A-to-Z checklist without any deviance. This was the more rigid way to teach someone to fly. The alternative, and Karen's preferred method, was to follow FAR Part 91, called General Operating and Flight Rules, which listed the required regulations students needed to learn and demonstrate, without specifying *how* Karen had to impart such wisdom.

Either way, entering the world of aviation and becoming a pilot does not come cheap. Pilots, by law in the highly regulated arena of aviation, are not autodidacts: "self-taught pilot" is a nonexistent euphemism. At the time, Karen's instructor rate was sixty dollars an hour for either ground or flight lessons. On top of that, students had to pay for the airplane rental and fuel, which varied from forty to ninety dollars an hour depending on the aircraft. At an average of 65 hours for most students to earn their private pilot certification, each student's tab was going to run $6,500 to $10,000 or more. To continue training and become a fully certified commercial pilot as Karen had—with the multiple required certifications—students could expect to shell out up to $100,000 or more. Karen had done the same only by spreading out her training, over almost eight years and two different airports separated by the Pacific Ocean and the western portion of the United States.

Being a flight instructor, to most pilots, is an uninspired stepping-stone to greater things aloft. Pilots between jobs can teach and continue to accumulate flight hours. Similarly, in the cyclical ebb and flow of commercial aviation, many are stuck being flight instructors simply because of a glut of pilots at any given time and no available jobs.

Karen, on the other hand, immediately enjoyed instructing. Unlike a soured old-timer with 10,000 hours who had done it all, Karen was much newer to flying, with far fewer hours, so she was still energized and inspired to share her passion. Teaching also reinforced her own burgeoning knowledge, which was a confidence booster. The most difficult element as a flight instructor was the impossibility of teaching good judgment, a critical skill for pilots. Students either had it or they did not, and the ones who did not tended to be overconfident and dangerous. As a result, some paid the ultimate price.

"There were parts of flight instructing that were nerve-wracking," Karen recalled. "It's like a parent-child relationship. You're walking a tightrope to let students make mistakes right up to the point where it could kill you both. Then you just have to take over the controls."

With anywhere from one to several ongoing students, and her full-time job as a flight attendant, Karen was working seven days a week. In hindsight, being a trained pilot and still working as a flight attendant was holding her back from progressing toward her ultimate goal. The more seniority she built as a flight attendant, the better her routes, schedule, and pay. She had also mostly escaped the clutches of being on reserve. That safety net of full-time employment was difficult to let go. Looking back, if she had just cut the safety tether and committed 100 percent, it might have accelerated her progress and career as a pilot.

When she was working as a flight attendant, she'd find reasons to venture into the cockpit, talk with the pilots, and absorb more knowledge. It never failed; the entire demeanor and attitude of pilots immediately shifted when Karen said she was also a pilot. It was definitely a man's, man's, man's world behind the cockpit door. There were very few early female pioneers and role models for Karen. Valerie Walker, a stunning, tall blonde, began working on the flight deck for Western Airlines in 1976 as one of the first two female pilots for the airline. In the early days she was a second officer, a flight engineer on the Boeing 727, and she later became a Delta captain. On one trip Valerie slipped Karen a note that read: *Don't worry: I'm just a pilot trapped in a female's body.* A male passenger boarding the plane had seen Valerie and commented on the fact that there was a female in the cockpit.

As the 1980s began, there were roughly eighty women in the cockpits of planes owned by the major airlines. While that sounded promising, there were roughly thirty-five thousand commercial pilots, which meant for every 438 male pilots, there was one woman. All new pilots, male or female, started as flight engineers. Like any worthy movement, progress to the captain's seat for women was excruciatingly slow. Going all the way back to Seneca Falls, New York, abolitionists Elizabeth Cady Stanton and Lucretia Mott first advocated granting voting rights to women in 1848. The suffrage movement was eventually successful, with passage of the Nineteenth Amendment on August 18, 1920, but the long battle had taken seventy years, which was 144 years after formation of the country.

It was not until 1976 that Emily Warner became the first female captain, at Frontier, on a nineteen-passenger de Havilland Twin Otter. A woman was finally at the controls. But still there were loud murmurs in the cockpit from male pilots, along with conspiracy talk: *Had the hiring standards for women and minorities been lowered under increasing pressure from the Equal Employment Opportunity Commission?* Because, concerned male pilots argued, such moves could put people's lives at risk!

Pioneering females had to endure other absurd challenges, such as male pilots openly positing whether a woman's menstrual cycle might diminish her ability to pilot an aircraft, especially in harsh weather or under other difficult scenarios.

Then again, how could women be taken seriously as capable pilots when the major airlines ran 1970s ad campaigns that portrayed attractive "stewardesses" as little more than airborne sex objects? One Continental Airlines campaign used the tagline, "We really move our tail for you." National Airlines used the even more blunt "Fly Me" tagline and followed up with an alluring stewardess who promised, "I'm going to fly you like you've never been flown before."

In this era the track to plum corporate flying jobs was almost exclusively through the old boys' club: retired military pilots. How could women who simply went to flight school be as proficient as pilots who had trained and worked under the proud red, white, and blue banner of American military might? Even more specifically, did the workplace label itself—cockpit—forever ban females from membership simply by their anatomical differences? In a word, no.

The term originated in the latter part of the 1500s, when recreational cockfighting used a round pit for blood sport. Shakespeare was alluding to a round, noisy theater and its inadequacies when Henry V laments:

> Can this cockpit hold, the vasty fields of France? Or may we cram, within this wooden O the very casques, that did affright the air at Agincourt?

Then later, sailors adopted the term to describe the lowest deck at the stern of fighting ships where, during battle, the surgeon and his medical mates set up because the space was least subject to blasts and ocean movement. Like all lower-deck areas on early craft, the space was hot, stuffy, confined, crowded, poorly lit, foul-smelling, and bloody. All of which was descriptive of the original rooster-battle venues. In the 1800s the term *cockpit* described the steering pit of sailing yachts. From there, by the early 1900s the steering area of an aircraft also had its moniker.

But almost seventy-five years later, there were still passengers who, after spotting a uniformed female on the flight deck, requested a transfer to a different airplane. Karen herself recalled being in a terminal in her pilot's uniform and hearing a male passenger exclaim: "Oh my God—it's a female pilot!"

In turn, all American women were under enormous pressure to do and have it all. This was the era of the superwoman, extolled in the Enjoli commercial, who could put the wash on the line, feed the kids, get dressed, pass out the kisses, and be to work by five of nine. And then, of course, she could "Bring home the bacon, fry it up in a pan, and never let you forget you're a man."

That campaign ran in 1978, two years after Warner became a female captain, which meant that, no matter what women might be achieving in the workplace, they were reminded of their ultimate daily duty: *never, never, never* let him forget he's a man. The standard practice in those days of Scotch-taping buxom pinups and Playboy centerfolds around the cockpit was just another reminder of a woman's duty, purpose, and place in the workplace hierarchy.

Those same men, in the cockpit, watched and waited for—*expected*—mistakes from their female peers. Simple procedural errors. Minor flubs. Major gaffes. The overt stares included the ongoing assessment of bra size, hair and makeup, waist-to-hip ratio, and overall suitability for a quick rut in the galley. Aviation into the 1980s was still a locker-room domain where obese, unkempt men could spray F-bombs within earshot of passengers while the female pilots were expected to look pretty, smell like flowers—*Enjoli!*—move with the grace, manners, and precision of being at a formal British high tea service, and be 100 percent flawless in their technical aviation execution. And *never, never, never...* It was an impossible expectation and standard to meet.

It had taken her forebears 144 years to rewrite US history in the twentieth century. Karen was not dissuaded by the institutionalized misogyny of her own era: she was determined to be a left-seat pilot.

IN late 1989, Dave Harker accepted a job offer from Smith's Food and Drug, a company hiring corporate pilots to be based in Phoenix, Arizona. Karen and he moved to an apartment in a quiet suburban community called Ahwatukee. Karen continued as a full-time flight attendant with Delta Air Lines and as a part-time flight instructor at three area airports, including Chandler (CHD), Phoenix Sky Harbor (PHX), and Falcon Field (FFZ) in Mesa. Karen continued to stack up pilot ratings, and by 1992 she had achieved:

- July 1, 1991: instrument instructor
- April 16, 1992: multiengine instructor
- August 27, 1992: airplane single-engine sea

The only two ratings she did not yet possess were "multiengine sea," which would give her the ability to fly multiengine planes affixed with floats instead of landing gear, and "airline transport," required for captains of any airplane exceeding 12,500 pounds. To captain a Boeing jet for her employer Delta Air Lines as she envisioned, Karen would still need her airline transport rating. But she was already qualified to be a copilot sitting right-front on such a jet, which is where every new pilot started anyway.

The dream was now hers for the taking. The Hawai'i girl who had started her flight training in the macho, macho man's world of aviation in the early 1980s had slowly and steadily worked her way through all the expensive and time-consuming hours.

Her plan was to build flight time as an instructor as she applied for pilot jobs. The early 1990s, however, was not a good time for Karen to be seeking her first pilot post: the glut of experienced pilots meant she was competing against people—men, mostly—with ten times as many flight hours. Another challenge during this era, too, was that the door had been opened for foreign nationals who were scooping up many of the flight instructor positions and squeezing out experienced American instructors.

The dream was close, but timing, market forces beyond her control, and gender would require another large measure of Karen's well-honed determination and persistence if she was to enter the cockpit and join the aviator boys' club. In the meantime, she would continue working aft of the cockpit door, the vertical manifestation of the glass ceiling in aircraft. There, at the back of airplanes, Karen earned her paycheck in the once female-only domain of a job originally titled "air stewardess."

At least by the early 1990s she and her peers, including more and more men, were "flight attendants," but the chasm between that post and the cockpit—in terms of training, pay, respect, and authority—was still as wide as the oceans Karen routinely crisscrossed.

EIGHT

Touching a Dream

IN THE EARLY 1990s, ONE GLOBALLY KNOWN CELEBRITY COUPLE traveled under a pseudonym: the Martin family. Those who knew the couple's identity and path to accomplishment, riches, and fame knew the code name gave a nod to someone in the inner circle who had been an integral part of the journey, and eventual superstardom, of one of the world's all-time greats.

This particular husband and wife traveled frequently between Los Angeles and Tucson, Arizona, where she had family connections and the couple had a second or third or fourth house. This was the secreted world of celebrity travel, the private jet charter that, at a hefty price tag, bypassed every annoying aspect of air travel endured by commoners. No big airports, parking hassles, curbside drop-offs, mile-long check-in lines, baggage checks, security lines, pat-downs, strip searches, or, finally, squeezing into hard plastic chairs at the gate only to hear a delayed-flight announcement.

For the well-heeled elite, once inside the aircraft there were no seats crammed side by side and stacked in endless rows of loud passengers and screaming children. No pitched battles for the cold, one-inch hard-steel common armrest. No line for a dirty lavatory teeming with bacteria and misplaced microscopic fecal matter. No lukewarm cold food or cold warm meals wrapped in foil. No gate changes or missed connections. No endless waits at carousels, no lost luggage, and no writing careful descriptions to get luggage delivered three days into a six-day vacation.

At $10,000 and up for short flights, and much more for transcontinental or transoceanic excursions, that long list of pain, endurance, and exhaustion simply vanished. Stepping away from the budget-saddled crush of humanity, welcome to the wonderful, wonderful world of private jet charter. In this cocooned world moved well-placed executives of large corporations, business and entertainment moguls, and other high-earning superstars in their respective fields: actors, athletes, entrepreneurs, musicians, and, eventually, people who got famous without doing anything except reality television. That is, money talks—everyone else flies coach.

The secret world of private charter flights begins in quiet, polished hangars with epoxy-coated floors cleaner and shinier than those in most people's kitchens. These private aircraft garages are usually located at smaller airports away from all the chaos and confusion of the huddled masses yearning to breathe free. Whether by traditional limousine or discreet private car with blackout window tint, travelers arrive at the hangar and climb out mere steps from the gleaming jet. There, as they climb the short stairs, the flight crew is all smiles and warm well wishes, with handshakes and hugs for the regular clients. It is a welcome reception among well-dressed travelers and aviation professionals alike, which once existed in the mainstream world in the early days of commercial passenger travel, but had unofficially disappeared by the time the Bee Gees were "Jive Talkin'" chart toppers (1975).

Eventually, mainstream air travel's dress code and decorum became on par with travel on the #7 cross-town bus: ratty T-shirts, ripped shorts, flip-flops, housedresses, muumuus, form-fitting Lycra, tracksuits, pajamas (*yes, pajamas*), and gray, stained sweatpants (the kind Rocky Balboa wore in 1978).

In that other moneyed, parallel universe mortals rarely glimpse, luggage magically moves from vehicle trunk to plane belly, unseen and untouched by the traveler's hands. The entire airport arrival, check-in, and boarding process in the private charter world totals about twenty seconds.

Welcome aboard!

Karen's entree into this vaunted world was via Kimberly-Clark Corporation, which arranged private charter flights for various clients. On one of those planned excursions, the scheduled flight attendant had to cancel at the last minute, leaving the pilot and copilot scrambling for the key third member of the flight crew. But a charter company catering to the Robin Leach set could not just plug in a mouth-breathing hack for such a critical task: a suitable replacement had to be flight-trained, professional, clean, pressed, and starched. Equally important, with global superstars as clients, the flight attendant had to be intelligent, savvy, polite, courteous, and capable of carrying on a conversation with a certain air of erudite sophistication, preferably in the Queen's English. A starstruck or agog fan asking for autographs simply would not do. For this particular charter and puzzle, the pilot knew immediately who would fit the bill: Karen Harker.

That pilot, Keith Lorch, was an FAR Part 135 charter pilot and also a friend of Karen and her husband Dave. Most charter operators ran under FAR Part 135, which was officially titled "Operating Requirements: Commuter and On Demand Operations and Rules Governing Persons On Board Such Aircraft." An FAR Part 135 certificate meant Lorch flew smaller turbojet-engine-powered aircraft with fewer than thirty seats, nontransport category turbo-propeller-powered aircraft with ten to nineteen seats, and transport category turboprops with twenty to thirty seats. Lorch knew he could entrust Karen in this very refined world of private charter. Lorch called Karen, who answered on the third ring, and asked if she'd be interested in the gig.

"Well, I've never done anything like that," she said. "I have no idea what would be expected of me."

Lorch gave her the rundown, which was actually pretty involved. Attending to the specific needs of celebrity clients went way beyond just showing up, smiling, and offering drink service. Long before departure, Karen had to arrange *everything* for the short flight. That included the catering—a major undertaking—along with purchasing certain newspapers and magazines. She'd have to contact a florist and arrange delivery of suitably fresh floral arrangements. These particular clients were also vegetarian, so all the catering needed to creatively accommodate such a diet. The preferred drink in this case was Johnny Walker Red, which needed to be available along with a full bar of other selections just in case. This all needed to be ordered, picked up and/or delivered, and stowed on the aircraft prior to the couple's arrival for departure, from Tucson International Airport (TUS), in two days. Karen considered it and then said, "Sure. I'll do it."

After hanging up, she was still smiling and shaking her head as she thought about the clients she would be meeting in two days. No question: she was a *huge* fan! But she was also a professional and promised herself she would not act like a star-glazed schoolgirl. And under no circumstances would she ask for an autograph. Besides, she told herself, Tucson–Los Angeles was a quick flight, so it was not like she was going to get to ask the million and one questions spinning through her head. Not that she would anyway: cool, professional sophistication would be the modus operandi. But still, as she went to work flipping through the Yellow Pages to find a florist in Tucson, all she could think was, *Wow!* The band had always been one of her all-time favorites, and she was going to shake his hand, and his wife's as well, in two days.

Just, wow!

Two days later, by the time the black limousine was in view, Karen had everything stowed on the Learjet as instructed. With almost military precision, she was standing with the pilot and copilot in her starched and pressed dark slacks and white button-down shirt. Her hair was up and pinned into a tight bun, her makeup and lipstick absolutely perfect.

It had been a whirlwind two days getting everything ordered and prepared. When the catering showed up, the eight hundred dollars' worth of food was a logistical nightmare to store in the small galley. But now everything was ready: fresh-cut floral centerpieces on the small foldout table. Crisp magazines and newspapers, aesthetically arranged, in the days before everyone carried their own ubiquitous small screens. The couple was flying this short charter to LAX before boarding a commercial flight to Scotland.

Karen definitely had some butterflies flitting through her belly, and she repeatedly wiped her palms at the sides of her pants as the limousine rolled to a stop. She had crossed paths with plenty of celebrities, starting with her fellow students at Beverly Hills High School and then as a flight attendant, so she was not typically starstruck. And she knew she wasn't going to ask something stupid. But still, these were two people who were one notch above "celebrity," in the rarefied air of a wholly unique level of status. Karen had thought of a few others she might put in this same category of talent, accomplishment, global reach, and all-around intangible cool factor: James Dean. Audrey Hepburn. Paul Newman. Elvis Presley.

The couple emerged into the Arizona sunshine and walked over. A final thought flashed through Karen's mind: *This is really happening!* She smiled, extended her hand, and mentally switched gears to work mode. There they were, in flesh and blood. She greeted them each by "Mister" and "Missus," out of respect, but was immediately told to dispense with such formalities and use first names only, please. After a nervous laugh from Karen, the couple walked up the stairs and disappeared inside the jet. Karen followed the pilot and copilot up the stairs, still feeling some nerves. She was in her element, aviation, but in a way totally foreign to her. And besides, *No, stop acting like a schoolgirl. Just get a grip,* she told herself. *Do your job.* The permanent smile, at least, would not leave her face for days as Karen had always loved the Beatles.

"I have to admit," she said years later. "Paul and Linda McCartney. That was a big deal to me."

Once under way and in the dull-roar cocoon of a sealed jet, Karen fell easily into her role and did not go through any more *Oh my God, that's Paul McCartney!* mental gyrations. He took his usual Johnny Walker Red, and they both had the Mexican vegetarian dish Karen had carefully ordered. Light conversation flowed easily. They asked Karen where she was from and where she lived. Karen returned polite answers and asked her own similarly innocuous questions. She stayed on message and avoided any queries into the music of the Beatles, Wings, or whether any of the "Paul is dead" clues on Abbey Road were real or imagined. Then the man who wrote "Yesterday" asked Karen Harker for a glass of milk. A pall settled around the travelers and their flight attendant, and all she could think was, *Eight hundred dollars' worth of food and drink, and I forgot milk.*

"I was mortified that I had to tell Paul McCartney I didn't have any milk for him," she recalled. But this was Paul McCartney, not some snotty rich kid whose dad's last name was stamped on an empire, so Karen didn't have to duck an airborne fork or endure a silver-spoon tirade. The Milk Situation was barely a blip in an otherwise perfect flight and interaction.

"The thing that impressed me the most was how genuinely nice and down-to-earth they both were," she said. "They were engaging and took an interest in me."

At the time, Karen did not make the connection to the McCartneys' "Martin family" code name. It was a clever nod, of course, to legendary Beatles producer George Martin, who regularly did the impossible, such as arranging a string section of violins, violas, and cellos on the evocative 1966 tune "Eleanor Rigby," from the Revolver album, without any traditional rock or pop instruments anywhere on the track.

Karen Harker, apparently, made quite an impression on Linda McCartney and the man who would later be known as *Sir* Paul McCartney. The iconic couple began requesting Karen for the Tucson–LAX leg of their journeys back and forth to Great Britain.

On subsequent charter flights for the McCartneys and other private clients, Karen worked aboard airplanes owned and operated by aviation legend Clay Lacy. Founded in 1968 by the accomplished eponymous pilot, Clay Lacy Aviation was an early player in jet charter on the west coast, with proximity to Hollywood's burgeoning entertainment industry. Born in 1932, Lacy grew up in Wichita, Kansas, and later served as an airline captain, military aviator, experimental test pilot, air race champion, aviation record-setter, and aerial cinematographer. Starting with a single Learjet in 1968, by 1990 Clay Lacy's namesake operation was a full aviation-services company including the discreet mission of transporting "the Martin family" above the browned tablescape of California and Arizona desert.

Karen could only pinch herself as she imagined the quick conversation: *Honey, I just got off the phone with George. He and Ringo want us to stop by for dinner when we get back. They want to talk about a project with Clapton. And love, get me Karen Harker!*

Karen did three more flights with them over the next few months. But as they continued to request her directly, it became awkward whenever she had to decline because of her regular work schedule with Delta Air Lines. After all, that was her job; Lifestyles of the Rich and Famous was just a fleeting side gig. In her best Robin Leach approximation she heard: *Life wasn't always peaches and cream for this affable young Brit from Liverpool. But by 1990 he was living the caviar dream of private air charter, with Karen Harker attending to his every champagne whim and gold-plated fancy.*

But still, Karen cringed every time she had to bow out: *Hey Jude, we need to let it be. Not that you can relate: Money, that's what I want. You know, funny paper? So let me introduce to you, your new flight attendant, the one and only ...*

The brief brush with a Beatle had been truly special. Yes, she had to admit to a fantasy or two of a new deep friendship with Paul and Linda that included intimate gatherings and private renditions of "The Fool on the Hill," with Linda whipping up exquisite vegetarian fare from her own published cookbook. But ultimately, Karen had more realistic visions on her mind. As far as the Beatles fantasies, she had to be content with a signed copy of Linda McCartney's cookbook, which she gave Karen on one of the flights and which Karen has to this day. Karen Harker's continued and all-consuming focus was on becoming a full-time pilot.

And in 1992, that dream would come true.

NINE

Taking Flight

THE INSTANT KAREN HARKER SAW IT, she was time-warped to the back of the Ducati and a certain gritty leather tang, her pulse quickening as she and her dad raced along a low cool spot in the road near a sweetly pungent orchard. Now, two decades later as an adult, she felt that same speechless awe, her mind spinning. This was a beautiful, sculpted piece of art that looked fast just sitting parked, a gleaming piece of modern machinery and true high-performance aircraft. It was propeller-less, sleek, and sexy. Still breathless, Karen moved closer and felt a twin pulse of awe and sweaty-palms fear.

The Learjet 24 was an American twin-engine that could hold two crew and up to six passengers. Powered by two General Electric CJ610-6 turbojet engines, the forty-three-foot airplane had a top speed of 545 miles per hour (473 knots) at 31,000 feet. It was 1991, and Karen was about to climb into the gleaming cockpit of this engineering marvel and, soon after, soar into the ether. And when she did, she would make the jump from the go-karts she had been flying to a Formula One race car, from prop planes to jets, which could flawlessly execute every maneuver she initiated or, with equally quick precision, end her life.

As this year had unfolded, Karen was working full time as a Delta Air Lines flight attendant and, on her off days, flight instructing to build her hours. Her husband's job as a corporate pilot with Smith's Food and Drug fell victim to the slow economy. When the company eliminated his post, he began picking up contract pilot jobs and was able to bring along his own copilot: his wife Karen.

For Karen, these contract jobs were a huge step up from flight instructing. Flight time in jets was imperative and would be immensely beneficial. An added bonus was that the pay was at least decent. The married couple each received a day rate, which was $500 for Dave as the pilot and $300 for Karen as the copilot. They operated under FAR Part 91, which was less strict than what was required for most commercial flights. The first of these jobs came in early August 1991, when the phone rang and Karen got the news from her husband. Executives at a company called Pensus wanted to hire the duo for a series of flights from Phoenix to Mexico, including several jaunts within Mexico, and then back to Phoenix. In preparation, on August 5 Dave and Karen drove to Scottsdale Airport (SDL), where Karen would begin ground training on the Learjet 24.

"I was thrilled to have the opportunity," she recalled.

She climbed the stairs, moved to the flight deck, surveyed the panel, and started mentally sorting the various functions and locations. The ground training portion had to be quick (but still 100 percent thorough), because they had to depart soon for Mexico. For her second-in-command flight check on the Learjet 24, they would have to go airborne with her demonstrating her competency. This would be the first jet she had ever flown.

On the check ride day, Karen was more excited than nervous. She had read everything she could find about the craft, and during her walk around she noted the Lear's unique gadgetry not found on other planes. Conspicuously located forward of the door was the angle of attack vane. She had also read in the manual that the radome, the domed structure that protected radar equipment, had a spray nozzle at the apex for emitting deicing alcohol. Satisfied with the exterior, she followed Dave up and inside. Like in a fine automobile, even closing the door offered a nod to precise engineering. It was similar in heft and feel to a bank vault door, and when fully seated the electrical drive unit demonstrated the precise machinery, hidden from view but audible, with a high-tech buzz as the lugs engaged. Impressive, she thought. And that was just closing the door!

After going through their preflight checks, radioing their intentions, and taxiing out to the designated strip of runway, it was time. As the captain, Dave gripped the thrust lever and slowly pushed to takeoff power. Dave's right hand was positioned on top of the thrust lever. As he advanced the power, Karen's left hand braced the thrust levers, just below Dave's hand, to make certain nothing inadvertently reversed the levers. These Learjet controls were all conventional, with cables and push rods.

She was scanning each of the large indicators, in the flash of seconds. Dave released his feet, which started the smooth machine gliding down the wide slab. That old familiar ghost mantra, *Here we go*, flashed through Karen's mind in a giddy blend of anticipation, excitement, focus, and measured fear similar to the emotional rush on a steep clackety-clack climb up the first big hill on a roller coaster.

Here we go ...

When the magical moment came, as gravity lost its battle to the correct speed of air over two perfectly shaped wings, the nosewheel lifted from the runway, followed by the main wheels, and they were in a perfect takeoff roll. Karen swallowed back the nervous anxiety in her throat as she watched the airspeed indicator. As first officer, she was responsible for callouts during the takeoff roll: *airspeed alive* ... *eighty knots* ... *v-one* ... That last one was the go/no-go point of no return. Then: *rotate*.

Immediately, the first and most impressive thing Karen noticed was the way the Learjet 24 climbed. In a lot of airplanes she had to step-climb, which meant ascending in a stair-step manner: climb, level off, and then climb again. In the Learjet the pilot just pointed the nose up and let it rip: in a dozen minutes they could top 41,000 feet. Karen almost had to rub her eyes when she repeatedly checked the altimeter, because it did not seem possible: less than five minutes into the flight they had blown past flight level two zero zero and were already pushing 25,000 feet.

This is one fantastic bird! The abundance of bare polished metal reduced paint erosion. Every system had a backup for the backup. If they lost hydraulics, for example, and had to drop onto a deserted road, they could press a button and blow the gear down using a bottle of compressed nitrogen. So when Dave gave Karen the controls to this million-dollar toy, it was a milestone high point in her aviation career.

The plane flew heavier yet was more responsive, a different piloting experience in every way. The ailerons were fairly light. She did not need to worry about rudder because the automatic yaw damper coordinated things unless she switched over to manual. She was bulleting through time and space, at flight level two six zero in excess of 400 miles per hour, but it was all so smooth, precise, and quiet that it did not feel like they were moving that fast.

When it was time to complete the flight, Dave took back the controls and made the landing approach. He had already briefed Karen on one Learjet quirk that she needed to experience firsthand. As their speed dropped down through 150 knots, the airplane started to Dutch roll ever so slightly. As it banked one way, Dave corrected, and the airplane went back the other way. Landing a Learjet required this certain deft waggle on the control stick. The key variable in the equation was learning how to limit the amount of aileron fed in during each correction. Karen watched and made her mental notes. Back on the ground, she had a permanent grin that would not leave her face anytime soon.

On August 6, they departed Scottsdale in the beautiful Learjet 24 and flew six passengers to Torreon, Mexico (TRC). Flying international had meant filing "general declaration" documentation, including details on each crew member and every item aboard the aircraft. They had also prepared knowing they would need bundles of US cash in small denominations, which even on official flights such as this was the unofficially official way of getting things done in Mexico. Brief meetings in cockpits, with the pilots pointing out their planned routes on a flight chart, ended with a rubber-banded cash bundle slipped to the Mexican official who would—*Of course, señor!*—file the flight plan.

From Torreon they flew on to Queretaro (QRO) and stayed in San Miguel de Allende. Then Queretaro to Guadalajara (GDL) to pick up a passenger and return to Queretaro. When they landed in Guadalajara and left the plane, Karen looked up to the tower where she saw two air traffic controllers peering down with binoculars. She knew immediately what they were thinking: *¡Dios mío! Una mujer en la cabina.*

Next was a round-trip, Queretaro to Oaxaca (OAX) with four passengers, on August 9. Karen detailed every leg in her flight log, handwritten in pen, and made notes of any eventful happenings: *Nearly hit a poor canine on takeoff roll. Weather and thunderstorms in Queretaro.*

On August 10 they left Queretaro and flew back to Torreon, then to Tucson to clear customs, and back to Scottsdale with the original six passengers. Karen wrote: *Will miss Mexico!* And although she did not write it in her flight log, during the entire trip she had two overriding thoughts. First, *they were paying her to fly this airplane!* And second, if marriage was challenging, then flying with one's spouse was even more difficult. Dave Harker was a crack pilot, and he pushed Karen to perform and rarely gave compliments. Any mistakes elicited stern reprimands. That challenge, however, was always overridden by the joy of her primary thought: *they were paying her to fly this airplane!*

BY May 1992, Karen and Dave were seamless as a husband-and-wife flight crew. Sometimes they got to ferry a beautiful airplane, which meant no passengers or other crew. They would take a commercial flight to their pickup destination, such as Albuquerque (ABQ), and get to fly back to Phoenix together in a fabulous airplane. Lots of married couples went out to dinner or the movies: Dave and Karen Harker flew jets together and bonded through the never-ending discussions and analysis that all pilots knew.

Overall, the marriage seemed to be working well. The two pilots were busy with flying—Karen as both pilot and Delta Air Lines flight attendant—and caring for their two parrots and two dogs. They had bigger plans, too: despite the endometriosis diagnosis and grim prognosis for pregnancy a decade earlier,

Karen and Dave had been trying for years to have children together. Frustrated, Karen went for another laparoscopy procedure to clean up any damage from the endometriosis. The gynecologist she had found in Scottsdale had reversed the earlier prediction and told Karen it would be possible for her to get pregnant.

Dave already had two children from a previous marriage, so, given Karen's medical history, she always assumed the inability to conceive was a problem with her. Still, even with another procedure Karen and Dave were unable to conceive a child. Determined, they went to a fertility specialist, but thousands of dollars later no one could give them any concrete explanations as to why they were unable to conceive. Karen resigned herself to the reality that the clock was ticking away; nature had passed her by. She worked on accepting that she was not ever going to get pregnant, but acceptance did not come easily. A family was something she had missed out on as a child. She was the lonely kid, with no siblings after baby Kathleen died, left to wander down to the beach alone and envision her own big, happy family someday. She longed for the craziness and closeness she suspected children would bring. Instead, with becoming a mom out of the picture, Karen turned her complete focus back to her pilot career, which was a perfect place to channel all her energy.

She was both eager and anxious about officially transitioning from being a flight attendant to working only as a pilot. Compounding the challenge was the reality in the early 1990s that charter and corporate pilots, with great-paying jobs, were also regularly cut loose and unemployed, which she had already experienced when her husband lost his corporate job. Being a pilot was a wildly volatile and unstable career compared to the steady reliability of her work as a flight attendant. And that job only continued to get better the longer she stayed and built seniority: better schedules, better routes, better pay, and no reserve.

Adding to her challenge was that pilots everywhere were always looking to move up, so there were few if any plum job slots in 1992. While her husband was applying to United Airlines and the other major players, Karen was focused on trying to get hired by a smaller regional airline, or fixed-base operation, as she continued to build her flight hours. She finally got the chance to prove her mettle with a small airline that had roots back to the roaring twenties.

IN 1928, William P. Cutter founded a company called Cutter Flying Service, Inc., based out of Albuquerque, New Mexico. The fledgling airline managed to survive the Great Depression of the 1930s and into the 1940s by taking passengers on air charters to ranches and tiny pinpoints on the browned landscapes throughout New Mexico, Arizona, and Texas.

When America entered World War II, much of the general aviation industry and supporting businesses ground to a halt. To survive, those at Cutter Flying Service reinvented their company as a training center for military pilots. Expanding west with a new moniker, Cutter Aviation, Inc. eventually located at Phoenix Sky Harbor International Airport (PHX) in 1959. In 1988, the company opened a new fixed-based operation facility at the same airport, consolidated aircraft sales, maintenance, and charter services to the new facility, and started providing fuel and line service. The new Phoenix facility became the company headquarters and, in 1992, the brass hired a new chief pilot named Dave Harker.

With that introduction Karen, too, had an inside track onto the company's roster of pilots. Once again, she would be the right-seat fill-in pilot as needed. She provided her Delta work schedule to Cutter Aviation each week and then hoped that on one of her off days as a flight attendant she'd get to suit up and strap in as a pilot. Her first such assignment was for Organ Donor Network, when she got a random call at 2 a.m., flew to Tucson, picked up a harvest team, and flew back to Phoenix with living human organs specially packed and iced.

As Karen's flight hours and experience mounted, she continued to check off new aviation milestones. It was during her time flying for Cutter Aviation that she stepped into one of the first "glass" cockpits, which meant the traditional steam gauges—big round dials with painted numbers and actual needles—were now small electronic screens with digital numbers and the instrumentation was all incorporated visually. A definite learning curve was involved getting comfortable in these aircraft, including the King Air and Beech 2000, nicknamed "The Starship." From day one at flight school she had trained on those tried-and-true classics: Cessna 152 and Piper Warrior. The Starship had odd design quirks, including propellers at the rear, a configuration that turned out to be an expensive and short-lived business flop.

At Cutter, Karen did other part-time flights on the Beech Bonanza. She also did ferry flights, to relocate aircraft within Arizona, and passenger flights, including taking a news crew to Montana to cover a raging forest fire. In January 1996, she did ferry flights for the well-heeled elite who descended upon Phoenix for Super Bowl XXX in a fleet of gleaming private jets. Once there, the gridiron showdown was played at Sun Devil Stadium in the Phoenix suburb of Tempe. Because of the number of aircraft and varied departure times after the big game (Dallas Cowboys 27, Pittsburgh Steelers 17), Karen and other pilots moved the toys of millionaires and billionaires among various Phoenix metropolitan airports for the postgame exodus.

On another assignment Karen took six employees of the machine manufacturer Caterpillar on a business trip from Phoenix to Salina, Kansas (SLN), which was just a fuel stop, and then onto Nashville (BNA), Amarillo (AMA), and back to Phoenix. It was quite a time in her life: one day she'd be at 35,000 feet serving Diet Coke to executives in her Delta Air Lines flight attendant uniform, and the next she'd be in her pilot uniform at the controls of a Learjet with Norwest Bank executives aboard and en route to various business dealings.

"Being a pilot at Cutter Aviation was an awesome job," she recalled. "It was always different planes, different passengers, and different destinations."

A big bonus for Karen was flying side by side with her husband Dave, who was a strict, accomplished, and hardcore pilot who pushed his wife to continually learn and develop her abilities. On many occasions, his challenges took her well beyond her comfort zone, such as the day they were ready to descend into Salina, Kansas. Strapped into a Cessna Citation jet, a sleek, turbofan-powered plane, they were battling brutal headwinds that were buffeting and rocking the aircraft.

"I'm not comfortable doing this landing," Karen told the pilot, her husband.

"You need to do this landing," he said, in that direct way that Karen knew meant only one thing: she was going to land this aircraft or die trying. Indeed, death was a real possibility if she screwed up; crumpling the million-dollar jet was another. *OK, this was going to be a handful.*

In heavy wind, she knew she had to compensate by dipping the wing into the wind, but then had to correct for the landing rollout. It was one thing to practice it on a Cessna 152 in the steady Hawaiian breezes; it was altogether another thing to have to do it for real on a Cessna Citation in brutal conditions. Even as she brought the jet down beautifully and smoked the wheels, it was an all-white-knuckle affair. Pulse pounding, she only exhaled when Dave said she had done a great job, a rare verbal nod. When they climbed down the short stairs to exit the plane, the wind was so extreme they could not walk upright.

With a great part-time position at Cutter Aviation, Karen was back to her repeating quandary: When should she cut the cord as a flight attendant and try to find a full-time pilot job? When she did, she'd lose her flight attendant salary and all her seniority. But the upside was that she would make herself available for more freelance jobs at Cutter and, eventually, a full-time post there or somewhere else. She needed to let go of the trapeze and fly to reach the other side.

But after a dozen years earning her privileges as a flight attendant, she was reluctant to give up her seniority. One pragmatic consideration for Karen was her steady, reliable paycheck as a flight attendant; it would be a big risk for her and her husband to live solely on his paycheck in the precarious world pilots inhabited.

Ultimately, she decided to continue straddling both worlds, as both a pilot and a flight attendant. In hindsight, Karen would later realize that this had been her last and best opportunity to make the leap of faith. She would realize, too, that the decision would eventually cost her the dream she had nurtured since those early morning blasts on the Ducati with her father.

THE unexpected call came in early February 1997: Karen's mother had fallen ill and was in the hospital. After all the intervening years and little communication, mother and daughter were not emotionally close in the ways Karen had always longed for as a young girl back in Redondo Beach. Regardless, it was still her mom, and Karen went immediately to visit her at the hospital in Bakersfield, California. Karen barely recognized her Mother, who had been admitted as Jane Doe. Karen learned that on a life rescue helicopter flight from Ridgecrest to Bakersfield her mother's heart had stopped, and her standing Do Not Resuscitate orders had been ignored. Her mother was comatose, and so bloated she looked like some other person. A small scar on her mother's left foot provided the needed clue to her identity. Karen leaned close and said, "I love you. If you need to let go, it's OK."

Being there brought it all rushing back … baby Kathleen, the endless loneliness and longing, growing up on the back of a motorcycle. Karen had no siblings to help carry the emotional load of this life milestone; the doctors had already told her to prepare for the worst. She went out for a quick dinner with her stepfather—a stranger, really—and to process all that was happening: should she take her mother off life support? When they returned, Karen's mother had already passed away. Karen was both sad and also relieved she did not have to make the decision herself.

Marsaline (Baio) Meyer died February 11, 1997, at just 55. Born in Roscoe, California, she had later become a choreographer and road manager for Creedence Clearwater Revival, the Grateful Dead, and other bands. She was a self-employed clothing designer, seamstress, and homemaker, and had married LeRoy Meyer, a nice man Karen had met but barely knew. Karen had also never known of her mother's interesting career path. During her life and after her death, who her mother had been would be, for Karen, always largely shrouded in mystery.

Dave Harker drove from Phoenix for the memorial service, which Karen had to plan without much direction, input, or help—an odd and somewhat eerie exercise after so many years of estrangement. One request was that her mother wanted to be buried next to baby Kathleen, but those plots had already been taken. Karen chose the closest available plot and then sobbed: the emotional distance between her and her mother first arose when baby Kathleen died. Now there would forever be a similar physical distance between the final resting places of mother and youngest daughter. And here was Karen, still around and left alone to plan and map it all out again on her own, a snapshot of her entire life. Rather than peace or resolution, her mother's death seemed a sad and open-ended coda to what had been and what would never be. Instead, Karen had found her way to her own new place, aloft in gleaming jets, anchored to the unchanging tenets of acceleration, motion, and physics.

Meanwhile, Karen's father Reinhold Vern Sommerstedt continued his life into the 2000s just as his eldest daughter had always seen him: highly intelligent, eccentric, and a jack-of-all trades. The second generation Californian eventually met his beautiful wife Zoya, a native of Ukraine, on an online dating site. Like Karen, they married on a Hawaiian island. They settled in Las Vegas where Karen's father ran his own company as an investment advisor who regularly held lectures to help others navigate the tricky world of offshore tax havens.

As far as motorcycling, he eventually traded in his two-wheeled machines for Unimogs, a multi-purpose, four-wheel drive utilitarian truck produced by Mercedes Benz, which would have been an equally unique method of getting Karen to grade school.

EVENTUALLY, Cutter Aviation executives wanted to retain full-time employees only. As a part-time pilot, flight attendant, and flight instructor, Karen did not fit the new profile. Her earlier decision to straddle two different career worlds was already coming back to haunt her. Although she did not realize it at the time, she flew her last flight for the company on February 26, 1997: Phoenix (PHX)—Palm Springs (PSP)—Mesa (FFZ)—Phoenix in a Cessna Citation for a group of Ford dealership executives. At some point, it occurred to her that no one from Cutter Aviation was calling with freelance gigs. Around this same time her husband, too, left Cutter to become director of operations for Swift Aviation, a new company being launched with Citation 10 jets and sparkling facilities.

Because Karen had never had a steady, full-time job as a pilot, she took the temporary employment lapse in stride and didn't give it a second thought. But larger events were afoot, including her almost imperceptibly unraveling marriage to Dave Harker. Like the unnoticeable but steady work of water that creates canyons over time, forces had started to erode the emotional connection between the high-flying duo.

TEN

House of Horrors

IN JANUARY 1998, KAREN HARKER TOOK HER NEXT PILOT POST, with Native Air Ambulance flying out of Williams-Gateway in Mesa, Arizona, now renamed Phoenix–Mesa Gateway Airport (AZA) with the closing of Williams Air Force Base. Her new mission: flying to remote reservations to transport sick and injured Native Americans for treatment at hospitals in metropolitan Phoenix.

In her previous post at Cutter Aviation she had been flying jets, so this new job was, at best, a lateral step: she would be flying the British Aerospace Jetstream, a twin turboprop with a pressurized fuselage that was notoriously difficult to land. Jets, despite the higher speeds and dazzling high-tech gadgetry, were surprisingly easy to fly. The Jetstream, which despite the name was not a jet, had no autopilot and would make Karen work hard. Additionally, Karen also took a steep pay cut. Her new salary at Native Air Ambulance was only $1,200 per month. Despite fifteen years of flight school and ongoing aviation training, multiple ratings, and steadily accumulating air time, she earned more in her job as a flight attendant.

And because she had that full-time job at Delta Air Lines, she scheduled all her off days as a Native Air Ambulance pilot. There were no official demographic profiles to check, but she was definitely a rare anomaly as both a flight attendant and an accomplished pilot.

Interestingly, for safety reasons pilots were under strict FAA regulations that capped their annual maximum seat time at 1,000 flight hours. But there was no such regulation covering combined hours aloft, such as being both a flight attendant and a pilot.

Despite all the challenges in her new post, Karen was energized by learning to fly the difficult Jetstream. She was the only female among three new pilots who began ground school together, where they spent four full-time weeks. Their ground instructor was an America West pilot who taught them every aspect of the British Aerospace Jetstream, including its specific oddities and unique systems. From the tip of the nose to the top of the tail, they learned the airplane inside and out. As a pilot, if a problem occurred in flight, pulling off the road and calling a mechanic was not an option. Pilots had to know their aircraft and what to do when mechanical systems went south.

To that end, Karen and the other two new pilots took numerous written tests to prove their understanding before ever sliding into the cockpit and taking flight. Those tests covered aircraft systems and limitations, meteorology, Federal Aviation Administration regulations, and company policies. There were endless pages of documentation they had to know cold. Every word, spelling, and punctuation mark in their written answers had to be perfect, because attention to detail saved lives. Fortunately, Karen was blessed with natural curiosity, an exacting nature, and a good memory, a tactical triumvirate for a pilot. An added challenge for her was once again being the only woman in an all-boys club.

"I was determined to get along with all the guys and not be overly sensitive," she said. Karen Harker was no pushover, but she was not a hard-charging, bra-burning feminist, either. Her strategy was to take the middle road; she would get along to go along. She never walked into new situations with a chip on her shoulder about being a woman. Of course she would stand up for the tenets of equal rights and pay for women, but her strategy also meant, at times, feigning a smile when the off-putting locker-room remarks flew. And fly they did.

What's the difference between a jet engine and a flight attendant? At the end of the flight the jet engine stops whining.

Karen could laugh. Was it sexist? Yes. Bothersome? Not really. Disrespectful? For Karen, it depended on the context and nuance. Welcome to the boys' club. But as the men guffawed, the gutter talk got old and inevitably crossed the line.

Perhaps it was her single-dad upbringing on the back of a Ducati, but most of it never bothered her. Almost every pilot she knew was a man, and the people signing the checks were men, too, all the way up the hierarchy. So instead, she chose a more subtle counterattack, which was to denigrate the entire gender with a few good jokes of her own that she kept tucked away: *How do you know there's an airline captain at a party? He'll tell you.* Her father had given her insight into being able to think like a man.

"Obviously I looked different, but I just tried to blend in with the guys," she said.

Once ground training was done, in April 1998 Karen took her first flight in the Jetstream and started to get comfortable in yet another new aircraft. The Native Air Ambulance fleet comprised two helicopters and three fixed-wing aircraft at its base in east Mesa, Arizona. As air ambulance pilots, Karen and the others worked twelve-hour shifts. From the time a call came in, they had five minutes to get airborne during daylight, ten minutes at night. When working, Karen lived in the crew area at the airport for each twelve-hour shift. She was the only female pilot out of the ten fixed-wing pilots on the payroll. Each shift started with a briefing in the dispatch area. Fellow pilot Gary May had also been a flight attendant, for Southwest Airlines, and joked with the medical crew, "Not sure how our flight will go tonight, but Karen and I can make a great cup of coffee."

The "green room" was the break area for each of the three pilot crews and three medical teams; each shift meant fourteen people awaiting the next call. They ate meals together, read aviation manuals, talked aviation, and watched movies. During the day shift they also chewed up idle time by meticulously scrubbing each airplane's entire exterior and then moving inside to clean the interior to perfection.

Day or night, when an emergency call came it was a thunderous bell that rattled all three crews, one helicopter and two fixed-wing, to attention. At night, from a dead sleep, Karen's heart raced as she waited to see whether her team was taking the flight. Each night that bell sounded five or six times, and it scared the living crap out of her every time. The noise blared over the loudspeaker and reverberated through the old military hangar, followed by a booming voice: "Fixed-wing seven juliet alpha, White River." That was the aircraft identifier and the destination. Regardless of who was going out, every call woke up everyone.

When Karen's identifier came up in the wee hours, she'd leap out of bed already partially in her jumpsuit. All she had to do was wriggle her arms down the sleeves, zip up, and go. They scrambled into the darkness in unison with the medical crew, climbed the stairs, strapped in, started flipping switches and pushing buttons, and readied for takeoff. When the ground crew member held up one index finger and circled the air with the opposite index finger, Karen started engine one. Then two fingers for engine two. They had been dead asleep one minute, and ten minutes later they were airborne and speeding toward Superstition Mountain to the east in pitch-black darkness.

Karen loved her new place in the desert Southwest, but could not know the future significance of the immovable rock fingers perched below her position at 5,057 vertical feet. Back and forth she flew over that mountain, in daylight and darkness, under blazing desert sunshine, through clouds and rain and the odd smattering of snow. The volcano that had anchored the range for forty million years was a postcard backdrop to her ascension toward a dream. The same mountain would one day be the epicenter of her worst nightmare.

Hand-flying the Jetstream, a real beast to manage, was just the type of aviation challenge she loved. Taking off out of Williams-Gateway and flying over the desert mountains always put her on alert. Most of the outbound flights to "the rez" were short, under forty-five minutes, so now they were on descent to another tricky landing spot, White River, which was down in a canyon surrounded by terrain with a steep drop at each end of the runway. Final approach in the Jetstream was like controlling a barge barreling down from the sky, no autopilot, and a heavy control wheel that felt like arm wrestling a grizzly bear all the way to the tarmac. Approaching the runway at 3 a.m., in the blackout conditions of a high-desert night—with only two strips of shimmering runway lights for visual reference—produced purified blasts of adrenaline unlike any other. Then, once on the ground, the end of the runway at White River fell off into the oblivion of a deep, dark canyon waiting to swallow an airplane. Karen could not see the abyss at night but knew exactly where the terrain became a black hole. For Karen Harker, this was just another typical "day off" from being a flight attendant at Delta Air Lines.

"That was one of my favorite flying jobs ever," she recalled.

ON June 15, 1998, Karen was summoned to Native Air just when she was starting to think she would finally get an actual day of rest without being in an airplane. One of the captains was out ill, which meant Karen would get that day off because she was not yet left-seat qualified at the required 1,500 hours of flight time and a type rating. But instead of staying home and sleeping, Karen was going to work to fly with a temporary fill-in, whom she was already cursing for stepping up. His name was Shawn Perry. He, like Karen, had a bad case of the aviation bug and, when not working as a pilot on passenger jets for America West Airlines, now moonlighted at Native Air Ambulance, where he had once worked full time.

At first glance, Shawn Perry reminded Karen of actor and director Ron Howard, with his red hair and freckles. Karen immediately thought he was cute in a boyish way. In the small fraternity of pilots, her husband Dave Harker already knew Shawn and had frequently talked about him. Shawn was introverted, almost reclusive. Karen had shown up early for briefing, and then wondered why Shawn stayed in the dispatch office for hours while all the other pilots and medical crew socialized in the green room. When a call came, Karen and Shawn flew to Tucson, where they had to wait in a pilot lounge.

Wanting some fresh air, they stepped outside where, away from the other pilots, Shawn opened up more about his previous marriage and girlfriend. Karen and Shawn talked and connected emotionally, as they both shared personal trials and tribulations. After that night, Karen flew with him only one other time at Native Air Ambulance.

"Shawn Perry was one of the wonder pilots who got all his ratings at a very young age," she said of the man whose surname she would one day take. "He was really sharp." His father, J. Leon Perry, had started a company called Ponderosa Aviation in 1974, when Shawn was a young boy.

By the summer of 1998, as an air ambulance pilot for Native Air Ambulance, Karen was one step away from being a pilot for a major US airline. As she continued looking, watching, and waiting for her dream job, she was not concerned whether it was her next post or two or three down the line. All that mattered was that she would soon achieve her ultimate target in the aviation world. Instead of serving drinks and fetching pillows at the back of a Delta Air Lines jet, she'd be in a crisp, starched pilot uniform on the flight deck of that same aircraft. With everything she knew and believed, it seemed a foregone conclusion that it was just a matter of time. What she did not know was that she would soon be fighting for her life, after coming off an all-night shift and slipping into a harrowing odyssey.

AFTER working the all-nighter for Native Air Ambulance, Karen usually woke up around 1 p.m. to begin her day and start preparing for her next shift at 7 p.m. But on July 1, 1998, as she stepped into the shower she was wincing from horrible stomach pains, which became so bad she was incapacitated. Soon she was yelling for her husband Dave to take her to the hospital. He drove her to the closest facility, which was Chandler Regional Hospital. Karen was in so much pain she fell to the floor in the emergency triage area and started vomiting. Dave dialed the number for Native Air Ambulance and told them his wife would be out sick that night.

After a round of tests, the doctor came back and told Karen she had appendicitis, they needed to operate immediately, and that by the next day she would definitely be feeling better, on the mend, and headed home. She'd then need another three weeks off work to fully recover.

As a trained pilot, it never once occurred to Karen to question the doctor's diagnosis or seek a second opinion. She operated under the assumption that doctors, like pilots, underwent strict training, endured long years of education, and, once licensed, were regularly tested and retested to demonstrate competency. On that last point, she was about to learn otherwise. At the moment of diagnosis her primary thought was simply immense disappointment because she would not be able to work for almost a month. This was a critical blow. She loved her pilot job.

Two hours after arriving at the hospital, still in horrible pain, she was finally slipping into the balm of general anesthesia. Surgeon Joan Kohr removed Karen's appendix, which a later pathology report would determine was normal, pink, and perfectly healthy. The next day she was sore and still not feeling well, but the medical staff reassured her that this was all normal after major surgery. The doctor authorized her discharge and sent her home to convalesce.

Over the next three days, her condition never improved. In fact, by July 4 she was just as sick as she had been before the surgery. She could not eat, had a blistering fever, and was doubled over on her patio, vomiting. She called the doctor back and left three messages that something was not right. Finally Kohr relented and said Karen could come to the office for a checkup; when she did, the doctor told her everything looked fine.

On July 10, her condition worsened. Her husband was away on a work flight to the East Coast and then overseas, so a friend came to stay with her. She took one look at her ghost-white friend and said, "You have to go back to the hospital. Except this time we're taking you to a good hospital."

Instead of driving to the same nearby hospital in Chandler, Karen's friend took the thirty-minute drive north to Scottsdale Healthcare Shea Medical Center. Doctors there were alarmed when they ran a blood panel: Karen's red cell count was off the charts. Things took an even more ominous turn when the emergency room doctor returned and Karen overheard, "Where's her family? They need to get here. She might not make it through the night."

Karen started to panic and tried reaching her husband to tell him not to leave the country as planned for his charter flight on Swift Air. He got the message, told his employer what was happening, and immediately caught a flight back to Phoenix. Sometime in the wee hours he arrived at the hospital. He was horrified when he saw his wife writhing on the hospital bed and near death.

She was beyond sick, delirious, and in excruciating pain. Baffled, the doctors could not pin down a diagnosis with any certainty. She had eight tubes draining necrotic septic fluid for one test after another. One theory was that she had suffered a punctured bowel during the appendicitis surgery, but they were not certain. Doctors ordered more and more powerful antibiotics, the big guns, to fight a nasty yeast infection that had spread throughout her body. Karen could not eat, and her internal organs were starting to shut down. She was about as sick as a person could possibly be and still be alive.

Doctors called in gastroenterologists and infectious disease specialists, but no one could determine the cause. Clinging to life by a thread and in critical care for three weeks, the prognosis was grim. No one, especially doctors, believed she would survive, because peritonitis is notoriously fatal. With her internal organs failing and her lungs clogged with pneumonia, Karen was in a drug-induced fog and could barely breathe or speak. In her delirium, the smells and sounds of her baby sister's departure came back. She hallucinated bugs crawling on the walls. Karen sensed she was moving toward that place to join Kathleen and her mother. As Karen's weight plummeted, now just 88 pounds, the veil between this life and the next was being pulled back. The daily updates from the doctors were completely disheartening: You *do* realize you're as sick as a person can be? Karen was 35 and terrified because they couldn't even come up with a diagnosis. Doctors said the only way to help her was emergency surgery.

"Either we do it, or you will die," a doctor told her.

When surgeons cut Karen from her breast line to well below her belly button, they found a gaping hole in her stomach. That gastric perforation, caused by an ulcer and misdiagnosed as appendicitis, came within hours of taking her life. The ulcer had leaked necrotic material throughout her system. The secondary peritonitis she had developed was an infection of her stomach lining.

Post-surgery, doctors had Karen on the antibiotic amphotericin B, which the nurses called "Ampho the Terrible" for its many potentially lethal side effects. The medical staff was checking her blood gas levels three times a day with multiple needle insertions on her inner wrist. Every time she saw the technician she started sobbing. She also had a PICC line, a peripherally inserted central catheter, which was a tube for administering medicine. A nasogastric (NG) tube snaked through her nose, down through her nasopharynx and esophagus, and into her stomach for feeding. She had pneumonia and fluid in her left lung which doctors had to drain daily with a painful puncture procedure.

"It was a house of horrors," she recalled. "The entire ordeal was absolute torture."

Her husband Dave stayed bedside around the clock and helped prepare and then host visitors, including Shawn Perry. Karen's work peers, pilots, and flight attendants started arriving to pay final respects and say good-bye. With pneumonia and little lung capacity, Karen could barely speak. Numerous tubes, lines, and compression leg wraps covered Karen's body. Shawn would only later tell his future bride that he had been certain that was the last time he would see Karen alive.

But Karen did not die, and gradually regained enough strength to fight for her life. The pneumonia slowly cleared. Her organs started functioning again, but she was still struggling to breathe and speak. The NG tube came out, and she started taking small amounts of liquid sustenance. Eventually, she was able to try tiny pieces of solid food. She was frail and could barely walk in a hunched shuffle. Karen finally left the hospital, which none of the doctors had thought she would when she first arrived in such an abysmal state. After six more months of painful, tedious, and grueling physical therapy, she had mostly regained the weight and physical strength she had lost.

She had not been able to work at either job—as flight attendant or pilot—for more than six months. As a reminder of the ordeal, she had a new twelve-inch zipper scar down her front that had deformed her muscle tissue including losing her belly button, and made it very difficult to stand straight. Later, in 2000, she would have surgeries to insert wire mesh in her abdomen so her intestines wouldn't pop out.

In December 1998, after the unplanned six-month leave of absence, Karen was back to work at Delta Air Lines and Native Air Ambulance. Finally among the living again, it was then that she received another devastating blow: a biopsy revealed that she had stage I invasive ductal carcinoma. To sum it up: Karen was 35, it was Christmas Eve 1998, and she had breast cancer.

E L E V E N

Pregnant Pilot

KAREN HARKER WAS IN THE GREEN ROOM at Native Air Ambulance when she got the phone call. She had gone in for her regular checkup at the gynecologist and asked for a mammogram just as a precaution. She held a manual she was reading for the new plane the company had acquired, a Pilatus PC-12 single-engine turboprop.

"Are you alone where you can talk?" Dr. Kathleen Frye said. Karen looked at the pilots and medical personnel milling around, making coffee, reading, and talking.

"Yes," she said, unconcerned.

"Your mammogram came back abnormal. We need to do a biopsy."

Two days later Karen went for the biopsy and, a few days after that, received the official diagnosis: invasive ductal carcinoma. The breast cancer was on the left side directly underneath the nipple, where lumps were difficult to detect. In an odd twist, after the near-death panic six months earlier and long recovery back to health, Karen had a new perspective that helped her process the devastating news. By comparison, this challenge seemed less daunting than what she had just endured. She had a clear diagnosis, they had caught the cancer early, and she knew the exact course of treatment she needed to undergo immediately. That was all preferable to writhing in excruciating pain, teetering near death, while doctors argued about what was wrong with her. Still, she had the normal "C-word" fears.

"I had been through so much already, I just thought, *here's one more thing*," she recalled. Another element of the diagnosis was that her pilot career would once again be interrupted.

In January 1999, Karen underwent a lumpectomy in her left breast. When the surgery was not successful, she underwent a second lumpectomy two weeks later. When she saw the results, a body mutilated, she was devastated. She then began radiation therapy. Chemotherapy was contraindicated because of the huge doses of medication that had ravaged her body and organs six months earlier during the peritonitis. The oncologist was concerned that chemotherapy could dangerously weaken her body. The alternative, radiation therapy, was the recommendation—with the caveat that it, too, had severe potential risk, including heart damage. Meanwhile, the FAA grounded Karen during her radiation therapy. Once again, she was on a medical leave and unsure when she would get her pilot career solidly back on track.

AS Karen was overcoming the cancer scare, two pilots she knew, Mike Glow and Gary May, had just left Native Air Ambulance to work for the start-up Farwest Airlines, a company that was snatching up good pilots with unbelievable salaries for an FAR Part 121 supplemental airline.

Founded in 1947, Biegert Aviation originally had large federal government contracts for crop dusting in the Midwest. Max Biegert initially defied that old adage about turning a profit with airplanes—*How do you make a million dollars in aviation? Start with two million*—by making a fortune with his eponymous company. Then he and his wife started another venture and, eventually, demonstrated the truth of the old adage.

After exiting the crop dusting business, they operated a profitable day-care business in Houston, Texas, which became the Children's World Learning Center and later KinderCare Learning Centers. When a loan they had made in another business deal defaulted, the Biegerts inherited the security collateral, which was the Grand Canyon Railway. Unexpectedly, the Biegerts now owned a tourist-based, steam-engine train service that carried passengers sixty-four miles from Williams, Arizona, to the Grand Canyon. Being more versed in air travel than rail, the Biegerts launched Farwest Airlines to taxi tourists from California, Las Vegas, Phoenix, and Flagstaff to Williams, where passengers could then take the rail line. As of April 1, 1998, Farwest Airlines LLC was officially issued a certificate of existence by the Arizona Corporation Commission.

Karen was intrigued; she applied to Farwest as a pilot and was hired. Karen reluctantly had to tell Chief Pilot Bill Umberger and Captain Dennis Morgan, of Native Air Ambulance, that she was leaving the company.

Once again, at Farwest Airlines she was the only female among the initial cadre of ten pilots, who were each earning around $75,000 in annual salary, an incredible pay jump from the $1,200 a month she had been making at Native Air Ambulance. In her new job, Karen would be flying one of the three de Havilland-7 airplanes in the fleet, an unusual plane that was somewhat rare, and the predecessor to the de Havilland-8, which she would fly at her next job. At Farwest Airlines, she would be flying to Flagstaff, Phoenix, and the Grand Canyon within Arizona, and to Las Vegas, Nevada, and Long Beach, California. By now, Karen had flown more than 30 different makes and models of aircraft.

The de Havilland Canada-7, known among pilots as the Dash 7, was a four-engine (Pratt & Whitney Canada PT6) turboprop airplane that first took flight in 1975. With the wings above the fuselage, the airplane held fifty passengers and had a range of one thousand nautical miles. Manufactured in Canada, this unique airplane was rarely seen in the Southwest. It was somewhat of a relic and, like a flying tank, was a challenging airplane to fly—which meant hard work and more fun for pilots. It was a big step up from the Jetstream and much different than the Pilatus PC-12.

"It was a great opportunity that fell in my lap thanks to pilots Mike Glow and Gary May, who recommended me," Karen recalled. "I had to go for it."

Six weeks of ground school started in January 1999 with the initial contingent of new pilots. Because Farwest was a new airline, company executives had a lot of boxes to check, under constant FAA scrutiny. Every day there was a federal air inspector sitting on site to observe the ground school training of the ten pilots and twenty new flight attendants. Farwest operated under FAR Part 121 supplemental, which meant the same standards as any major airline. The only difference was that Farwest flights were nonscheduled. Along with all the other bureaucratic hurdles, the nascent airline pilots also had to do proving runs with FAA inspectors to demonstrate operational proficiency.

Karen smiled the first day she saw everyone assembled: all the flight attendants were female, and all the pilots were male. Except her: she had crossed the dividing line. To maximize her potential as a pilot, Karen made another strategic play when she took a second consecutive six-month leave from Delta Air Lines. Without having to juggle two jobs, she could focus exclusively on being a pilot. The experiment worked so well that she would take two more six-month leaves in succession.

In her new job the ground instructor was Ron Clark, an ex-military pilot who later became an aeronautical professor at Embry-Riddle Aeronautical University. Ground school was a full-time, eight-to-five grind, with courses in the Phoenix suburb of Chandler at the small Gila River Memorial Airport (LO7), located on the Gila River reservation. As always, the collection of assembled aviators was eclectic and inspiring. There was a retired Air Force pilot who had flown the Dash 7 in the military, and who would become one of Karen's favorite captains. Another was a crusty old Australian pilot with a thick accent, who was immediately skeptical of his first officer's gender. Coupled with Karen's temporary abstinence from alcohol for health reasons and the corollary sports-and-locker-room bonding talk of men, she was like some alien being. Another retired Air Force pilot was a chauvinistic know-it-all and, for unknown reasons, was afflicted with frequent and rancid flatulence. In an attempt to spare his fellow pilots, he'd stand in the corner during ground school.

Mentally and emotionally, Karen was over the moon as a new pilot hire at what promised to be a great company. Karen told her new employer about her cancer diagnosis, and they were very supportive. Physically, however, she was barely recovering from the six months of health battles and now two more surgeries related to the breast cancer. She would be undergoing radiation five times a week. That radiation therapy was scheduled as a six-week regimen, but it took more than two months because her body was not tolerating the treatment. In the hospital, she was surrounded by people battling cancer, which was depressing. She'd put on a robe and be wheeled into the large metal cylinder. On those days, she had permission to be late for class, and her instructor passed the information along to the federal examiner. After treatment and sitting in ground school, she feared she might vomit because she was constantly nauseous. She was exhausted, too.

"I tried to put on a happy face, but I felt like crap," she said. "Regardless, I still had to perform at a top level."

Meanwhile, as Karen had spent six months convalescing at home during the illness, she had had a lot of time to mentally sort through things and come to the sad conclusion that her marriage with Dave Harker was failing. The high-flying duo was suffering from a malaise common in the industry: AIDS, or Aviation Induced Divorce Syndrome. With scattered schedules, frenzied lives, and long hours, days, and weeks apart, their connection had snapped.

Neither had any major or overt complaints about the other, but they had become, more or less, roommates who shared a love of aviation. By the spring of 2000, Karen and Dave were separated. That summer, Karen made a phone call that changed the entire trajectory of her life. Such drama was not hyperbole: by the time she hung up, everything had changed.

"Let's get together and hang out," she said. "Maybe meet for a drink?"

Shawn Perry agreed, and they had that drink at Rainforest Café at a local mall. A casual friendship ensued. Karen may have been newly single, but she had also been through hell and back physically, so she had no designs on anything romantic. He was a pilot, too, which made conversation easy. In fact, their entire friendship revolved around exactly that: their respective fascination with airplanes and all topics related to flying. Shawn was now a pilot for America West Airlines, and they liked to bounce ideas off each other and debate how to handle various airborne scenarios. Although their personalities were quite different—Shawn was more introverted, while Karen was an extrovert—they shared a love of airplanes.

BY summer 2000, Farwest Airlines was officially suffering under the old aviation truism, as a river-trough of red ink flowed from the company coffers. Owning, maintaining, and operating even a single airplane was incredibly expensive. Anyone who owned a small fleet of such gluttonous, cash-guzzling machines, such as Biegert did, faced steep uphill odds in recouping all those costs and returning a profit. As it turned out, the economics of an airline that existed solely to transport tourists to ride a train did not pan out.

"We'd fly ten passengers up to the Grand Canyon on a plane that could hold fifty," Karen said. "And they paid us whether we flew or not, which is probably why they went bankrupt."

Farwest Airlines folded in summer 2000, which meant once again Karen was without a pilot job. On September 2, Karen's divorce to Dave Harker was final. She bought her own place in Gold Canyon, a rugged spot near Superstition Mountain almost an hour from downtown Phoenix. Because she had accepted that she'd never have children, she never once considered what school district came along with the twelve-hundred-square-foot home on Vera Cruz Way. Within a couple months Shawn Perry moved into Karen's house. What had started as one drink and a great friendship had quickly progressed to something Karen never had expected.

The next month, in October, a small regional outfit hired Karen as a pilot. Mesa Airlines operated under FAR Part 121, which meant she would be trained to the same standards as every pilot flying jumbo jets. That experience was critical. She would be a first officer, right-seat, on the twenty-five passenger de Havilland-8, which everyone called the Dash 8.

Karen was glad to have a new pilot job, but leery as well. Among pilots, she had not heard good things about working for this regional, where the pay was a poverty-level insult at $12,000 per annum. The supply-and-demand market economics of the aviation field were entrenched: too many pilots for the much fewer and finite number of jobs. The working hours were even worse than the pay and bordered on indentured servitude. The only mercy was that the FAA capped pilots at 100 hours of flight time in any given month, and a total of 1,000 hours annually.

Because most pilots aspired to be with the major airlines, jobs at regional airlines were often the necessary minor-league-grind stepping-stone to the fatter paychecks, benefits, and better schedules of the big leagues. For Karen, the job was critical for keeping her proficiency and skills, so it was useful on that front. Her other option would be to go back to flight instructing, which she thought would be a lot worse than whatever any regional airline could throw at her. By the time her run at Mesa Airlines was done, however, she would have to amend that assessment.

ON Halloween 2000, Karen arrived at a facility near Sky Harbor International Airport to begin her training on the Dash 8. Eight years prior, the same year Karen began flight school, Larry Risley and his wife Janie founded Mesa Airlines, named for its location on a windy plateau in Farmington, New Mexico. The company exclusively operated several of the small regional outfits that flew under larger corporate logos, including America West Express and United Express. So while the airplane she was flying might be stamped "America West Express," Karen's paycheck was from Mesa Airlines.

On the first day of training, there were four new pilots: Karen, another woman, and two men. The other woman was Tiffany Saunders, a former flight attendant at America West Airlines who had an engineering degree and had also worked at Boeing in Seattle. When the instructor walked in, he looked at the two blondes and said, "The flight attendant training is down the hall."

Was this pre-1920s America, before the suffrage movement helped usher in a new era with passage of the Nineteenth Amendment, gaining women the right to vote? No, it was not: welcome to America, in the year 2000, where gender bias was alive and well in the aviation industry and throughout the working world.

As a pilot on a small regional airline, Karen's daily destination list was like an inventory of towns from Hollywood westerns: Aspen, Durango, Grand Junction, Flagstaff, and Tucson. Heading west to California, Mesa Airlines took passengers to Bakersfield, San Luis Obispo, and Santa Barbara. Despite her poverty-level salary, Karen was keeping all her flight ratings current and continuing to develop her aviation skills. Her boyfriend Shawn Perry's job as a pilot with a larger airline brought the household income up to a sustainable level. After ten years of marriage and then divorce, Karen was in no rush to get married. She was working exclusively as a pilot while on leave from Delta, and watching and waiting for her opportunity with a major airline. But life was about to deliver another major curveball she never saw coming.

BY summer 2001, when Karen Harker missed a couple periods, the only thought she had was that, at 38, she was young for menopause. Since the endometriosis diagnosis in her twenties, her body had also been through the wringer and back with the near-death illness and then the cancer scare. And she and her ex-husband Dave Harker had tried for ten years without success, so there was simply no way she was pregnant. But just to eliminate at least one variable, however unlikely, she bought a home pregnancy test.

When she saw the results, she was dumbfounded, elated, and in a state of shock before she could focus solely on being excited. She was pregnant! She was 38 and on the fast track to her dream career. One way or another, she'd figured within five years she'd be a first officer on the flight deck of jumbo jets at a major airline. From there, she wanted to be a captain before 50. *Pregnant?* It just did not compute initially. Her boyfriend Shawn, 29, was excited, but was initially shocked.

For two successful pilots looking to expand and cement their aviation careers, the unexpected pregnancy was a game-changer. As the one earning a much smaller salary, it was Karen's career aspirations that were immediately thrown into chaos. Initially, she was determined to have it all, baby and career; not once did she consider giving up her pilot career, a determined and noble promise to herself that she would not be able to fulfill. With her pregnancy, the clock was now ticking on her career as a pilot. Within six months, after twenty years of training and hard-won experience, it would all be over.

THERE had been one big advantage to being blissfully unaware she was pregnant: by the time Karen found out, she was already beyond the worst of the morning sickness. Immediately, she became very careful and conscientious with anything that might affect the baby. Along with no alcohol or other medications, Karen would not even take an aspirin if she had a headache.

During this time, especially post-9/11, the embattled major airlines began offering long-term leaves to employees to cut costs. At Delta Air Lines, Karen could choose either a three- or five-year leave. The last of her several consecutive leaves was almost up, so she decided to put in for a new five-year break. This would allow her the time and space to be a mom and continue her career as a pilot without trying to juggle the impossible with a second job as a flight attendant.

Not surprisingly, Mesa Airlines did not have an official uniform for pregnant pilots. So instead, she went to Gap, at a time when "pilot" shirts were in style. She bought a white stretch maternity shirt, carefully removed the epaulets from her Mesa Airlines shirt, and sewed them onto the shoulders of her new Gap shirt. Black slacks with the wide stretch maternity waistband completed the ensemble. The first time she wore the uniform to work a young girl at the airport pointed and said, "Look, Mommy, there's a pregnant pilot." Male captains and other first officers, too, gave Karen sideways scowls when they saw her waddling around places in airports and airplanes once solely reserved for the silk-scarved macho men who had carried the banner since Orville and Wilbur first took to the skies.

For her part, Karen had no desire to work while pregnant. But, as one of the few women in cockpits, she wanted to prove she belonged.

"I felt like I had to prove myself in every aviation job I had," she said.

Her gynecologist assured Karen that flying, especially at the lower altitudes of a small regional airline, would not endanger the fetus in any way. But Karen knew being a pilot was a physically difficult job in many ways. On her worst shifts, she might fly eight legs in nasty weather. That meant multiple plane changes, up and down stairs, lifting bags, walking through airports, and sitting for long periods.

As she had heard before even starting the job, working as a pilot at a regional airline was anything but glamorous. The pilots and flight attendants got worked harder than the lavatory-door hinges on a packed Airbus A380 out of Bangkok besieged with food poisoning.

"They flew the hell out of us," Karen said. "It was absolutely exhausting. Looking back, I would never do that again pregnant."

A typical day as a pilot on a regional, as noted in Karen's flight log: Grand Junction (GJT) to Phoenix (PHX), back to Grand Junction, back to Phoenix, up to Aspen (ASE), again back to Phoenix, and then finally ending in Bakersfield (BFL). The FAA-mandated maximum was eight hours a day, which they regularly pushed up against. Some days, during instrument approaches or bumpy flights Karen could feel Morgan kicking like crazy as though she, too, didn't like getting bounced all over the place.

Before her new baby daughter was even born, Karen was already emotionally torn and struggling with how to balance being a pilot and a mom. She was over-the-moon excited about her impending motherhood, but being a mom was also never a part of the plan. She had been working for almost twenty years to achieve her dream as a pilot. Now, would she be able to do both?

In November 2001, Karen had to go to Seattle, where she'd sit in a simulator for her FAA-mandated one-year check ride. Now six months pregnant, she could have rescheduled and done the check ride after maternity leave. But if she did that her certification would expire, so when she came back to work she'd have to jump through all the hoops of initial training again. She also felt uneasy about letting her certification lapse and giving her employer any reason not to bring her back after maternity leave. Again, being a woman—and a pregnant one at that—seemed to put her at an immediate disadvantage with the mostly male pilots competing for limited pilot slots.

As the day for the check ride arrived, Karen did not feel well. Her pregnancy-related anemia was making her light-headed and fatigued. As she always had, she steeled herself to do what she had to do, which was push through, pass her check ride, and start counting down the days until she could take maternity leave. As she left her hotel, she might have taken the roiling Seattle gloom as an ominous sign, but she barely noticed as she climbed in the taxi, gave directions, and tried not to pass out or throw up.

Once inside the building, as Karen waddled along pulling her own luggage (the line check airman had not offered to help), he walked ahead of her, opened a door, and then let the door slam in her face. From these first interactions with the line-check airman, Karen's skin went cold and a wave of intuition told her this was all a bad idea. Whether it was her pregnant waddle, her gender, her hair color, all of the above, or something else entirely, for some reason the line-check airman did not like Karen Harker.

Every pilot had to endure these annual check rides, and not even the most masochistic among them enjoyed the agonizing process. For starters, flight simulators were much more sensitive than actual airplanes, so what worked flawlessly in the real world might blow a check ride in the simulator. Typically, at most airlines pilots get one dry run, a check ride that does not count, just to get a feel for the simulator. To cut costs at Mesa Airlines, pilots received no such leeway. No warm up. And no test run in a simulator she'd never flown. She had to strap in and fly cold, live in the simulator her first time. Karen never played the female card, but she sensed it: she was blonde and pregnant, and this guy was giving no mercy to prove women did not belong in the cockpit. So it was no great surprise when she busted the check ride.

It was a pride-swallowing, embarrassing disappointment that happened to nearly every pilot at least once in a career. The check airman told Karen she'd have to extend her stay for another two days. The following day she would undergo one training session on the simulator and then a second check ride the day after. If she failed that, she'd be grounded and fired. Spending another two days alone in a dreary Seattle hotel room was not what Karen had envisioned. And doing a second check ride was an agonizing prospect. But she had no choice. Either she passed, or she lost her job. Rain was plentiful, but sleep was a rare commodity for the next two long nights she spent in that simulator in Seattle.

TWELVE

Smashing the Glass Ceiling

TWO DAYS LATER, Karen busted her second check ride. Just as a final indignation, Mr. Weasel actually looked at her, with a crooked smile, and said, "I am woman, hear me roar!"

On the flight back to Phoenix, Karen was furious. It was hard to get past the reality that no pregnant woman was going to pass a second check ride with that weasel-faced check airman who, from the moment he had seen Karen's distinctive six-month gait, had been out for blood. Not even the fantasy wonder-pilot offspring of Amelia Earhart and Charles Lindbergh would have been green-lit *with child* by that pedantic cad. Of course, none of that mattered. The reality was that Karen was about to have her first baby, and her hard-won career was hanging in the balance. On top of that, the blown check ride was now stamped on her record for the next five years. With that inglorious smudge, if the brass at Mesa Airlines decided to dump their plump pilot, she was now adorned with the scarlet letter of the aviation world, a decided badge of shame that would make it exceedingly difficult to get hired elsewhere. At the next job interview there would be an application with a simple and unavoidable question: *Have you ever failed a check ride?*

Unfortunately, too, this was not an essay question wherein Karen would have a chance to articulate the attendant mitigating circumstances. Instead, answered with a flat, gray-toned "Yes" or "No," the question was the aviation equivalent of, "Have you ever been charged with and/or convicted of a felony crime?"

Yes, but I can explain ... My lawyer screwed it up and, no question, the prosecutor was out to get me! The judge hated me, too. It was a kangaroo court all the way. And that jury was pure evil. So, yes, but no, not really, I mean you have to understand...

Once a pilot answered in the affirmative when asked about a blown check ride, any explanation thereafter was like so much cloud vapor being sucked through turbines in flight: white-noise nothingness.

Back in Phoenix, Karen had to go sit face to face with the chief pilot at Mesa Airlines, who would make the final decision on her status. He dispensed with any small talk and opened with: "If you want to quit, we'll make you eligible for rehire later."

Bullshit! she thought. *Not after I worked so hard.* Karen was resolute: "No."

"No? You don't want to be eligible for rehire?"

"No, as in I'm not going to quit. You can fire me, but I'm not quitting."

There was a pause that stretched into an uncomfortably long silence. Neither flinched, but each knew what was etched in the silent subtext. In the vernacular of corporate attorneys everywhere who had researched such scenarios, firing a woman who was six months pregnant, one with a solid flying record, would invite untold legal and fiduciary exposure. They had to carefully finesse this situation.

"OK," he said. "We'll give you one more chance. If you don't pass, you're fired."

"And there's one other condition," Karen said. She didn't have any leverage to make demands, but she had no choice but to try.

"What's that?"

"I won't take the check ride with that same check airman."

He weighed her demand against the other—*untold legal and fiduciary exposure*—and nodded. "OK. One more chance with a different check airman."

With that agreement, and Karen's impending childbirth, they scheduled the final check ride for two weeks later. Karen would be flying back up to Seattle, to Last Chance Saloon, where everything would be on the line. But before that, just to add a little more pressure, stress, and anxiety to the entire scenario, she and Shawn Perry were flying to Hawai'i for their already scheduled wedding on December 12, 2001.

It was a simple Hawaiian ceremony on the beach, north of Kona, with the only guests Lance and Gwen Lau and their kids. The wind was blowing so hard Karen had to apply a shellac coating of hair spray. Seven months pregnant, she wore a simple Hawaiian dress she had had altered. She wore a traditional *haku* lei on her head, and each wore a lei around their necks. Hers was made of ginger, and Shawn's of maile and ginger, draped like a scarf. Shawn wore a Hawaiian shirt with slacks and Top-Siders without socks.

The return to the islands was magical for Karen, the place where her ascent into the skies had officially begun. The combination of the water, the light, and the steady temperate breeze was familiar and unlike any other place she had found. Thankfully, those special memories were never interrupted or punctuated by any flashbacks of working along the loud, rancid conveyor belt at Rocky Road egg farm in Waimanalo, with cockroaches scrambling up her arms, under the menacing gaze of the locals as she tried to keep pace. That imagery had blissfully faded away.

Meanwhile, in every spare moment, Karen was studying for the check ride. Because this was a third attempt and, she sensed, the company was looking for an out to dump her, she had to be ready to answer questions that would go way beyond reasonable; she'd have to demonstrate her proficiencies with letter-perfect precision. Passing any check ride was largely a mental exercise: could she stay cool under pressure and perform by the book, even if the book didn't have much relevance in the real world—in real cockpits? The check airman wanted to know that if she were piloting an airplane full of passengers and an engine caught fire, she wasn't going to collapse in tears. So while the pressure to perform was part of the job, the stress level on this check ride would be amplified a hundred times: pass, or her entire nineteen-year career was all but over.

Of course, in six months, after maternity leave, she could get her ratings current on her own dime and then apply, interview, and start training back at square one. Then she'd have to try to convince an airline to hire her fresh off the blown check ride, which would follow her for five full years. It would be like trying to get a job as an airship pilot if, during her last logged flight, she had been at the helm of the Hindenburg.

Further, with limited available jobs, she was always competing against legions of pilots with vast amounts of flight hours and military experience including, increasingly, more capable females. Even with all things aviation being equal, female pilots had to be better in every way to prove their gender was not a liability.

With all that swirling in her mind, Karen kissed her newlywed husband, waddled onto her flight seven months pregnant, and landed six hours later in Seattle, where the city was bone-chillingly cold under a blanket of steady gray drizzle.

On December 19, 2001, she walked into Flight Safety International for her final check ride. When she got to the simulator, she shook hands with the new check airman and felt a rush of relief that the other weasel was nowhere to be seen. But whatever lessening of anxiety she might have felt was immediately replaced with stunned silence as she looked around the simulator. Apparently, this check ride had garnered lots of interest from various parties, and Karen would be under the scrutinizing glare of her own check airman in the left seat, a fixed video camera manned by another check airman, an FAA inspector, and a union representative. What, no clowns, dancing bears, and mariachi band?

Breathe, she thought. *They can only bust me if I make a mistake. You can't fail if you don't make a mistake. So you can't make a mistake.*

She had to be flawless from the moment she slid into the full-motion, level-D simulator seat and buckled her safety belt. Amazingly, Karen learned that she would not be required to repeat the two-hour oral examination, an unexpected bit of good news that seemed to tilt the odds back in her favor ever so slightly.

While Karen sat inside the simulator, which moved and tilted to mimic actual flight, the examiner sat at a nearby control panel to run the scenarios. Karen carefully ran through her preflight checks and then fastened the safety harness. Each metal click reverberated in her mind as a reminder that she had barely started. *Oh, how easy it would be to bust another check ride!* For the next two hours, every movement she made would be scrutinized. She worked through her before-start checklist and her start checklist.

So far, so good, she thought, taking a deep breath. Then she felt a little kick and momentarily placed her right hand on her round belly. Another little kick made her smile and washed away the anxiety; there were far more important things than this check ride for a regional airline. Morgan's well-timed reminders boded well, and two hours later Karen was unbuckling the clasps and climbing out of the simulator. If she passed, she'd have a mediocre job awaiting her after her maternity leave ended. If she did not, well, she'd be forced to recertify but, hopefully, would find a better post at a larger airline. When the results came, the drama had already played out and resolved in her mind.

"I totally nailed it," she recalled of the check ride, which, in the vernacular of aviation, meant a flawlessly smooth performance. "There was no way they were going to push me out of the profession."

That meant Karen could continue to work right up to when it was time to have the baby. On January 13, 2002, with a very plump belly, Karen did a Phoenix–Aspen (ASE)–Phoenix–Palm Springs (PSP) turn. The next morning she returned to Phoenix. On January 17, she flew Phoenix–Durango (DRO) for an overnight and then returned to Phoenix on January 18. As they made the final approach, the captain nitpicked Karen on every fine detail. She said nothing, but steeled her resolve: this was going to be the best landing she had ever made, and it was going to be for the little girl she felt kicking around in her belly.

Perfectly smooth landings in the Dash 8 are as rare as female captains, but Karen pulled it off. The captain told her it was about as good a landing as he had ever seen in the Dash 8. Karen smiled and said, "That was for my daughter." She did not know it at the time, but that was her last flight for Mesa Airlines.

The next month, February 2002, Karen was on reserve and in the final month of her pregnancy when she got a call from the scheduling department at Mesa Airlines: she had been assigned a trip. Today, no airline company would schedule a pilot to fly who was in the ninth month of pregnancy. But in the long-ago medieval times of 2002, this was common practice at regional airlines that grinded employees harder than the baggage handlers working the Jeju (CJU)–Seoul (GMP) route who heft ten million Samsonites a year. Likewise, Karen would not get a paycheck unless she was in uniform and working. Then she got more good news: company executives were scheduling her for a line check, with the one-and-only evil examiner Mr. Weasel (!), who would be riding as captain for the entire three-day trip to evaluate her every move. It was all very suspicious and felt like a planned trap.

Karen hung up the telephone, her heart racing. Then she did the only sane thing she could, which was to call in sick. There was no way she'd undertake this doomed scenario three weeks from her due date. More infuriating was that only captains were required to have line checks. Karen called her union representative to ask why she was being asked to do the line check, but no one seemed to have any plausible answers.

Karen's intention was to have her new baby girl, then take her six weeks of maternity leave under the Family Medical Leave Act, and then return to work as a pilot for Mesa Airlines and begin immediately looking for another job. But after her little bundle Morgan arrived, Karen would never fly another flight for Mesa Airlines. Nor would she ever complete her studies at Embry-Riddle Aeronautical University, where she was enrolled in the four-year degree program.

In fact, little did she know—Karen would be a new mother whose career as a pilot was over.

PART II

THE CHILDREN—

MORGAN, LOGAN, AND LUKE

THIRTEEN

Beautiful Baby Girl

WHEN MORGAN LEIGH PERRY ARRIVED, the first child and daughter of Karen and Shawn Perry, she was a miracle baby who appeared to be perfect in every way. She was born February 24, 2002, at Scottsdale Healthcare Shea Medical Center; the miraculous part was that Karen had finally accepted she was unable to conceive and yet, at 39, she was a mom. She had done all the recommended ultrasounds and an amniocentesis, all of which showed the in vivo Morgan was normal and healthy, which her birth seemed to confirm. Morgan, seven pounds and three ounces, had an almost perfect APGAR score: her activity, pulse, grimace, appearance, and respiration were all ideal.

After a few days, the luminous glow of a new warm bundle gave way to a common and more pragmatic question for the first-time mother: *Will I ever sleep again?* Additionally, for a process that was supposed to be as natural as breathing, breastfeeding was a painful ordeal for Karen. Whether it was the radiation treatment she had undergone, genetics, or both, her milk production was low. Determined to do everything right, she tried every folklore remedy to boost milk production, along with numerous sessions with lactation specialists. Those experts seemed particularly militant that breastfeeding was a mother's duty and was to be pursued to the ends of the earth. Karen followed their marching orders and soldiered on through raw, blistered nipples and a screaming infant who was not getting enough sustenance.

Karen resorted to the Medela supplemental nipple system, with a tube carrying formula from a bottle to a plastic holder that works by gravity. To mimic nature's way, Karen taped a tiny tube to her upper chest. To set up this contraption every two hours throughout the night and get the formula flowing, with Morgan screaming for milk, was nightmarish at times. Shawn even gave it a go and taped the holder to his chest when Karen needed to collapse from exhaustion. Shawn had taken time off work and was hands-on with everything from simulated breastfeeding to diaper changes.

Together, in the first weeks, they were two new parents lost in the emotional roller coaster of bringing home a tiny human being: bliss and anxiety, serenity and exhaustion, laughter and tears, frustration and excitement, and the slow creeping madness of cumulative sleep deprivation. At the center of it all, however, was an impervious core of pure joy: Morgan was a beautiful baby girl who had already stolen two hearts.

Then, without pretext or warning, the light and perfection were blotted in a particularly cruel way for the first-time parents. At just six weeks old, Morgan had her first epileptic seizure. The nightmare began on April 3, 2002, and would haunt Morgan all the days of her life. That day, Morgan had been blinking repeatedly. Karen thought perhaps her baby's eyes were irritated, a common occurrence in the dusty desert. She called the pediatrician, who told her to take Morgan to the emergency room if the incessant blinking did not stop.

Then, after carefully monitoring her baby's motions for a full day, Karen noticed that Morgan had a tick movement in unison with each blink. Morgan would tilt her head to one side, over and over. Karen gasped: her infant daughter was having seizures. She didn't know *how* she knew, but as the mother, she knew. Karen rushed Morgan to the emergency room at Scottsdale Healthcare Shea Medical Center, which is where doctors had delivered Morgan and also had saved Karen's life.

Initially, the ER doctors did not necessarily agree that Morgan was having seizures because they were difficult to diagnose in an infant whose primary symptoms were erratic eye movements. But the hard scientific image of an electroencephalogram (EEG) confirmed Karen's motherly intuitive sense: seizures, and a lot of them.

That initial finding started a cascade of emergency airlifts, hospital admissions, specialist visits, and treatments that forever changed the course of Karen's, Shawn's, and Morgan's lives. Morgan would have up to forty seizures a day as a tiny infant, toddler, and little girl. She valiantly contended with the affliction, as her mother and father suffered emotionally right alongside her during each episode.

"Morgan experienced every type of seizure known," her mother recalled, "along with some that were not identifiable in any medical publications."

During that first emergency room visit, Morgan's condition worsened. Doctors decided Morgan should be transported to Banner Desert Medical Center, which has a renowned pediatrics unit. It was a Native Air Ambulance helicopter that transported Karen and her daughter back to the hospital where Karen had undergone radiation for her breast cancer. Under different circumstances Karen would have pondered these connections—especially being a passenger traveling with a patient for an emergency service she had once provided—but Karen's full focus was on Morgan.

As a favor, Shawn's childhood pediatrician and longtime family friend came to Banner Desert Medical Center to examine Morgan. When he was done he could only shake his head. This was going to be a tough nut to crack as Morgan developed more severe and longer-lasting seizures. Doctors discovered that she had an intracranial hematoma, a brain bleed, with no clear answers as to the cause. They thought the hematoma might be the source of the problem, which meant that as soon as the bleed resolved so, too, would the seizures. For the distraught new parents this news was a tremendous relief. But when the bleed resolved and the seizures continued, Karen and Shawn were back to an anxious state of limbo. Delicately, Morgan's physicians repeatedly asked Karen and Shawn if the baby had been dropped, and the parents assured them, *No, she has not been dropped! Not once, not ever.*

These were heartbreaking days for the new mother, who watched her infant suffer, helpless to do anything about it. For the long six weeks of hospitalization that followed, Morgan mostly slept, awoke for feedings, and had seizures. Some were so severe that even with medical intervention the seizure would not stop. One seizure lasted thirty-four minutes. For Karen and Shawn, it was torture to watch little Morgan repeat this cycle over and over and over again. Doctors recommended transferring Morgan again, to Phoenix Children's Hospital, and when no one there could successfully diagnose the source of the seizures, to Banner Good Samaritan Medical Center in downtown Phoenix, in an ongoing attempt to help Morgan. Nothing was more wrenching for the new parents than watching their infant writhe and convulse, the uncontrolled electrical activity in her brain producing the outward physical symptoms they could see and, perhaps, scary thought disturbances they could not.

Meanwhile, another lesser dilemma loomed: Karen was scheduled to go back to work at the six-week mark. In tears, she called Mesa Airlines and said there was no way she could return to work now because she needed to be at the hospital with her infant daughter. Instead of empathy, compassion, and understanding, Karen's employer offered a more direct ultimatum: *Come back to work, or lose your job.*

Karen didn't hesitate and snapped back with, "Then fire me, because I'm not coming back. I'm not leaving my child." When a woman from human resources called back hours later, she told Karen the company was granting her a two-year leave of absence as a pilot for Mesa Airlines. Concurrently, Karen was still on the five-year leave from Delta Air Lines. Flying anywhere, as pilot or flight attendant, was not on Karen's radar. She was able to exhale a bit: any immediate pressure to return to work was gone, and she would be able to dedicate her full focus to Morgan. However, the Mesa Airlines leave of absence was another domino to fall in the slow toppling of Karen's pilot career. Of course she had no idea, as she and her husband were getting a crash course in epilepsy treatment.

Doctors classify and divide seizures into two broad camps: partial and generalized. Partial seizures affect a specific part of the brain and are further defined as either simple or complex. Generalized seizures affect the entire brain and also include several types: generalized tonic-clonic, or grand mal, seizures cause the entire body to alternately stiffen and jerk and can cause loss of consciousness. Myoclonic seizures cause lightning jerks in the muscles, usually on both sides of the body. During absence, or petit mal, seizures people lose awareness and exhibit a blank stare. Atonic seizures disrupt muscle response and cause collapse. Unfortunately, Morgan suffered every type and others doctors could not identify.

"There was no rhyme or reason to Morgan's seizures," Karen said. "They would come and go, and we never knew when she would have one."

One identifier as a trigger was sickness or excitement—good or bad—as they lowered Morgan's threshold for seizures. Karen said, "I remember one Christmas Morgan was so excited, and it triggered a seizure. Standing upright looking at her wrapped gifts, she fell flat on her face."

Karen spent her first Mother's Day in the hospital with her daughter. They had airlifted Morgan to UCLA Medical Center in California on, again, Native Air Ambulance. Karen knew the plane type well and had flown it often, a Pilatus PC-12. She knew the pilot, too, who asked if she wanted to strap in and help fly. While it was a well-meaning gesture and nod to her experience, Karen graciously declined, thinking, *Hell, no, I don't want to fly.*

Shawn made the six-hour drive west in his truck so they'd have a vehicle while in California. Towed behind the truck was a fifth-wheel camper trailer, courtesy of Shawn's parents, that would be their home for however long they needed to stay. Karen and Shawn were both on leave from work, and with the medical bills rapidly mounting, they could not afford a hotel.

Life had become a dismal blur of medical tests: magnetic resonance imaging (MRI), computerized axial tomography (CAT scan), lumbar punctures, EEGs, and others, none of which were providing any answers. A procession of premier physicians and specialists at multiple hospitals were all mystified by Morgan's condition.

"We were living a nightmare that seemed to have no end," Karen said. Worst of all for the new parents, their daughter appeared to be suffering with each horrible episode. "It was certainly not the life we wanted for our daughter," said Karen. "We were devastated."

Within the first week after arriving in California, the head of neurology at UCLA recommended that Karen and Shawn consider a hemispherectomy for Morgan. They'd need to wait until August when Morgan would be six months old. The doctor explained that this was a very rare surgical procedure, wherein part of the brain was either removed or disabled, with the aim of also removing the localized source of the epilepsy within the brain. This was a procedure reserved solely for extreme cases such as Morgan's, where the seizures had not diminished with medications.

This sort of massively invasive surgery could only be performed on very young patients, during the "window of plasticity" between infancy and age 7, before the neuron pathways in the brain were fully wired, interlinked, and established. If done correctly at the right time, Morgan's brain would treat the surgery as an injury and be able to adapt and create new connections among neurons to compensate for any brain damage caused by the hemispherectomy.

Karen and Shawn listened intently, and were equally amazed and horrified. While there might be positive results from such a surgery, it also sounded like some grim sci-fi experiment. But without much hope elsewhere, they reluctantly agreed to the surgery and scheduled a date near the end of summer.

THE stress of living in hospitals, and now a trailer, was taking a toll on Karen and Shawn's marriage. There were arguments about treatments, fights about petty things, and a lot of tears from the constant anguish. On one occasion Karen watched while five different nurses attempted to get an intravenous needle into Morgan's tiny arm. They stood around her crib and stuck her repeatedly without success. Then all the nurses started weeping along with Karen. There was anger, sadness, and the sheer physical exhaustion of it all. There was the overwhelming sense of helplessness at not being able to alleviate their baby's suffering. Depleted emotionally, physically, and spiritually, the couple often turned on each other to vent their fears and frustrations.

At the UCLA Medical Center, doctors continued the search for a medication to reduce the frequency of Morgan's seizures. Karen painstakingly recorded each seizure in a log—the time of day, symptoms, and duration—to provide data for physicians to sift through and use in their treatment of Morgan. Each painful event, up to forty times a day, was another piercing dagger into the mother's heart and soul. For the infant Morgan there was also the potential that the cumulative episodes were causing permanent damage to her brain's development.

The next drug on the list was zonisamide, an antiseizure medication and a powerful one for an infant. Karen was instructed to pull each capsule apart, mix the tiny beads with juice, fill a syringe, and slowly dispense the mixture into Morgan's mouth. Another day, another week, another new drug. Karen was precise in following each instruction to the letter, but emotionally was more robotic than hopeful as she dispensed the medication. So far, nothing had worked. Why would this be any different?

And then, a miraculous thing happened: the number of Morgan's seizures started to drop dramatically. She went from as many as forty a day to thirty, to twenty, and eventually to ten. A smattering of days here and there were 100 percent seizure-free. The new parents were hopeful, as Karen prayed that a miracle had ended the seizures that had dominated every facet of their lives. After months and months at hospitals in two different states, Morgan was finally able to go home. Along with the breakthrough, however, was a scary downside: the efficacy of the new medication was rooted in reducing neuron activity in Morgan's brain, which in turn reduced seizures. Reducing neuron activity in an infant's brain, however, meant inhibiting Morgan's development. It seemed Karen and Shawn only had dark trade-offs to consider no matter what course they chose.

Karen, along with Shawn's mother, Sandra, who went by Sunny, flew back to Arizona with Morgan via Shawn's employer, America West Airlines, while Shawn made the six-hour drive across the desert with the truck and trailer. By the end of May 2002, the family of three was back home in Gold Canyon near the towering desert mountain. Shawn went back to work the next month, as the intense roller coaster of emotions eased somewhat. The angry showdowns and stress about Morgan's next course of treatment also lessened as Karen found some normalcy with her little newborn.

In August, Karen called the head of neurology at UCLA and cancelled the hemispherectomy. The doctor had serious concerns about doing so and offered grave warnings about what a disservice this would be to Karen's daughter. He went on to say that Morgan was simply going through a "honeymoon period" with the medication. The doctor flatly guaranteed the seizures would return. Without the surgery, he said, Morgan would never walk or talk and would likely be in a vegetative state the rest of her life. Karen was once again torn between bad alternatives, wedged between the cold logic of science and her own strong sense of motherly intuition. Karen chose to heed her own inner guidance.

"All I knew was that while Morgan was not having seizures, there was no way I was going to let a doctor cut her head open, take half her brain, and send her on her way," Karen recalled. Against more dire predictions, Karen held firm and thanked the doctor for everything he and the medical team at UCLA had done.

Despite the ominous prognosis, Morgan lived an entire glorious year without another seizure. The threesome spent that year enjoying their time together as a new family while Karen continued to read about and study the development of the human brain. It was a special year with just Morgan, no siblings, no work for Karen, and few other distractions.

"I thought a miracle had happened," Karen said.

Karen stayed in touch with her pilot friends and peers, but she was ecstatic to be on leave and at home, finally, just being a new mom with her baby. She did not think much about work, but did have her plan mapped out. Eventually, to restart her career as a pilot she'd need to get "paper current," which meant three takeoffs and landings in ninety days. After her leave was up, she'd have to retake initial training, too. Because she was already on the staff, she would reluctantly go back into the meat grinder that was flying for Mesa Airlines. No question: Karen missed flying, the challenges it brought, and the attendant brain simulation. She missed the adrenaline surge of belly up and skyward.

As far as being a Delta Air Lines flight attendant, she missed her large cadre of friends and meeting interesting passengers. She did not miss all the other mundane and utilitarian aspects of the job. Career-wise, her only plan was to return to work as a full-time pilot and move on to bigger and better employers, airplanes, and paychecks. With Shawn a first officer at a major airline and earning a low-six-figure salary and good benefits, things were looking up in the Perry household in late 2002 and early 2003. But the relative serenity was to be short-lived.

WHILE the seizures had finally abated, another grave concern was confirmed as Morgan started missing her developmental milestones. At four months old, she was like a rag doll, with little muscle tone; she could barely lift her head. The seizures and medications had already taken a toll on the baby and her ability to develop properly.

Morgan Perry qualified for state-paid help through an Arizona Early Intervention program that included physical, occupational, and speech therapies and an early intervention specialist. With Shawn gone at work for half of each month or more, Karen was on her own much of the time, watching her daughter's delayed development.

Meanwhile, after all the seizures, tests, and endless anxiety, doctors finally had what they considered an official diagnosis for Morgan: focal cortical dysplasia. The condition was an abnormal development of the brain cortex that caused focal epilepsy and, even worse, progressive neurological deterioration. Morgan's abnormality was located in the left occipital lobe of her brain. The prognosis for Morgan was not good: she would likely suffer a lifetime filled with seizures. Doctors also determined the condition was nongenetic.

Morgan tired quickly of the rigorous schedule of various therapies. As Morgan began recognizing these various activities as work, Karen had to be creative. She got Morgan involved in hippotherapy on horseback, and swimming, so Morgan could have fun and still realize the benefits of therapy.

Morgan's first year of life was a blur as they celebrated her birthday in February 2003. One of the first words Morgan learned how to say was "mountain."

She already knew she lived by the mountain. Later, while driving, Karen would frequently point and ask her three kids if they knew the name of the mountain. In unison they'd all say, "Superstition Mountain." For the volcanic anchor, forty million years in the making, the next eight years would register barely a change, nearly imperceptible on the geologic time scale. In 2003, after everything they had been through with Morgan, Karen and Shawn's field of focus was elsewhere when they got a surprise that stunned them both: Karen was pregnant again.

FOURTEEN

Beautiful Baby Boys

DURING KAREN PERRY'S SECOND PREGNANCY, she gained seventy-five pounds. Navigating the world, she felt like a 4-H blue-ribbon watermelon on legs. She had an insatiable appetite and ankles swollen so badly that, toward the end of her pregnancy, she could barely walk at all. With the birth of their second child looming, Karen and Shawn took one last family trip to Kona with Morgan in September 2003, which would be Morgan's only trip to the Hawaiian Islands. Once again, the land and sea were magical to Karen as she returned now as a mother. The watery light and fragrance of flowers immediately transported her back to all she had achieved in this special place, another stepping-stone in her march to independence. Kona had become a pinpoint in Karen's evolution. During this trip, Morgan's face lit up with excitement wherever they took her.

Back in Arizona, Karen was positively rotund. When she went to a local pumpkin festival in those final weeks, her friend had to push Karen around in a wheelchair. With Morgan's continued developmental delays, she too was unable to walk, which meant Morgan rode in the wheelchair on her mother's lap.

Other than a few routes to Mexico and Costa Rica, Shawn was flying domestic US flights as first officer and instructor on the Airbus 320. During the months he worked as a simulator instructor he enjoyed a regular nine-to-five schedule and was home for dinner, bath, and bedtime stories every night with his daughter. As always, he was a great dad to his daughter and was always in the trenches changing diapers and taking Morgan to her never-ending therapy appointments when his work schedule allowed.

LOGAN Jay Perry was born one week late and had to be induced, on October 31, 2003, at Scottsdale Healthcare Shea Medical Center. Logan was a chunk of an infant, at eleven pounds. That he was born on Halloween may have been a nod from the universe, because Logan was a true character, with a natural flair for creating live theater, comedy mostly, and infusing levity into the Perry household. But like his sister Morgan, Logan began life with some challenges and had to wear a cranial orthotic device for a year to correct his misshapen head. He also suffered from chronic asthma and was allergic to just about everything, which seemed to be a common malady for children growing up in the dusty and ever-blooming warm climate of southern Arizona.

"I thought things were challenging with Morgan, but Logan turned my world upside down," Karen recalled. "He was a handful from day one."

Aside from those early challenges, Logan gradually developed into the healthy, happy, "normal" middle child, sandwiched between an older sister and the eventual baby brother who would also have demanding special needs. But "normal" was not an apropos adjective to describe the unique Logan Jay Perry. Karen and Shawn sensed immediately that their bouncing toddler was an old soul, with a razor-sharp intelligence and wit, trapped in a little boy's body. Indeed, Logan grew into a mini bon vivant, a colorful personality who could hold center stage and have everyone in the room laughing and adoring.

Logan's unique intelligence was apparent by age 1, when he knew how to operate every electronic device in the Perry household. When Karen needed to change the settings on the television, she turned for help to Logan, who somehow always knew what to do. At twenty months, Logan knew how to lock his mom out of the house. While getting Morgan to ingest food was an ongoing daily battle, Logan was a gleeful chowhound who plowed through multiple servings with all the decorum and grace of a famished trucker straight off a long haul. Between Morgan's rounds of doctor and therapy visits and Logan's appointments in downtown Phoenix to monitor the development of his head, Karen was running an unofficial health care transport service with daily stops. In what seemed like the blink of an eye, more than two years had passed since she had first become a mother, and Karen was staring at the red "X" she had long ago marked on the calendar. It was April 2004, decision time.

Karen's two-year leave from Mesa Airlines was nearing its end. The high drama of the blown check rides and the big showdown in Seattle, with her first basketball-sized baby bump, was like some distant dream, devoid of the emotional charge it once held. Relieving the suffering of her epileptic baby girl, and raising her effusive son, was now the epicenter of her universe. With a son and a daughter who were going to require a lot more time, attention, love, and dedication than most toddlers, Karen made an easy decision and quit her job as a pilot with Mesa Airlines. Longer-term, of course, she planned to go back to work as a pilot. At the time, rather than feeling disappointed, Karen felt calm and purposeful.

Working the grind of being a regional airline pilot was certainly near the bottom rung on the employment hierarchy. The "regionals" were notorious stepping-stone jobs, and Karen had done her step and was ready for the next rung up the ladder. The decision to stay home was not without concern. With the medical bills piled high and deep from all Morgan's appointments, airlifts, surgeries, and treatments, Karen and Shawn filed bankruptcy in 2003. With a clean slate, they resolved to do better and, once the kids were both in school, Karen would get back into the cockpit. That was the plan, at least.

SHAWN and Karen now had two bouncing toddlers in the household; Morgan

Perry was their beautiful, sweet girl, and such a fighter. The parents did not want their daughter defined solely by her seizures and endless treatments. To inject some lightness into the routine and to spend time around other children, Karen entered Morgan in some baby beauty pageants. All dressed up in different cute outfits, Morgan won several crowns and trophies at Hawaiian Tropic and various other Arizona baby pageants. What Karen loved most was that Morgan's epilepsy was unknown and unseen by any of the pageant judges and other parents. At the height of her short-lived baby modeling career, Morgan was even featured in a television commercial for Cord Blood Registry (CBR).

Karen liked taking Morgan to Gymboree a few times a week. Morgan loved it, but for Karen it was difficult to watch her little girl struggle with her awkward gait and poor coordination. While other parents were getting excited as their kids accomplished new feats, Karen watched Morgan struggle to do even the simplest moves.

But eventually, although behind schedule, Morgan started ticking off the milestones the UCLA neurologist had warned would never arrive if they skipped the hemispherectomy: Morgan walked, talked, laughed, and ran. Karen later learned through testing that a hemispherectomy would have actually been a contraindicated approach for Morgan after all. Motherly intuition had trumped science, and Karen and Shawn felt like they had dodged a bullet. They also continued trying anything they thought might help Morgan, including chiropractic treatments, herbal tinctures, traditional Western medicine, Eastern medicine, and craniosacral therapy.

"We were so desperate to help her, we would try anything," Karen recalled.

Craniosacral therapy was a gentle, hands-on approach that purported to unwind deep body tensions to relieve pain and dysfunction and improve whole-body health and performance. Pioneered by Dr. John E. Upledger at Michigan State University, the therapy calls for practitioners to use a soft touch—about the weight of a nickel—to release restrictions in the soft tissue surrounding the central nervous system.

Karen and Shawn surely never planned to have a third child. They had their girl and boy and, at 41, Karen certainly did not want to get pregnant again—but that's exactly what happened. When she confirmed it with an at-home test, she shouted aloud, "Oh shit!"

With the financial doom of Morgan's mountain of medical bills wiped clean, Karen and Shawn's situation improved quickly, and in December 2004 they were able to move into a beautiful new custom home they had built at 7499 East Cliff Rose Trail in Gold Canyon. It was essentially the "captain's house," before Shawn was a captain, which they both assumed was a foregone conclusion. When Karen returned to work as a pilot, too, their annual household income would hypothetically surpass $200,000. Unfortunately, "hypothetically" was the operative word: Shawn never became a captain, and Karen never returned to work as a pilot. They purchased the new house during the steady buildup of the real estate craze and market bubble when, even barely a year after bankruptcy, almost anyone standing upright with a pulse could get a new home loan for almost any amount.

Their new four-bedroom home was just over three thousand square feet, with a nice yard for the kids. When the family moved in, Morgan was 2, Logan was 1, and Karen was four months pregnant. Barely in the new house, and taking advantage of fast and loose credit rules, Shawn took out a home equity line of credit to pay off some other bills. These moves created a burdensome mortgage and the imperceptible initial fissures that, combined with other pressures, would unravel a marriage and foreshadow the darkest of chapters, yet to come.

AFTER that blissful seizure-free period, Morgan's seizures returned. By the time she was almost 3, she was old enough to know something was wrong with her. She often did not remember the seizure episodes. Some lasted only a split second, like a jolt of electricity that made her tense and shudder. The most severe "drop" seizures went on for five minutes or more.

In another attempt to help Morgan, Karen and Shawn enrolled their daughter at the Infant Child Research Program at Arizona State University at an off-campus site in Tempe, a suburb of Phoenix. With Karen pregnant and Logan tagging along, Morgan was placed in a program for autistic kids. Morgan was also having difficulties with her feet, which were flat and pronated inward. Simple walking was difficult for her, which prompted her awkward gait that was emotionally painful for Karen to watch. Morgan went to another specialist to be fitted with supra-malleolar orthotics, or SMOs. Her orthotics supported the leg just above the anklebone and helped Morgan maintain a vertical, or neutral, heel, while also supporting the arches of her feet. The goal was improved standing, balance, and walking. These SMOs were hand-cast specifically for Morgan's feet and ankles, and she had to wear them every day.

LUKE Devon Perry was born June 19, 2005, at Scottsdale Healthcare Shea Medical Center, the third child of Karen and Shawn Perry. Now with three young children, Karen was immersed in motherhood and the odd combination of joy and isolation motherhood can bring. Shawn was doing well in his career and keeping the household aloft financially, which meant he was gone half or more of each month on trips. Thankfully for Karen's sanity, there was one silver lining to Morgan's disability, which was that she qualified for benefits under Arizona's Department of Economic Security/Division of Developmental Disabilities. Strict policies dictated who qualified and who did not, with long lists of regulations and piles of required paperwork and documentation. Karen had persevered through the process, and at three months old Morgan had been approved by state officials for benefits, with an assigned case manager. Sadly, from that first assessment it was clear that Morgan would likely be eligible for state assistance for the rest of her life. This was not a condition to be overcome, from which she could heal and move on to full functionality and independence. Her way of being had been stamped for life. Karen was gradually finding acceptance of that reality, but she was completely unprepared for another difficult diagnosis.

By the summer of 2006, Luke seemed like the perfect 1-year-old boy. He had a sweet disposition from the start and appeared to be meeting his milestones right on target. Karen and Shawn had held their breath at each stage: one month, two months, three months ... and slowly exhaled with relief as everything appeared on track after going through such agony with the infant Morgan. Unfortunately, however, it became evident that Luke was speech-delayed.

After enduring Morgan's missed milestones, Karen's motherly radar was on high alert for Logan and then Luke. She was on the lookout for any small quirk, tic, movement, or indication that something did not seem quite right. Shawn insisted Logan and Luke were both perfectly healthy, that Karen was being overly paranoid, and she was trying to find things wrong with their children. Karen firmly disagreed; she was keeping her head out of the sand and refusing to pretend otherwise when she could clearly see a deficiency in Luke's speech ability. Taking up the charge further, Karen worked for a year with Arizona's Children Association and helped disseminate a large child development milestone chart and informational brochures to smaller doctor's offices in several Arizona counties. Clearly, monitoring child development had become deeply personal.

Contrary to Shawn's objections, Karen had Luke extensively evaluated, at eighteen months old, by a developmental specialist who had seen Morgan. A week later Luke underwent a second evaluation with a second specialist. The two experts then compared their respective notes and conclusions from the sessions. Then came the blow: Luke was autistic. Karen and Shawn were devastated. The silver lining was that Luke was on the mild end of the autism spectrum. Karen did not know how the condition would manifest in Luke, so she studied the typical features. She learned there could be problems with social interactions, impaired verbal and nonverbal communication, patterns of repetitive behavior with narrow, restricted interests, and a number of other associated symptoms. Luke might have difficulty using language, forming relationships, and appropriately interpreting and responding to his external world. *Sounds like the story of my life*, Karen thought in a dark comedy moment of parental exhaustion.

A specialist explained Luke's perception of the world to Karen: that Luke had the amazing ability to memorize hundreds of individual pieces of a puzzle, yet he had no concept of how those pieces actually fit together in any meaningful way.

No, no, no, NOT my baby Luke. How could this be?

Once again, it all seemed so unfair. She and Shawn could not imagine it to be true, because Luke was so bright; likewise, none of their friends believed he was autistic. Most times, Luke seemed like any normal boy. But he was autistic and diagnosed "higher functioning" and a prodigious savant—someone with extraordinary mental abilities in a specific area of intellectual functioning, similar to the character Dustin Hoffman played in the film *Rain Man*.

Like his sister Morgan, Luke qualified for physical therapy through state-assisted programs, along with speech and occupational therapies. As Karen and Shawn learned more, a positive prognosis started to emerge for a relatively normal life for Luke. Along the way, they learned Morgan was autistic, too, which manifested as angry outbursts and getting stuck on tasks or outcomes. When things did not go as planned, legendary meltdowns ensued that became dark nightmares for her parents to help her navigate.

Soon days, weeks, months, and years had slid by, and Karen was staring at the calendar again: in August 2006 her five-year leave from Delta Air Lines would be over. If she wanted to leave that job and return to work as a pilot, how was she going to manage that with three children? FAA regulations would first require her to go back for a condensed refresher-training course. Beyond that, she was emotionally torn because working again would give her some time, space, and perspective from a 24/7 world of sippy cups, diapers, doctor visits, and temper tantrums. Somehow, one minute she was a new mom for the first time and now, more than four years later, she was the mother of three.

The high drama that sometimes came with working for an airline was back in play by late summer 2006. Karen received a letter from Delta Air Lines detailing how her career re-entry process would unfold. On a designated day, she'd get a phone call. If she did not answer immediately, she'd have only a two-hour window to return the call, or her job slot would be given up to someone else. For someone with twenty-two years of seniority, it all seemed somewhat cloak-and-dagger. But with the benefit of almost total autonomy to arrange her work schedule every month, Karen was not going to miss that all-important phone call. Just to be sure, she and Shawn cancelled a planned trip to Mexico so she could wait by the telephone and respond immediately, which she did.

Ring.

Hello? Karen said.

The chicken is in the pot.

Cook it.

Dead air, then: *The package is in play.* Click.

Well, that's not what was said, but at least that's how it all *felt*: very spy-novel mysterious.

Nonetheless, Karen was reinstated and soon airborne again as a Delta Air Lines flight attendant in November 2006. She and Shawn bid opposite schedules, which meant when one was working the other was caring for Morgan, Logan, and Luke. Under that schedule, the only "break" they each got was to go to work. Shawn would have preferred Karen stay home, which would have meant less total income but help with the kids when he was off work. So the day Karen went back to work, another crack formed in the marriage. It was difficult for Shawn to be alone with the kids while Karen worked. But Karen needed to get back into the workforce after more than four years away. At that moment, being a pilot would not work because the job required too much time, training, certification, and commitment—that would have meant choosing her job over motherhood. Ultimately, Karen sacrificed her own career as a pilot in deference to Shawn, who already had an established pilot career. Slipping back into her flight attendant job was much easier and provided immediate income, and, eventually, a transition path back to the cockpit. At least that was the plan.

My mother Marsaline Sommerstedt holding me as my journey began in Anaheim, California, in 1963. Below is me with Mom holding my baby sister Kathleen, who died when I was 4. My father Reinhold Sommerstedt, in spring 1972, taking a break with his 1971 Ducati RT 450 motorcycle on a trip to El Rosario in Baja, California.

All images courtesy of Karen Perry family archives unless noted otherwise.

After the death of my younger sister and my parents' divorce, I spent a lot of time by myself. My Tennessee walking horse Gus B was the apple of my eye and came with my dad and me when we moved from Oregon back to Southern California in 1976.

Living in Hawai'i was magical. At left I'm in O'ahu in 1982, age 19, sailing a forty-eight-foot Cheoy Lee yacht. Above I'm on the SS Independence, at sea, near the Hawaiian Islands in 1983. As crew we were not allowed in the passenger areas, so this was one of the few areas reserved for crew only.

I'm sitting on a PA-28 Piper Cherokee at General Lyman Field in Hilo, Hawai'i, in 1983. This was the same flight school and airport where I first soloed. Fast-forward to 2000 (at left), I was a pilot with Farwest Airlines, 37, and two years away from becoming a mother for the first time. Standing behind me, from left to right, are Captain Mike Glow and Captain/Check Airman Jim Powell. The women were the flight attendants on our crew. Below is the Pilatus PC-12, the single-engine turbine that I flew while working at Native Air Ambulance.

At top, in 1998, I'm standing next to the Jetstream BA-3100, which was one of the airplane types in the fixed-wing fleet I flew for Native Air Ambulance. At left that's me, in 1991, standing by the Learjet 24 I piloted on a five-day chartered trip to and throughout Mexico. My logbook records indicate that I have flown more than 30 types of aircraft. The cockpit is the same aircraft during a stop in Guadalajara.

Image courtesy of Eva Morgan ©2015.

Shortly after Farwest Airlines folded in summer 2000, I was single again and bought my own house in Gold Canyon almost an hour from downtown Phoenix. Ever since, Superstition Mountain has been a looming presence and a force in my life.

Shawn Perry and I married December 12, 2001. It was a simple Hawaiian ceremony on the beach, north of Kona. Our beautiful baby girl Morgan Leigh Perry (below) was born February 24, 2002, and appeared to be perfect in every way. Her seizure disorder first appeared when she was six weeks old.

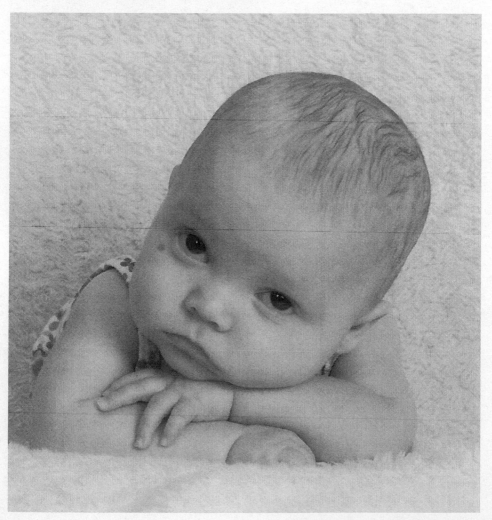

From the outset, Shawn was a loving father who doted on his baby girl. Below is Morgan, in the backyard of the first house we bought in Gold Canyon, with our cocker spaniel Max. Morgan loved being with animals.

Logan Jay Perry was born one week late, and had to be induced, on October 31, 2003, and thereafter he was a real character! The little helmet (left) was for plagiocephaly, or flat head syndrome. Unlike his siblings, Logan was free of any special needs. I'm certain, with his personality and intelligence, he would have excelled in life.

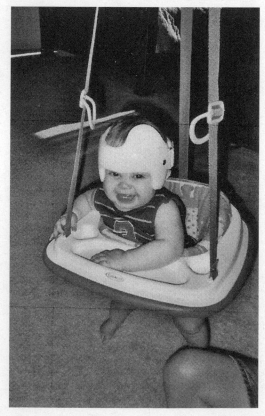

I had my hands full, literally, with Morgan and Logan. Luke Devon Perry (below left) was born June 19, 2005. After he turned 1, at right, we received the official diagnosis that he was autistic.

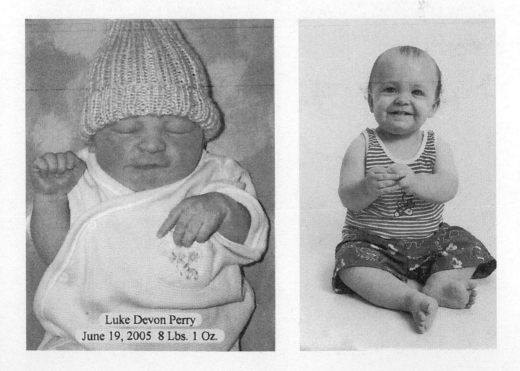

Luke Devon Perry
June 19, 2005 8 Lbs. 1 Oz.

Happy times for Shawn and me at SeaWorld in San Diego with (from left) Logan, Morgan, and Luke.

Morgan was my only daughter and little angel, who had her share of challenges in this lifetime. It was always precious when she was doing well and able to find her smile.

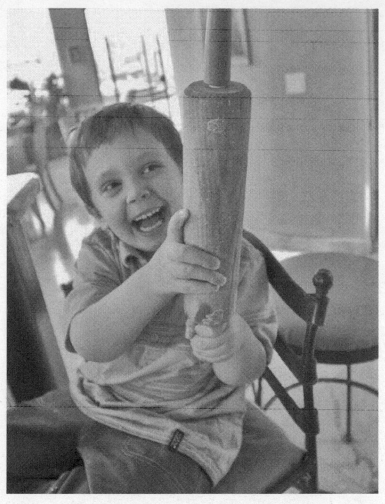

Logan was my little man, the love of my life, who brought so much joy, laughter, and levity to our family.

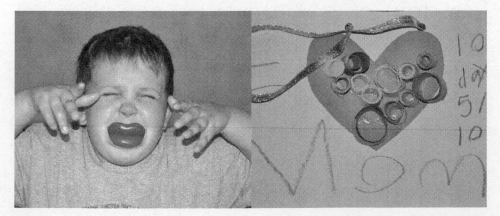

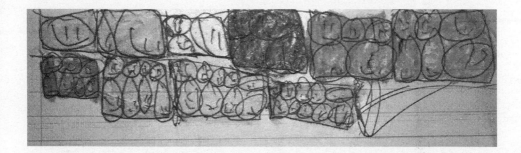

Luke was my sweet, innocent boy who, like many autistic children, had an early affinity for numbers.

One of Luke's favorite expressions of his creativity was self-portrait photography. He took thousands of images, many of which I have yet to see.

Logan (left) the principal character with his thoughtful understudy Luke.

It might be the greatest wish of every parent to freeze time so that
we may treasure our children's innocence just a little bit longer.

Image courtesy of Eva Morgan ©2015.

My loves, my life, and the way I will always keep them close in my heart.

Image courtesy of AirTeamImages.com. Reprinted with permission.

Above is the type of plane that later carried my children, their father, and two other adults on November 23, 2011: a turbine Rockwell Commander 690, a high-performance twin turbo-propeller aircraft with an operational ceiling of 31,000 feet. Below, on Thanksgiving morning 2011, first responders approached the crash site by helicopter and were immediately struck by two facts: how close the airplane had come to clearing the mountain and what a treacherous scene this would be to investigate on such a steep slope.

Image courtesy of Pinal County Sheriff's Office. Reprinted with permission.

From the air, it was impossible to imagine what a horrific crash site they were about to encounter. Upon landing with the first team to set safety lines, they began the wrenching ordeal of recovery of the six victims, evidence collection, and investigating the scene.

Even the most experienced first responders, normally inured to gruesome crash sites, were emotionally drained after spending three full days amid the wreckage. The crash impact was so violent (below), the wreckage barely resembled an airplane.

Sculptor Louis Longi is incorporating this piece of landing gear, one of the few pieces of recognizable wreckage, along with other remnants, into his "Ribbon of Life" bronze memorial, which will be a permanent, fifteen-foot-long, two-thousand-pound outdoor installation at Superstition Mountain Museum. Below, the outpouring of support from family, friends, and the community was overwhelming and sustained me through the darkest times.

Image courtesy of Pinal County Sheriff's Office. Reprinted with permission.

Image courtesy of Eva Morgan ©2015.

Unbelievably, 150 of my peers arrived in full uniform for the memorial and lined the long stairwell at Gold Canyon United Methodist church. It was a stunning sight that day for what we called a "Celebration of Life," and I was so moved by the love and support of these wonderful people. That my employer Delta Air Lines chartered their own Boeing 757, to shuttle everyone from Los Angeles to Phoenix, is simply unprecedented in the airline industry. At right and below, we gave hundreds of donated toys to the local W. Steven Martin 911 toy drive. Less than a month after my kids died, Eva Morgan and I helped at the 2011 event delivering toys, along with police officers, to children throughout the eastern suburbs of Phoenix.

Images on this page courtesy of Eva Morgan ©2015.

Image courtesy of Larry Andrews ©2015.

After the memorial service, guests wrote messages to my kids on each balloon, and then we released them all together. It was really a magical moment thanks to a woman, whose daughter had recently died, who donated the balloons.

Image courtesy of Pinal County Sheriff's Office. Reprinted with permission.

Past, present, and future: Living in Gold Canyon, I came to love Superstition Mountain more than a decade before it became the site of a gruesome tragedy. Today I continue to live in the mountain's shadow and beauty, but with new hope as Eva Morgan and I focus on helping children through our nonprofit, 3 Wings of Life. Along with many other approaches, including equine therapy with my new horse Dixon, our aim is to bring smiles to the faces of many children.

Image courtesy of Eva Morgan ©2015.

FIFTEEN

1234567

ANY FLEETING SPAN OF NORMALCY the Perry family might have enjoyed ended abruptly in late 2006, when it became apparent Morgan was going to need brain surgery. Doctors had exhausted every possibility for eliminating the source of Morgan's seizures. Surgically removing the damaged brain tissue was the last remaining, and most feared, option.

In preparation, Morgan went into an epilepsy monitoring unit (EMU), where doctors could observe her seizures in a controlled environment. The process began with a surgery during which doctors cut through Morgan's skull to place electrodes directly on the surface of her brain. Then they sewed her up with the electrodes in place. She spent her time in the EMU in a playpen of sorts where she couldn't fall. Either Karen or Shawn had to be with her 24/7. When she had a seizure, one of her parents pushed a button to start the wall-mounted camera recording. Meanwhile, the electrodes were capturing brain functions and recording the data onto a graph. The video and data provided a visual and graphic roadmap of each seizure's originating point and those areas of Morgan's brain being affected.

At times, to induce seizures, doctors carefully decreased her medication for direct observation and recording. The EMU was a complex medical and restrictive physical environment, so it was emotionally difficult to put Morgan there. The withdrawal of her medication, too, introduced other possible risks and physical reactions. Morgan had depth perception issues, which made it difficult for her to distinguish where her body was in relation to the world around her. In turn, this uncertainty caused a lack of confidence and decreased gross motor skills. Morgan frequently walked into walls, tripped, and fell down. (As if she did not have enough challenges with which to contend, Morgan also had hemiparesis, a muscle weakness affecting her upper right extremities, and her entire body was hypotonic, which means low in muscle tone.) Thankfully, Morgan made it through the EMU phase and was scheduled for surgery.

In December 2006, 4-year-old Morgan was at St. Joseph's Hospital and Medical Center in Phoenix for her first brain surgery. The entire buildup to the moment was scary for Karen and Shawn, who had left Logan and Luke with a babysitter. Hours before surgery, the neurosurgeon and neurologist were still differing and arguing back and forth about the procedure and exact plan, which did nothing to calm or soothe Morgan's parents. One of the risks of pursuing surgical solutions was that once they started down that road it might necessitate more surgeries. But they were out of options.

The first step of the procedure was to cut Morgan's scalp open to prep her for the six-hour surgery.

"Watching Morgan go into surgery was hideous and nerve-wracking," Karen recalled. She had been through it herself with her own near-death scare, which had trained her to be her daughter's advocate. Since shortly after Morgan's birth, Karen had been researching the human brain and studying neurology.

After a long, stressful day, with her parents waiting, Morgan pulled through, woke up, and was in good spirits. Morgan and her parents spent a total of ten days at the hospital before they could take her home. Karen was trying to get more extended time off work for Morgan's aftercare, but she had just come off the five-year leave at Delta Air Lines.

Unfortunately, Morgan's condition improved only marginally after the surgery. It did reduce the seizures temporarily, but then they gradually returned to previous levels and intensities. The risky approach had not produced a long-term solution. Morgan continued to have seizures so severe that the episodes scared Karen, Shawn, and her two brothers.

As feared, Morgan's first surgery had not been sufficient to treat her condition, and she would require more invasive procedures. Within a four-year period through 2010, Morgan had a total of five brain surgeries. Each time surgeons were, literally, removing more of Morgan's brain. Through all of her struggles, one of Morgan's gifts was the unconditional love she offered; she had a way of bringing people together, which is exactly how a very special person came into Karen and Shawn Perry's lives in 2008.

BORN in Reno, Nevada, Eva (Clark) Morgan was the oldest of three children. Her mother was from Norway and her father was a comedian and keyboard performer, all of which meant frequent travel as a young girl. The family eventually settled in Omaha, Nebraska. Eva wanted to be an artist and started community college with an eye toward commercial art, but the travel bug had already bitten her at a young age. She came to Arizona in 1983 and, in 1984 started with America West Airlines as a flight attendant, a position she has held up to the present day through various mergers, acquisitions, and company name changes (now American Airlines). She married Greg Morgan in 1991, and together they had three sons.

In 2008, after returning to her earlier artistic aspirations through the medium of photography, Eva was selling her images at a local arts fair in Gold Canyon. At the table next to her was Karen Perry, who periodically sold jewelry at the same craft market.

"Wow," Karen said, "It's a small world! I work for Delta, and my husband flies for America West."

Without anyone saying the name "Shawn Perry," Eva made the connection: "You're Morgan's mom."

Eva had a niece who, similar to Morgan, had struggled with the same seizure condition, and who had lost that battle at age 18. Eva remembered seeing fundraising flyers about Karen's daughter and thinking, *Someday I need to meet that family*. From that day at the art fair forward, Eva Morgan became a close family friend to both Karen and Shawn Perry, and an unofficial surrogate mother to Morgan, Logan, and Luke.

Soon Eva was enjoying Morgan's innocent and heartbreaking charms as she crawled on Eva's lap to be held and hugged. Morgan had a little chipmunk toy that would say, "Hello, gorgeous," which made her laugh to no end. At night Morgan would pull Eva outside to look at the moon, which Morgan called "La Luna."

All the kids loved Eva's Jeep, but especially Luke, who would commend her driving with "Good job, Eva." And Logan? Well, it was as though he had his own cellular phone with Eva Morgan on speed dial, because he called her multiple times a day with one funny tale after another.

The bond between the Perrys and Eva Morgan and her family grew and, one day would be especially helpful for Karen and Shawn alike, as their common friend deftly straddled the terrain of supporting both through a difficult time: not once would Eva Morgan take either side in what would become a difficult divorce. She was an emotional sounding board and support system for them both, and would become Karen's permanent rock of stability after the crash.

ONE of the gifts Logan Perry brought to the household was comedic relief amid the challenges. One summer day a postal worker rang the doorbell and was waiting outside for Karen to sign for a package. She was bouncing her infant son Luke in her arms and went outside, where it was a ghastly 115 degrees. Once standing on the sizzling sidewalk, she heard the door swing shut behind her and then the unmistakable sound of the latch clicking shut. Logan had locked his mother and brother out of the house. Then he stood at the window laughing and pointing at them. Just 3, he knew what he had done, and he thought it was hilarious. Karen was less amused. She secured the package she had come out to get and went to the backyard. Down on her hands and knees, she carefully shoved Luke through the dog door and then somehow squeezed through herself, which is when she, too, relented and joined Logan in uproarious fits of laughter. That was just his way: he made people smile, laugh, and happy. Whenever he knew he was in trouble, Logan would grab the Bible and hold the book with outstretched arms to defuse his mother's anger.

The next year, on Christmas morning when Logan was 4, Karen awoke to find him on the top bunk bed surrounded by the family's Christmas gifts. Except, instead of piles of carefully wrapped presents, there was a mess of shredded paper. He had opened them all, every single gift. And not just his, but everyone's presents to each other!

Logan wanted to be a sheriff when he grew up. He loved playing soccer, learning karate, and swimming. But most of all he loved movies. From a very young age, when Logan wanted to see a new movie he'd go online and research all the theaters in town. Then he'd print out the show times, present the page to his mother, and ask which show they would be able to attend. Karen could only laugh: How could she say "no" to a child like that?

Even as a 5-year-old, Logan had culinary flair. One Christmas Karen surprised him with an Easy-Bake Oven. While Karen was purchasing the oven, the store clerk remarked about her excellent choice of gift for her daughter, and her friends said the same. Then she'd break the news that it was actually for Logan. Shortly thereafter, one weekend Karen awoke to beeping sounds coming from the kitchen. It was still dark, but she immediately thought, *Logan*. Barely able to move, she asked Shawn to check to see what their son was doing. Shawn left, returned to the bedroom, and crawled back into bed.

"You don't want to know," was all Shawn said as he buried his head in the pillow.

Karen got up and, armed with her video camera, joined her messy little cake baker in the kitchen.

AROUND this same time, in 2008, Luke's autism was manifesting in various ways. Once Karen noticed that on the outside of her bedroom door Luke had written the word "OPEN." This writing ability and understanding was beyond the reach of most 2-year-olds, but clearly Luke possessed it.

One morning Karen noticed Luke writing something with chalk on the block wall surrounding their yard. When she looked closer she saw he had written *1234567*. Beneath that he had written it again, *1234567*, and the same thing over and over again. Luke loved flash cards, and he would carefully arrange them in a very particular order. Logan, knowing just how to push the right buttons, would toss Luke's ordered stacks in the air and then sit back to enjoy his younger brother's wild reaction. Like his stacked cards, Luke had to have a certain order to his life and the world around him. Predictability and routine were critical to Luke, and he did not do well with change. Even small moment-to-moment changes tilted Luke's world in distressing ways. To pull him away from a task or toy could immediately devolve into a meltdown for Luke and a nightmare for his parents. Karen eventually learned to prepare Luke for change by setting a timer to define the completion of certain activities.

"Luke, when the timer goes off in five minutes you will be done using the computer," she'd say. With the timer now part of the planned sequence and ordered precision, when the time ran out Luke could walk away from the computer without issue.

It was difficult to find the right school situation for Luke because he was a challenging mix of high intelligence and scattered social skills. When he was 2, Luke taught himself sign language and how to read and write. Karen had a full plate with three kids, so she had no idea how Luke learned to do these things. Once while in an office lobby waiting for yet another doctor appointment, Luke picked up a children's book and started reading it aloud. Karen was dumbfounded. A woman watched and listened to Luke, too, in disbelief.

"Is that your boy?"

Karen nodded and smiled.

"He's reading that entire book," the woman said. "How old is he?"

"He's 2." Karen did not mention that Luke could also count from one to one hundred, and he could do it by fives and tens, too. Eventually Luke followed his brother to Mountain Brook Montessori School for prekindergarten and kindergarten. Morgan and Logan were at Peralta Elementary in Gold Canyon. Morgan was there for first and second grades and Logan for first.

One Thanksgiving, in 2008, Morgan was very sick. She stayed home with her father, as they had promised the boys a special dinner out. Karen drove Logan and Luke almost an hour to downtown Phoenix, where they went to Compass Arizona Grill, a revolving restaurant atop the Hyatt Regency Phoenix hotel. The biggest highlight for Luke was a laminated card with Phoenix facts and photographs. He studied it intently throughout dinner and memorized everything on the page. Meanwhile, true to form, Logan was running wild through the elegant buffet and eating his way, left to right, through every dessert.

Luke, after a series of evaluations by developmental specialists, qualified for state assistance similar to his sister Morgan. He started weekly speech, occupational, and physical therapies that Karen now knew well.

Sixteen

Family Split

BY 2008, KAREN WAS BUSY AS EVER with three toddlers ages 6 (Morgan), 5 (Logan), and 3 (Luke). Morgan, unfortunately, was still battling seizures. One day when Karen was picking the boys up at school, Morgan slumped forward with her arms drooping, turned white, and stopped breathing, which she had never done during a seizure before. Karen scooped up the boys and rushed Morgan to the hospital, but like all her episodes, the condition soon resolved.

That was why when someone from Morgan's school called to tell Karen that Morgan had suffered a seizure, Karen would say, *OK, thanks for calling to tell me.* To the teachers she might have seemed indifferent, but Karen knew there was nothing she or any doctor could do. Rushing Morgan to the emergency room would not help.

During other similar times Karen elicited reactions and glares from complete strangers. Karen had a disability sticker on her car because of the summer heat in Arizona and Morgan's difficulty walking. One of Morgan's medications, zonisamide, prevented her little body from sweating, a dangerous symptom in the desert heat. So as Karen piled in and out of the car parked in a handicapped spot, with three seemingly normal and bouncing toddlers, she often received glares and heard muttered comments. Morgan's disabilities were not always obvious to everyone; Luke's autism was completely invisible to the untrained eye. And Logan was, well, the life of the party.

Still desperate to help their daughter, Karen and Shawn had even made a final attempt to avoid more surgeries with a drastic change for Morgan. The ketogenic diet, recommended by physicians at Johns Hopkins Hospital in Baltimore, was a high-fat, adequate-protein, low-carbohydrate diet used to treat difficult cases of epilepsy in children. The diet forced the body to burn fats rather than carbohydrates, which mimicked aspects of starvation. By reducing carbohydrates, the diet forced the liver to convert fat into fatty acids and ketone bodies, which passed into the brain and replaced glucose as an energy source. The goal was an elevated level of ketone bodies in the blood, called ketosis, which reduced the frequency of epileptic seizures. That was the theory, anyway, but this particular subject was a stubborn 6-year-old girl who resisted every attempt at this extremely rigid diet. Morgan would have taken home the championship trophy as the pickiest eater of all picky eaters.

Karen and Shawn traveled to Baltimore with Morgan and went to Johns Hopkins Hospital in hopes of consulting with renowned neurosurgeon Ben Carson. They were buoyed by what they heard: after two years, more than half the children on the ketogenic diet were cured and completely seizure-free. The approach went back to Biblical times, when epileptics were thought to be possessed by demons and therefore were cast out and starved. By chance discovery, the severe calorie reduction lessened their seizures.

The extremely rigid diet, therefore, was quasi-starvation and had to be adhered to exactly to have any chance of success. Children had to be hospitalized and carefully monitored for several days to even start the diet. All Morgan's food was measured, weighed, and computed to provide an exact four-to-one ratio of fat to combined protein and carbohydrate. However, while it might have proved successful with others, Morgan immediately rejected it outright. At 6, Morgan had already endured her lifetime quota of hospitals, doctors, emergencies, treatments, therapies, evaluations, assessments, orthotics, medications, side effects, and symptoms. A highly restrictive diet was just too much for her.

Morgan wanted only to be a little girl. She adored all animals, and going to the zoo was one her favorite activities. She was particularly interested in the giraffe and butterfly exhibits. She also loved horses, cats, and dogs. She responded well to the therapy dogs during her various hospital stays. Sometimes the therapy dogs were the only way her parents could get her to cooperate when she became stubborn or depressed from being hospitalized. But Karen and Shawn could not very well ply Morgan with a rollicking new puppy or two to keep her on the ketogenic diet. Brain surgeries followed, as the last option to stop her seizures, and she would undergo five, total, by 2010.

LOGAN Jay Perry, 6 years old in 2009, had a real affinity for talking on the telephone. He'd slip out of bed while everyone else slept and start making impromptu early morning calls to his young friends, his parents' friends, and even his teachers. If no one answered, he'd leave a long rambling message. People diplomatically suggested to Karen and Shawn that they employ a pass code to keep Logan off the phone. Yes, Karen had tried that, but Logan figured out that he could still make at least one call, without limitation, simply by dialing 911. Karen made *that* discovery very early one morning when a Pinal County Sheriff's Office deputy showed up at her doorstep. Karen sheepishly told the officer that there was no emergency, but that as soon as she got ahold of her 6-year-old son there might be one. For him, at least. There wasn't, of course, because Logan's smile was always immediately disarming.

Logan was also quite proficient at sending text messages. Using Karen's cellular phone, he'd send a message to his teacher: *Hey, this is Karen Perry. Logan won't be coming to school today.* He was also proficient using Skype on the computer, which Karen discovered after the names of Logan's various girlfriends showed up on her account. Logan was so smart that Karen had to continually remind herself that he was a child. When Karen left on work trips for Delta Air Lines, Logan often called and left long messages. Usually his calls and messages started with a dramatic introduction: *Mother, you are not going to believe this!* Karen could only imagine what was next: Was the fire department at her house? Had he brought home three stray dogs? Bought a used car online? Ordered new patio furniture? *Well, mother, there is a scorpion in the garage and it is CRAWLING ALL OVER THE PLACE! And ya' know what, mother? I called animal control and guess what… they will NOT come out!*

One time Karen got a call on her cellular phone from a man asking to speak with Logan. *Creepy*, Karen thought, considering her boy's age.

"Who is this, and why do you want to talk to my son?" Karen said firmly.

"Well, er…" the man stammered. "He signed up online for continuing education."

"Are you sure you have the right name and number? My son Logan is only 6 years old." Then they both broke out in simultaneous laughter.

Logan could not pass a DVD kiosk without asking if he could rent a movie. He asked so often that Karen's automatic response was, "No." On one such occasion Logan loitered near the kiosk as Karen continued shopping while peeking from the aisle to keep tabs on him. Moments later she saw him talking to a very attractive woman, maybe in her twenties, with long blonde hair, a miniskirt, and knee boots. Astonished and amused, Karen watched as she rented a movie for the little charmer no one could deny.

Logan had a cadre of little girls who adored him. His "girlfriends" would call and leave long sweet messages for him. They would tell him that they loved and missed him, starting from about the time he was 6. When he was 7, Logan told his mother that he thought 8-year-old girls were really "hot." *Older women*, Karen thought. *Not surprising*. Then he matter-of-factly informed Karen that as soon as he finished high school he was marrying his girlfriend Keila and moving to Chicago with her.

Once in a play area at the shopping mall—that is, the bacteria zone—Karen noticed Logan eyeing a woman's ice cream cone. Karen turned her head briefly to check on Luke and Morgan, and when she turned back around Logan had the woman's ice cream in his hand and was eating it. She had given it to him!

It must have been time for *snack*, which was how Logan referred to the ingestion of any food outside normal meal times. *Mother*, he'd say, *is it time for snack?* Logan never missed a main meal, but he especially enjoyed "snack." On his first day at soccer practice, the team was only minutes into their first drill when Logan reached down and picked up the ball, which was taboo in the sport. Then he asked the coach, "Is it time for snack?"

On another occasion Logan had a group of senior citizens at the grocery store howling with laughter. It was a Friday night, and a long line of people had formed after they'd each ordered pizza. Karen and Logan had been waiting for some time, too, along with the others. All of a sudden Logan peered back into the kitchen and yelled, "Hey mister, where's my pizza?" Logan's charm, voice, and delivery only came off as tender and endearing, rather than rude. Everyone within earshot roared with laughter while Karen, once again mortified by one of her children, hid her face in embarrassment. Then Logan started dancing as he broke out with a paraphrase of the song from the film *Madagascar*, singing, "You got to move it, move it. You got to move it, move it!"

UNFORTUNATELY, for Karen and Shawn the fissures that had started to appear in their marriage had grown into untenable structural damage. In the autumn of 2009, Shawn moved out. At ages 7, 5, and 4, respectively, Morgan, Logan, and Luke did not fully comprehend what it all meant. They certainly sensed something had changed, but they were not exactly certain what or why. The divorce was finalized by early the next year, on February 5, 2010, Karen's forty-seventh birthday. Karen realized it would take some time for the kids to fully process the marriage dissolution when Logan said, "What? You and dad are divorced?"

On the health front, Karen had planned on getting reconstructive breast surgery. When she went for the consult, however, her physician recommended a double mastectomy because of her cancer history. Karen reluctantly agreed and underwent a double mastectomy one week after her divorce was finalized. Getting the surgery was the right move because during the procedure doctors discovered she had cancer on the right side.

Unfortunately, that operation left Karen with $30,000 in unpaid medical bills. Karen stayed in the house with the kids, along with the hefty mortgage in her name. While Shawn had agreed to shoulder responsibility for the credit card debt they had amassed, he filed bankruptcy again and the creditors started calling Karen. From her modest flight attendant salary, creditors started garnishing a portion each month. For Karen, the financial ship was sinking fast.

SEVENTEEN

Custody Battle

BY THE MIDDLE OF OCTOBER 2010, the stress had completely drained every last energy reserve from Karen Perry. Motherhood, divorce, and work had squeezed out everything she had. Her job alone could do that even to fresh-faced flight attendants twenty-five years her junior: twelve days in a silver steel tube cutting troposphere at 500 miles an hour. Outside at altitude, the pressure wave carved an invisible wake of ice crystals and supercooled water droplets. Inside, the human bodies packed tight had not yet evolved to pitch, roll, and yaw in such three-dimensional leaps of time, speed, and distance. Until Kitty Hawk, for tens of thousands of years humans had been as if ankle-tethered, wandering in a defined two-dimensional radius.

The human ability to aviate, to catapult through the atmosphere, had been a fantastic possibility for barely more than one hundred years. On the geological timeline, that was *Homo sapiens* rooting nests for eggs one night and, next morning, breaking the sound barrier in a glistening aircraft. On Earth, in the dizzying evolution to modern aviation, it was a full two hundred thousand years before humans created flying machines. To have been airborne for only the last ten decades of that timeline puts us in the infancy of aviation.

But stacked on top of the job was modern motherhood and three kids—including a daughter with epilepsy and an autistic son—a sad feud with the ex-husband, and toeing the cliff of financial freefall. Karen Perry's fatigue had devolved into something more encompassing, a force beyond description that penetrated down into her bones and pulsed back out through her ravaged center. There was tired, and then there was *tired*, the drop-dead exhaustion of an entirely different stripe. Karen Perry was *tired*.

God help me. How will I make it one more minute. If only… sleep… beautiful sweet elusive balm. Just take me now.

It was the cumulative toll of keeping it all together as a single mom with only a modest paycheck to fund the kids' medicines, endless co-pays, school extras and fees, Luke's Montessori tuition, and food, shelter, and clothing. On the worst days Karen made tough choices: gas in the car or lunch. The kids had to go to school; she could skip a meal and survive until dinner. The needle on the fuel gauge hovered in the red zone like a travel-edition game of Russian roulette.

That was why she took the hard fifteen-thousand-mile round-trips to Sydney (SYD): those grinders maximized what she could earn in three and a half days. Once there, the entourage of fifteen—four pilots and eleven flight attendants—would stride into the Four Seasons in Sydney. While the scene might have conjured the halcyon days of exotic and moneyed international travel, Karen was often flat broke, without even a single dollar bill in her purse. Before disembarking, she'd have the foresight to stow some snacks and fruit from the airplane galley. At the hotel, the crew usually started making sightseeing and lunch and dinner plans, but Karen always feigned exhaustion; she certainly was exhausted, but that was not why she stayed behind. Some adult conversation with Sydney's famous backdrops would have been tremendous therapy. Instead, she was too embarrassed not to be able to pay for her own twenty-dollar meal.

Karen did not even have a credit card she could use to float incidentals until payday; the divorce and second bankruptcy had destroyed her credit standing. Karen Perry had cash, or she had nothing. Tucked away in her five-star hotel room halfway around the world, at least she had shelter, food, and water. On occasion, some hotels offered a free breakfast, and taking a tour of the spa area sometimes garnered a few more pieces of fruit for the room.

In a losing battle to stay solvent, she was flying back-to-back-to-back-to-back trips: a two-day and then a three-day, followed by a five-day and another three-day, twelve straight days that blurred one into the next including back and forth across the international dateline to Sydney. Because of their respective epilepsy and autism, Morgan and Luke received state assistance through the Department of Economic Security Division of Developmental Disabilities, which helped offset child-care expenses. But the net amount she brought home from Delta Air Lines every two weeks did not go very far. She was caught in the trap faced by every parent in the modern world trying to have it all: paying someone else to raise her kids while she worked to earn money to, well, pay someone else to raise her kids.

Since 2010 Karen had entrusted that duty to Jaleesa Shelton, a twenty-something single mom and former hairdresser whose creative hair colors prompted "What happened to your hair?" questions from the kids. More important, she was very patient, dependable, and 100 percent trustworthy. Karen had to feel comfortable that when she was in Sydney, Australia, thousands of miles from home, her three kids were safe, loved, and being nurtured.

Karen was returning stateside November 1, 2010. Morgan had finally been released from the hospital a week earlier; she'd been laid up there a full two months. The brain surgery in August, number four in eight years of life, had accomplished the objective: to reduce her seizures. But then Morgan had a scary setback when she developed a MRSA infection in her brain. The methicillin-resistant *Staphylococcus aureus* was a stubborn bacteria, resistant to most antibiotics and potentially fatal. Morgan was hospitalized while doctors treated and eventually defeated this virulent infection, including another surgical procedure to flush the MRSA. Make that *five* brain surgeries in eight years of life. It had been a tense two months, only worsened by outright hostility between the parents: nurses walked Karen and Shawn in and out of Morgan's hospital room to make sure that if, by chance, their paths crossed, neither lingered long enough to start an argument. When Morgan finally returned home, it was with an internal PICC line (peripherally inserted central catheter) for her extended antibiotic therapy via intravenous access. Morgan was essentially quarantined at home for several more months to reduce the risk of infection to her diminished immune system. She could not go to school or be around other children, which was difficult.

After working these twelve days in a row, up and down to 35,000 feet more times than she could count, Karen was coming back a frazzled shell of her best self. Her body was battered from the altitude, zigzagging the international date line, and trying to re-clock to the eighteen-hour time changes. Any circadian rhythm that might have lingered, with codependent false hopes after twenty-six years in aviation, finally just packed up and left Karen's body permanently. *Girlfriend, you are on your own!* The joie de vivre had jumped bail as day, date, and time all blurred.

Once her flight landed in Los Angeles (LAX), taxied to the gate, and all the passengers disembarked, Karen's brutal run was, at least officially, done. But she still had to commute home, which meant non-revving back to Phoenix on Southwest Airlines or US Airways. "Non-rev" flying was the golden-ticket benefit of working for the major airlines: free airfare to any destination. At first mention people immediately conjured the panache and possibilities of such largesse: New York–Paris for lunch. Chicago–Geneva for a ski weekend. Los Angeles–San Francisco for the opera (that was a private charter in *Pretty Woman*, but same idea).

These "free" flights, however, came with heavy strings attached: space available. As much as an airline's marketing communications might have touted that "Our employees are our most prized assets," there was fine subtext: those same freeloading hordes lined up *behind* all the paying customers and, if there were no seats available, parked their prized assets in hard plastic at the gate to try again on the next flight. And one other pedantic detail, straight from the sophomoric 1970s "Ass, grass, or gas" bumper sticker: no one rides free. Employees still paid an annual service fee that covered most flights on US carriers and a reduced service charge on international carriers.

When the non-rev game played out in the right combinations, Karen could walk onto the first flight she tried— *Blackjack!*—and return to Phoenix without a glitch. On the worst days, every first card was a low-ball two or three and every hand busted: boxed out of every flight on every airline. On those days Karen spent another five, six, seven hours, officially off work but still trying to get back home. Free flights, indeed.

On this day, she caught the first Southwest flight she tried and landed in Phoenix at 8:30 a.m. From there, she took a van to the parking lot, and then it was a forty-five-minute drive to Gold Canyon just beyond the far eastern edge of sprawling metropolitan Phoenix. As she headed east on US 60 in her white Plymouth PT Cruiser, the thick concentrations of stucco homes and strip-mall suburbia gradually thinned and the freeway lanes winnowed from six to five, four, three, and then two each way.

Likewise, as she headed east with the radio pumping Top 40 tunes to keep her awake, the cool monolith of the mountain appeared to gradually inch higher. The Apaches believed the opening to hell, the lower world, was hidden there near Superstition Mountain. The choking dust storms that swept across the region in towering waves of sandblasting grit, told the legend, emanated from the hot breath blowing straight out of the darkness. Others believed the hidden portal led the opposite direction, to heaven. Whichever it was, Karen and her children lived in proximity to the mystical gateway, which would continue to sit silent, holding its secrets for the next 379 days.

Finally, mercifully, as she pulled up to her house, the twelve-day blitzkrieg fell silent. She turned off the car and exhaled. The dull roar of a jet at altitude echoing in her head gave way to an unbelievably expansive silence that had a different roar of its own. Karen looked at her ex-husband's white Dodge truck and sighed the deep release of full surrender. For self-preservation, she sent forth intentions for a quick, clean, and uneventful handoff. He'd need to explain Morgan's medications—frequencies and dosages—and how to clean and operate the PICC line. If he tried to pick a fight, she'd let it go. She had no will or energy to spare.

"I was as exhausted as a person can be," Karen recalled. As bad as it was, the heavy fatigue was only a precursor to even darker times.

Inside, there was no confrontation. Shawn explained everything, gave her some written instructions, and was gone in minutes. To nurse her sore throat, Karen poured a glass of Courvoisier and sipped at it while she tried to flush Morgan's PICC line. After numerous attempts, Karen made the mistake of calling Shawn and asking for his help. He did not answer his phone immediately. Karen knew the nurse would be there in the morning, and Morgan would be all right: the PICC line could wait until morning. Karen got her kids ready for bed. Shawn called back later, but Karen had slipped into a dead sleep right there in Morgan's bed.

What seemed like minutes was actually a few hours, when barking dogs and loud banging on the front door thumped at the edges of Karen's near coma of exhaustion. Then more banging on Morgan's bedroom window. Morgan woke up first, in the din, and climbed out of bed. Barely conscious, and confused by the ruckus, Karen awoke and walked to the front door, opened it, and stood there trying to process for a few seconds. *Why is my ex-husband standing here with two deputies from the Pinal County Sheriff's Office?*

"Have you been drinking?" one of the deputies asked.

"Drinking? What? No," she said, still confused. *I've been sleeping.*

One of the officers pointed to and asked about the half-glass of brandy sitting on the counter, which Karen had barely touched hours earlier. They asked whether her daughter had gotten her meds. Karen was still half asleep as the full story came out: Shawn had become concerned when he called back and couldn't reach Karen. He just wanted to make sure Morgan and everyone else was all right.

Still standing there in her pajamas, Karen explained her sheer exhaustion, the few sips of brandy still on her breath, and falling into a sleep of oblivion. Any potential standoff quickly de-escalated, and the officers and ex-husband climbed into vehicles and drove away. Karen was still so exhausted she just wanted to cry, but she was afraid if she started she might never stop. Little did she know that, in the next hours, as part of normal department procedure, this innocuous encounter would be officially documented into a Pinal County Sheriff's Office incident report, which would then become public record. Later, mere days after her three children had died in a plane crash, in the feeding frenzy of a hot local story, the frothing media would dig up this incident report, along with two others.

For now, after they left all Karen could envision was sleep, a recharge, and trying to be the best mother she could. Part of that plan was asking Shawn to come back and pick up Morgan, too, so Karen could slip into a much-needed deep slumber.

On November 2, 2010, at approximately 10 a.m., there was another unexpected knock at the door.

"What now?" Karen thought as she went to answer.

It was two process servers, and one said, "Your children will not be returned to your care. They are officially being removed from your home and going under the care of their father."

"What?" Karen said. "What are you talking about?"

Karen didn't hear anything they were saying, because the world was spinning around her like some maniacal carnival ride. Alone, exhausted, and dizzy, there was nothing she could do. No matter how ridiculous, the law had intervened and taken her children. The only way to get them back now would be through the court system. A big boost on that front would be Karen's volunteer efforts, advocating for children, with numerous agencies over the years.

That moment of panic was followed by a horrible two months that included court paperwork, custody hearings, and supervised visits with her own children. When the dust finally settled in January 2011, Karen was given primary custody, with Shawn getting visitation. As a devoted father to his three children, Shawn was heartbroken. He scheduled visitation every other weekend. Shortly thereafter he declared himself unfit to fly in his job at US Airways, which voided his medical certification, and he moved to Safford, Arizona. Shawn never fully explained to Karen why he had declared himself unfit to fly. The stage was now set for the Mesa–Safford flight, on the moonless night of November 23 later that year.

EIGHTEEN

Fleeting, Precious Time

IN THE SUMMER OF 2011, KAREN WAS SEARCHING for a school that would be a good fit for Luke and the challenges his autism brought. Parents of special needs children learned quickly that the one-size-fits-all approach did not work. Luke had followed his brother Logan, who was in third grade, into an excellent charter program at Edu-Prize. The school, however, used an intensive, structured, fast-paced program that did not fit well with Luke's abilities and sensibilities. In fact, Luke's teacher and the school principal politely suggested Karen remove Luke from their exclusive program after only one month of attendance. Meanwhile, Morgan had found a good fit at Leading Edge Academy, in their offshoot program called Pieceful Solutions. This was after long battles with Apache Junction Unified School District administrators and teachers over how best to educate Morgan. Karen had to fight every year for the needed services.

Morgan had an individualized education plan, and Karen was always watchful to make certain the district administrators and teachers were complying.

For years the public school psychologist had told Karen and Shawn that their daughter was mentally retarded. That child care professional, along with other school officials, wanted to place Morgan in a program that basically warehoused all the "short bus" children who did not fit into the mainstream profile. Karen and Shawn vehemently disagreed. They accepted that Morgan's development was delayed, and she was heavily medicated, but she was not MR, which is designated by an IQ below 70. Karen even had Morgan undergo a special test called quantitative EEG (QEEG), with the results showing Morgan's IQ was approximately 110, hardly MR. Karen refused to back down, and successfully advocated for Morgan so that she was not forever labeled and filed away somewhere.

With that experience as backdrop, by her third child Karen was an unflappable advocate for finding the best education. For Luke she finally found a Montessori school in Gilbert, a far-flung eastern suburb of metropolitan Phoenix. The school curriculum balanced structure and flexibility to let Luke gravitate toward subjects he found interesting. Luke, age 6, started attending the new school in October 2011 and, although he had some initial struggles, switching to half days allowed him to start finding his way. His teachers and fellow students immediately found Luke to be a very sweet, loving little boy who enjoyed being around people. Although his social ease was less common in someone with autism, Luke had other identifiable autism characteristics, including his speech delay and obsessive-compulsive behavior. All factors considered, Luke's ability to interact socially reduced Karen's fears about dropping him off at a new school.

On one occasion, when Karen was with Luke in a waiting room full of people, she watched as he methodically walked from one person to the next. He'd stop, look into each person's eyes, hold out his hand, and say, "Hi. My name is Luke. What is your name?" After they replied, Luke shook their hands like a seasoned pro on the campaign trail. And then, unlike a politician dispensing manufactured charm, Luke would tenderly kiss the new acquaintance on the cheek and move on to the next person. Karen was equally embarrassed (*Oh, my*

God!), concerned (*We don't kiss strangers!*), and touched by his kindness (*What a sweet, sweet boy...*).

Luke loved to draw with markers. As an artist, his chosen mediums were fabric, as in Karen's couch and bedspread, and Sheetrock, as in the walls at home. Luke was also fascinated with photography, and he took hundreds of pictures. His favorite subjects to shoot were ceiling fans and his own feet. Sometimes he managed to superimpose his feet over ceiling fans. He also used the camera on Karen's computer to photograph himself. While he was using the computer, Luke also figured out how to log into Karen's Facebook account and change her profile picture to a random, obscure image. Karen never did unravel how Luke learned such things, but she would one day be grateful beyond measure that Luke stubbornly ignored her repeated admonitions to stop taking photographs of himself with her computer. He left behind a treasure trove of hundreds of images, videos, and musical pictorials that he made himself, many of which Karen did not discover until years after the crash.

Another one of Luke's obsessions was roller coasters, and he'd mimic with his arm movement someone riding on one. For years Karen thought he was flying an airplane through an aerobatic routine, but then she realized he was on a roller coaster in his mind. Like 90 percent of young children, Luke was also a picky eater and only liked bananas, French fries, and pizza—the cornerstones of any nutritious diet. So, surprisingly, one of the last things he said to his mother was, "Yay, I love Thanksgiving!"

BY the time Logan turned 8, on Halloween 2011, he was already very independent. Karen started giving him short episodes of responsibility by letting him be home alone for twenty minutes while she ran a quick errand with Morgan and Luke. She'd tell Logan that under no circumstances was he to open the door for anyone, unless it was one of her close friends who Logan knew. On one occasion when, twenty minutes later, Karen returned from the errand, she was horrified to find Logan out on the sidewalk by himself, where he had already set up his kid furniture and was selling lemonade. Karen was furious and told him that he was obviously not ready for the responsibility with which she had entrusted him.

Logan smiled and, like a refined litigator making precise delineations to a judge, said, "Mother, you said not to let anyone *in*. You did not say that I could not go *out*." Karen's neighbor from across the street later told her that he had asked Logan how much for the lemonade. Logan told him two dollars. *Pretty steep*, the neighbor thought as he plunked eight quarters in the jar and received half a glass of lemonade. He asked Logan why two dollars only bought half a glass. Logan informed him cheerfully that it was all the lemonade he had left, since he had already consumed most of the pitcher.

Along with overpriced lemonade, Logan was well known in his neighborhood for Movie Night. He'd carefully prepare invitations using the computer and *mail* them to neighbors without telling Karen about the plans. Karen would only discover what was happening as the RSVPs began coming back. One surprised mother told Karen how professional Logan's invitations looked! Whenever Karen heard noises in the middle of the night, she knew it was Logan. She'd find him perched on the living room couch with a bowl of popcorn, enjoying a movie.

Wherever Karen went with Logan, he knew people. Karen used to ask him how an 8-year-old knew more people than she did? *Well, mother... I do not know!* At every social gathering, Logan was the consummate entertainer. He was very social and never needed an excuse to throw a party. He'd prepare and set up place mats and food for all the kids. Then he'd plan the entire event with activities and times, carefully writing everything down and posting it for all to see.

DURING the last two years of Morgan's young life, she was becoming increasingly difficult to handle. She was very strong physically, and her behavior was often over the top. As she grew, it was getting more difficult for Karen to handle her. It took an exhausting amount of patience to be around Morgan for any period of time. She was on a dizzying combination of medications, and her behavior was bizarre at times. The main side effect listed on one of her antiseizure medications was psychosis. While most children acted out and then moved on, Morgan would dwell on things for hours.

Morgan had certain food obsessions, and she'd get stuck in a specific rut for months at a time. One of these kicks was for refried beans, and that was all she wanted to eat all day, every day. Then it was Amy's frozen macaroni and soy cheese. If Karen tried to slip in a different brand of the same food, Morgan wouldn't touch it and refused to eat. Sometimes Morgan would see flies that were not there, and cringe and scream. The only way Karen could calm her was to put her in the bath for a few minutes. As painful as it would have been, Karen had considered putting Morgan in an assisted living facility where professionals could better attend to her 24/7 care and demands.

Like her younger brothers, Morgan loved people and was very friendly. Of course, whenever her younger brothers were acting out Morgan would scold them with, "You are naughty! You go to timeout." And like Luke, she had boundary issues with strangers. She'd sit on any man's lap whether she knew him or not, which made Karen extremely uncomfortable. Morgan was blissfully ignorant of any peril surrounding her. She loved to sing and could memorize every single word of the lyrics to songs she heard on the radio. Morgan was a beautiful little girl who would never be completely independent. Her mother only prayed that she'd find some small purpose and direction in life.

ON Logan's eighth birthday, Karen took him to Circus Circus in Las Vegas. The prior year they'd gone to Universal Studios in Burbank. He had asked Karen if they could drive to Burbank instead of flying. When Karen asked him why Logan said, "Because, Mother, flying scares me to DEATH!"

"Logan, come on, your mom and dad are both pilots," Karen said.

Karen reassured Logan that she would never let anything bad happen to him and was able to talk him into taking a commercial flight on US Airways; Logan white-knuckled his way through the short flight. He was in the window seat and closed the window shade. He tightly gripped both armrests and had a crazed look of fear. But Logan faced the fear and never again expressed any fear of flying.

The week before Thanksgiving 2011, Karen was stopped at a red light when Logan reached over to hold her hand.

"Mother," he said, "if I die next week does that mean you will still be my mother?"

Karen was stunned at his question and wondered why he was asking it. She squeezed his hand tight, smiled, and said, "Of course, Logan. I will always be your mother."

PART III

THE CRASH AND AFTERMATH—

LEARNING TO FLY AGAIN

Nineteen

Zero Hour: Crash Site

ON THE DAY BEFORE THANKSGIVING, November 23, 2011, around 10:30 a.m., three friends set out on a rigorous and scenic day hike up Superstition Mountain east of Phoenix. Joseph Garrett, Jeffrey Hunt, and Jordan Viramontes planned to trek up Siphon Draw Trail to the Flat Iron peak sitting almost one mile above sea level (4,860 feet). The highest peak on the mountain was even farther up, at more than 5,000 feet.

For even avid hikers, the trail was quite grueling, with more than 3,000 feet of elevation gain up through a scenic and rugged desert canyon. Those seeking a wide, well-groomed path with gentle switchbacks best look elsewhere: this trail went straight up, over, and between solidified rock. For the entire last two-thirds, any trail disappeared completely, with only faint paint blotches on rocks to mark the steep climb. It was the type of hike where quality gloves were as crucial as proper footwear, since the arms and hands were constantly called into action. For a fit and experienced hiker, it was a strenuous two-plus hours from the bottom to top. For most others, the ascent alone could take three, four, or five hours, which is why so many hikers got into trouble when the daylight dwindled.

Along with the ankle-twisting and arm-breaking potential of the terrain, the other big challenge was the bone-brittle desert climate, which posed a constant threat of dehydration and heat stroke when the core body temperature topped 105°F. Once afflicted, hikers were beset with complications involving the central nervous system: nausea, seizures, confusion, disorientation, loss of consciousness or coma, and even death. The hike itself was difficult enough, but to stay hydrated and lucid meant lugging sufficient stores of water up the steep rock climb, which added a lot of weight to the equation.

The three hikers scrambled up sloped rocks on all fours, using their arms to climb up, through, and over narrow rock wedges. While the climb was physically grueling, the landscape and views were stunningly beautiful. They worked their way up through ravines that were surprisingly thick with trees and foliage that also scratched arms and legs as they climbed. Loose scree was abundant, too, so they had to carefully watch their footing so as not to slip and slide backward down the mountain.

Near the top, the final obstacle was a fifteen-foot rock wall they had to traverse to access the scenic plateau. They'd been wedged in this rugged canyon for hours, mostly in shade, and then they each cleared the vertical ledge into brilliant sunlight. Straight ahead were the highest points—spidery rock fingers called hoodoos—and to the right the imposing Flat Iron. They had triumphed, and they took a brief moment to stare down the forty-million-year geologic timeline of what they had just scaled. They had no way of knowing they were standing near what would soon be the epicenter of a violent flash explosion. Time to impact was now marked in minutes.

Like most mountain climbs, the descent was much more difficult than the ascent. The terrain was steep and slippery, so the choice was to either shuttle backward at the many steep points, which was awkward, slow, and unnerving, or essentially crab walk and/or slide down across the scattered, slippery loose rocks. The terrain, and their already fatigued legs, made for slow going. The last really tough section was Siphon Draw, a beautiful solidified lava flow that was deceptively dangerous. To see it was to glimpse another epoch and imagine flowing rock solidifying into a motionless canyon river. It was impenetrably solid, with no loose shale, and sloped at about thirty-five degrees, which made descending in the fading light extremely precarious.

In other words, Siphon Draw was too steep to just saunter down. So once again, it was either shimmy backward or crab walk, which really put the burn in throbbing quadriceps muscles. As the slope angle decreased slightly, they could finally stand upright again and walk slowly by cutting back and forth laterally across the face, which really pounded and strained their jellied legs. As darkness settled on the beautifully rugged slab, the friends realized they were in trouble. Under the black cloudless banner, the way down the mountain would disappear completely. With the desert temperature rapidly headed toward the thirties later that night, staying out minus the proper gear was not an option.

They used a cellular phone to contact the Pinal County Sheriff's Office to send help. In Arizona, search-and-rescue activities fell under the domain of the sheriff's office in each of the fifteen counties. The rugged terrain in which the hikers were stranded was in Pinal County, which put their rescue under the jurisdiction of the sheriff's office there, headed by Sheriff Paul Babeu (pronounced *Bab-you*).

AS a kid growing up in Massachusetts, Paul Babeu knew his destiny. He wanted to serve as a protector who was there to help people in times of crisis.

"I always looked up to cops," he said. His uncle was chief of police in a nearby town and another family member was a police officer, and so the mold was cast. Born February 3, 1969, in North Adams, Massachusetts, Babeu went on to earn a bachelor's degree in history/political science at Massachusetts College of Liberal Arts and a master's degree in public administration, summa cum laude, from American International College.

By December 2002 he had migrated west, where he landed his first police officer post with the city of Chandler, a metropolitan Phoenix suburb. By the time he graduated with class 376 from the Arizona Law Enforcement Academy on April 25, 2003, he was ranked the number one overall police recruit by staff and also voted as the exemplary recruit by his class peers. He'd go on to receive two medals for saving lives in the performance of his duties as a patrolman, be selected by his peers to represent them as head of the Chandler Law Enforcement Association, and be on the board of directors for the Arizona Police Association.

After seven years as a patrol officer, Babeu won his first term as sheriff in 2008, in a historic effort as the only countywide elected Republican in the 133-year history of Pinal County. He started his post as sheriff January 1, 2009, and in 2011 was "Sheriff of the Year," as selected by his colleagues in the National Sheriff's Association.

He oversaw an operation with some six hundred full-time staff, more than two hundred sworn deputies, and more than four hundred volunteers. Pinal County deputies patrolled almost 5,400 square miles, an area larger than the state of Connecticut, and serviced a population of 375,000 people. During 2011, the Pinal County Sheriff's Office (PCSO) search-and-rescue (SAR) deputies and volunteers responded to 137 calls—mostly, as in this case, for missing and injured hikers. There were four full-time search-and-rescue deputies with 4x4 trucks, along with a team of trained volunteers ready to respond.

On November 23, 2011, the hikers were stranded right below a spot called the Waterfall, which was a forty-five minute hike up for fit, trained, and experienced search-and-rescue personnel, each of whom carried a forty-pound backpack supplied with night gear, first aid, and other survival necessities.

After 6 p.m., Deputy Scott Abernathy, a search-and-rescue coordinator with PCSO, got the call from dispatch about the hikers. At that moment, Abernathy was about thirty-five miles south of the mountain, in Florence, conducting a training session with fellow SAR deputy Jeff Love. Abernathy left the training session early and climbed in his PCSO-marked truck to head north to help get the hikers off the mountain. He called Louie Villa, an SAR posse volunteer, and asked him to start assembling a team to hike up the mountain in the dark. Abernathy hadn't eaten all day, so he wheeled into a McDonald's drive-through to grab some food for the drive. With the day before Thanksgiving 2011 fading, and now in complete darkness on a moonless night, the next search-and-rescue call would be on an altogether different scale.

Meanwhile, Karen was at home, fighting illness, in a fevered sleep, and isolated from the outside world.

DOWN at the base of the mountain, at 6:31 p.m., Jason and Jacob Costello had just left the Mining Camp Restaurant and stepped into the chilly, moonless night. They wanted to try a smartphone application to view star constellations, so the pitch-black backdrop was perfect to skygaze. With the phone aimed aloft, they noticed an airplane pass through their view and then disappear for a second. Then they saw a large bright flash.

Back up the mountain, as the three hikers were making their way to the Waterfall, southwest and down from Flat Iron, they had watched the same airplane fly directly overhead. The hikers, too, were immersed in the dark moonless night, and so the blinking lights on the wings were especially prominent. Jordan Viramontes said he did not notice anything unusual about the plane other than he thought it was flying low. Nor did he or his two friends ever hear the engine roar increase. Then the plane disappeared because of the steep visual angle up the mountain and, less than a mile from where they stood, there was a loud explosion. When they looked up they saw flames climbing toward the heavens. Officially, Pinal County Sheriff's Office incident number 111123199 occurred at 6:31 p.m.

"When it happened (the hikers) were horrified," said Deputy Love.

Karen and Shawn Perry's close friend Eva Morgan was at home that evening when one of her three sons came running into the house yelling, "A plane just hit the mountain!" They stepped outside and could see the glow. After living in Gold Canyon for more than a decade, Eva had become very connected to the mountain spiritually. As she stood watching what must be certain death in the silent orange glow, she felt an overwhelming need to get up the mountain and try to somehow help. Of course that was impossible, but she was feeling the pain of loss for the victims' families, who would soon receive devastating news. She had no idea her empathy would soon turn to bottomless grief for herself and her dear friend.

Almost immediately, numerous 911 calls flooded the dispatcher, and at 6:32 p.m. the call went out to first responders. While sitting in the drive-through line with his truck idling, Abernathy heard the radio call about a plane crash into Superstition Mountain. Abernathy backed up the four-wheel-drive diesel Chevrolet and raced north on Highway 79 without ever ordering food. Deputy Love responded too. Already, even from Florence, some thirty-five miles away, the enormity of the incident was visible.

"As soon as we got on Highway 79 we could see the fires up there," said Love, who joined PCSO in 2004.

Abernathy advised dispatch to contact other agencies for assistance, including the Maricopa County Sheriff's Office and the Federal Aviation Administration. Abernathy used his cell phone to call Louie Villa again to tell him they now had a second and much more serious incident on the same mountain. Abernathy simply said: "We need everybody you can get." That meant scrambling as many PCSO search-and-rescue volunteers as possible for a plane crash into Superstition Mountain. Within six minutes of the crash, Abernathy and five other PCSO deputies were headed to the scene. Abernathy also called Sergeant Brian Messing, his immediate supervisor, to alert him.

"My phone blew up when we got the call," said Messing, who oversaw the search-and-rescue function for the Pinal County Sheriff's Office. Messing, who lived in Oracle, just north of Tucson, and was at home at the time, instructed Abernathy to start organizing. Initially, a call about a plane crash could be anything or absolutely nothing. Every week of every year, concerned citizens called the sheriff's office to report what turned out to be either minor situations or nonexistent incidents. One of the most frequent nonincident calls: *There's a light on the mountain*. But it didn't take long for everyone hearing the call on the radio to realize this was no light-on-the-mountain fabrication. Said Messing, "As soon as I came out of Oracle I could see the glow."

At Phoenix Fire Station 41, some fifty miles west of the mountain, a two-man Arizona Department of Public Safety (DPS) crew was preparing to depart in a Bell 407 helicopter. The pilot that night was Ron Banning, who was paired with Russ Dodge, an officer-paramedic with thirteen years at DPS. They were on a typical twenty-four-hour shift and had been called out to investigate an explosion, possible plane crash into Superstition Mountain. Any other details were scarce. Within ten minutes of getting the call they were airborne, headed east, and flipping down their night-vision goggles. Said Dodge, "When we saw the glow from where we were, it was unusual."

For everyone responding, the increasing likelihood that an airplane had crashed raised numerous immediate concerns: With a fire that large, were they dealing with a downed major commercial jet? If so, how many hundreds of casualties were scattered atop the rugged terrain? And how many survivors awaited rescue under the black banner of this night?

From Oracle, the ninety-mile drive normally took Sergeant Messing about an hour and a half, but as the sense of urgency surged he hit his lights and siren and made it to Lost Dutchman State Park in less than an hour. Along the way he, too, was mobilizing resources, including the US National Guard and other personnel.

Twelve minutes after the crash, Sam Pacheco was the first PCSO deputy to arrive near the trailhead to Superstition Mountain. He stopped in the parking lot at Lost Dutchman State Park, which for the next three days would be the incident command post.

Within twenty minutes of the crash, Deputy Jeff Love was headed to the scene when he heard over the radio that the DPS Ranger helicopter was overhead the fiery crash site at more than 5,000 feet elevation. No one yet knew what type of aircraft had crashed, or how many passengers were aboard. At 6:52 p.m., Deputy Kevin Letteer was the second to arrive on scene and he, too, could see the large flames at the top of Superstition Mountain in the area of the Siphon Draw Trail, which faced west to northwest. A minute later, Deputy Sean Lennon arrived.

As Banning and Dodge approached the scene in the helicopter, they encountered heavy smoke pouring into the night. They could see flames lashing up from below as the fire hissed, popped, and exploded. They still weren't even certain that it was an airplane crash because it was difficult to distinguish much in the rage of swirling fire and heavy smoke. If it was an airplane, from the sheer size and intensity of the fire, they determined it was not a small, single-engine plane that had gone down. That realization raised other concerns: Were they dealing with a military aircraft loaded with potentially deadly explosives? A large commercial airliner? A wide cargo plane stocked with hazardous materials? They were getting radio updates as Banning circled the mountaintop that was very familiar to them both from numerous search-and-rescue operations. They learned of the missing hikers stuck somewhere below in the darkness. They also realized that any sort of ground response to this crash site would be two to four hours out because of the rugged terrain and difficult night ascent. The sense of urgency started to ramp up; if there were any survivors down there, the only way to help them would be to get someone on the ground immediately from the air.

With precious time ticking away, the airborne team made a critical decision: Banning would land to the north where he knew there was a saddle, a rocky outcrop far enough away from the flames to not put the helicopter or their own lives at risk. From there, Dodge would venture out alone to make a quick assessment and search for any possible survivors. They needed some sort of baseline assessment to help organize what might be a massive rescue operation.

Flying a helicopter on a moonless night into a slot canyon was tricky under the best conditions. As he circled the scene, Banning was also dealing with poor visibility from the ever-shifting cloud of smoke, and his infrared was rendered inoperable by the intense heat below. Banning waited, and when he saw the smoke clear he made an approach toward the saddle. But as he brought the helicopter in, the wind shifted and obscured what little visibility he had behind a thick cloud of disorienting smoke. He had to take evasive action and fly away at that point. On his second attempt, Banning was able to set the helicopter down on that saddle, at right about the same altitude as the flaming crash site.

"We could see and hear things exploding in the wreckage," Dodge said. Banning would stay on the ground, with the rotors whirling, to function as both radio relay for all the other agencies and to watch his partner and be ready for a quick exit if needed. Dodge climbed from the helicopter in gloves and a Nomex flight suit, a high-quality, flame-resistant coverall worn by US military personnel, law enforcement first responders, and civilian air crews. He had his survival backpack, a GPS unit, and handheld radio. From where he was he'd have to walk 150 yards, straight into the choking and swirling smoke cloud, to the lower north edge of the debris field that was intensifying into a deafening inferno of twenty-foot flames. He lowered his head and very carefully found each foothold as he methodically moved toward the pulsing wall of heat.

Due south of the fire, at the lower elevation of the desert floor, Deputy Abernathy was driving north and using his cell phone and radio simultaneously. Like all law enforcement, fire, and emergency medical agencies responding to the call, Abernathy assumed the worst and instructed arriving deputies on scene to start establishing staging areas including a helicopter landing zone (LZ) for multiple back-and-forth passenger extractions from the crash site, a triage center, and a designated media area. Abernathy, meanwhile, radioed for the official mobile command post vehicle, which arrived on scene later that night.

Lieutenant Blake King, of the Pinal County Sheriff's Office, was also at home when he got the call from Sergeant Messing. King immediately jumped into his marked vehicle and, at 6:56 p.m., raced to the base of mountain. Along the way he called Sheriff Babeu.

"Have you seen the MI?" King said, dispensing with pleasantries in reference to the major incident. Babeu was in uniform but off duty at a friend's house in Florence so, no, he had not yet heard. King told him all they knew: there had been a plane crash on Superstition Mountain, with a large fire now burning. Babeu asked all the right questions, but they still did not know what type of aircraft or how many people had been aboard.

Babeu hustled to his black unmarked Chevrolet Tahoe, turned on the lights and siren hidden in the grill and windshield, and sped toward the scene thirty-five miles to the north. Just before 7 p.m., three PCSO units were already on scene at the base of the mountain and seven more units were en route.

At precisely 7:00 p.m., Deputy Abernathy, as search-and-rescue coordinator, wheeled his truck into the parking lot at Lost Dutchman State Park, followed closely by Deputy Love. They oversaw setting up the incident command post area, which for the moment centered around their trucks. They also marked off the helicopter LZ, triage center, and media area. Deputy Abernathy had been with the Pinal County Sheriff's Office since July 2006 and was certified in search and rescue, as were his peers Deputy Love and Deputy Brian McGinnis. Everyone was still operating under the assumption that a large jetliner had hit the mountain, with the potential for untold numbers of injured and casualties. Abernathy called James Langston, the statewide coordinator at EMSCOM, Arizona's Emergency Medical Services Communications, which provided a communications link between field emergency medical services personnel and local medical facilities. At 7:08 p.m. Deputy McGinnis, too, talked with Langston, who said he would check with personnel at the US Air Force and local flight towers to potentially determine the aircraft type and size and any passenger information.

By now, all requested resources were being deployed, including the DPS Ranger helicopter landing at the crash site, surrounding fire departments, medical crews, air transport on standby, the volunteer Pinal County Sheriff's Office search-and-rescue posse, Apache Junction Rehab Truck, Mesa Police Department, Maricopa County Sheriff's Office helicopter, Maricopa County Sheriff's Office search-and-rescue coordinators, and rope rescue teams, which might be required if survivors were trapped on steep slopes.

When Deputy Love arrived at the command post, he assumed incident command, as the most experienced responder. He, too, was in contact with Langston. Priority number one was determining how many dead and injured were atop the mountain and how to deploy medical rescues. Also en route to the command post was PCSO Detective E. Scott Leonard, who requested Identification Technician Jennie Randall be on scene in about twelve hours, at 7 a.m., on Thanksgiving morning. Properly photographing and documenting casualties would be impossible in that terrain at night, so they were already preparing for the grim task awaiting at first light.

AROUND 7:15 p.m., Karen Perry had awoken from her nap and thought it was odd that none of her three children had called after landing in Safford, which they always did. She double-checked the time and was thinking they should have landed safely by 7 p.m. She sent Shawn a text just to make sure everything was all right.

Atop the mountain, it took Russ Dodge five careful minutes to walk from the helicopter to the edge of the debris field and its intense fire. The slope was steep and covered with slippery scree, so he had to move carefully as the fire roared. He started walking up the south side of the debris field and yelling into the inferno: "Is anybody there? Can anybody hear me?" He also blew a rescue whistle repeatedly because the high pitch better cut through the wall of noise, a rumbling churn like standing next to a massive waterfall.

"Fire is a noisy animal, especially when it's fuel-fed," Dodge said.

As he worked his way up the steep slope, Dodge started seeing what he knew to be human remains. Not intact deceased people they could identify, but much more gruesome parts and pieces of human beings. Similarly, under the roar and choking smoke, Dodge was not finding much that resembled an airplane, but rather shattered mechanical rubble. Then he saw a wheel and strut, a thick leg of the aircraft that had been sheared clean from the fuselage and was resting away from the fire, where Dodge kneeled to assess it more closely. The wheel was the first piece of helpful evidence in determining the size of the aircraft: it was too small for a commercial airliner but larger than a single-engine Cessna. Dodge radioed his finding to Banning, who put it out to everyone listening on their radios. The specter of a crashed large commercial jet and hundreds of casualties and injured had been eliminated. And based on the violent scene he was observing, Dodge was thinking there was a zero percent chance anyone had survived. But in search and rescue, the unbelievable can and did happen with regularity, so Dodge continued calling out and blowing the rescue whistle. It was an eerie and lonely place for Dodge to be trying to find any indication of life. But with each desperate plea into the flames—*Is anybody there? Can anybody hear me?*—all that came back was the bleak roar of the massive blaze.

Dodge knew, too, that the smoke was a dangerous consideration, because excessive inhalation could render him unconscious before he even realized what had hit him. He was coughing and having trouble breathing. The flames, too, seemed to be intensifying as the fire found new sources and wantonly fed on fuel, wreckage, and vegetation that popped and sizzled all around. He turned and couldn't see Banning sitting in the running helicopter 150 yards away. Dodge still had to walk back across the steep slope, and through the smoke, for extraction. The situation was getting more dangerous by the second.

"It was almost unbearable," Dodge said.

Still determined, Dodge tried one last futile pass. But as he found more and more severed human remains the depressing reality hit: there was almost no chance anyone had survived the violent impact. He could see and hear exploding hydraulic cylinders, too, which were launching white-hot debris twenty-five feet through the air. A direct hit from any one of these missiles could be fatal. With the wind shifting the flames and smoke and the fire burning hotter and hotter, Dodge realized the risk of staying there any longer was now much greater than any benefit they might derive. Although he wouldn't discover it until later, the heat was singeing his arm hair even through the thick sheath of his flight suit. He was in immediate proximity to a massive, shifting blaze atop a windy mountaintop that could easily take his own life.

If they required further confirmation that they needed to get out immediately, it came when Dodge went to look at a piece of debris and a rock under his foot gave way. Dodge fell and slid down about ten feet into a burning pile of debris that singed his boots and flight suit. Dodge collected two panels he found with airplane identifiers still visible, which would be helpful, and carefully made his way back to Banning in the helicopter. Dodge's risky insertion had provided valuable information: they were able to estimate the size of the aircraft, which eliminated many other more dire scenarios, and they had determined, sadly, that there were no survivors.

AS Banning and Dodge approached the designated LZ, Sergeant Messing was just arriving at the command post as the Bell helicopter touched down. Messing climbed out of his marked PCSO truck and entered the chaotic scene, where multiple uniformed deputies were working out of their trucks. A large cluster of media personnel was already there with their remote vans, cameras, and lights. With Banning's call going out over the radio, everyone involved was quickly losing hope that there were any survivors high up on the mountain under the veil of blackness.

Banning and Dodge climbed out of the helicopter and met with Deputy Jeff Love and others. Dodge handed over some of the panels he'd found at the crash location. Dodge said that after looking at the crash site there was a zero percent survivability rate. He said there were body parts and human remains spread all over the scene, and that the crash site would be burning for some time due to all the fuel on the ground.

Sheriff Babeu arrived at the scene command post for the first large-scale airplane crash within the jurisdiction of the agency he'd led since January 2009. With a swarm of media people already looking for answers, Babeu was resolute not to put out any information until investigators had confirmed facts. There was a buzz of activity around the mobile command center as deputies made plans to secure a perimeter around the crash site by blocking all access trails to the area. Whatever had happened up there, investigators would need to carefully identify, document, preserve, and collect all evidence. There were other logistics, too, such as making arrangements to get food supplies and water to the command post for what promised to be a long around-the-clock stay.

"It was organized," said Abernathy, "but it was chaotic." The normal protocol for such a major incident was to immediately marshal all possible resources and then release people and equipment if not needed. Abernathy worked out of his truck, using his computer, cell phone, and radio to gather information. He talked to personnel at Sky Harbor International Airport on possible identification of the downed aircraft. He briefed Lieutenant King. Then came another key piece of evidence: Sky Harbor International personnel confirmed the aircraft had not originated from the large metropolitan airport, which confirmed Dodge's assessment of the aircraft size based on the sheared landing gear he'd found.

"That helped us determine it wasn't a large commercial airline," said Abernathy.

Around 8 p.m., Eva Morgan's husband Greg had seen Karen Perry's number on the caller I.D. and told his wife, "Logan called."

Logan Perry, 8, called Eva almost daily with his wild schemes, tales, and hilarious anecdotes. But almost immediately, Eva knew something wasn't right; Logan wouldn't call her this late. Eva dialed Karen's cell phone number, which went to voicemail. Then something told her to call Shawn Perry, her close friend with whom she hadn't talked for more than a month. Same result: voicemail.

Eva thought back to a few days earlier, on Sunday morning, when Morgan and Logan's little brother Luke, 6, had called saying, "Church, Eva. Church, Eva. Church!" She took Logan and Luke to services that morning at Gold Canyon Community Church. She smiled at the recollection of how protective Logan had been of his brother that day, whether holding his hand or wrapping an arm around his shoulder.

Unable to reach anyone, Eva went to the couch and prayed for the families of the victims on the mountain. Then the phone rang, and it was a close friend of Eva's.

"Are you sad about the plane crash, too?" the friend said.

Silence. *What did she mean?*

Then the friend said, "So you haven't talked to her?"

Eva knew instantly and screamed. She dropped the phone and ran out to her Jeep. Before her husband could stop her she was racing to Karen Perry's house.

AT 8:05 p.m., Deputy Brian McGinnis met with Incident Command Deputy Jeff Love. It was during the briefing that McGinnis learned of the three hikers and began to coordinate efforts to find them. At 8:22 p.m., McGinnis made contact with the three hikers via cell phone. One of the hikers said they were coming down Siphon Draw trail but needed assistance. McGinnis mobilized a three-person PCSO search-and-rescue posse to start up Siphon Draw trail to make contact with the three hikers and bring them off the mountain.

Just before 8:30 p.m., PCSO Detective Leonard pulled up to the command post and found Sergeant Messing, who briefed the detective. They could clearly see the fire burning on the mountain west of Flat Iron as they talked. Messing explained that a search-and-rescue team was hiking up to the Waterfall to get the hikers off the mountain. After the briefing, Leonard called Detective Sergeant Philip LeBlanc and briefed him on the situation and current assessment.

At 8:30 p.m., Sergeant Messing got a phone call from James Langston with official notification of the passenger list: three adults and three children. The airplane was confirmed as 690SM, registered to Ponderosa Aviation out of Safford, which had departed Falcon Field Airport (FFZ) in Mesa at approximately 6:25 p.m. The plane was occupied by three adults and three children, as confirmed by Falcon Field ground personnel. The grim facts were surfacing: no survivors, all six passengers dead including three children.

KAREN Perry's earlier text message—*Did you make it there all right?*—remained unanswered. Then came a phone call from her nanny Jaleesa Shelton, the woman who had earlier dropped the three children off at Falcon Field Airport. Shelton told Karen that a friend of hers was watching the local television news and saw a story about a plane crash, The reporter had mentioned Ponderosa Aviation, which got Karen's attention but didn't immediately instill panic: Ponderosa Aviation had multiple planes, and early news reports were not 100 percent reliable.

Karen called her friend Eva Morgan, who didn't answer, and then called Mikel Hardy, the brother of the pilot and Ponderosa Aviation Co-owner Russel Hardy. Mikel's only response to Karen sent a chill through her body.

"The sheriff hasn't gotten there yet?" he said.

"No," Karen said.

"Well, he will."

Karen's world started to spin uncontrollably. Still alone and battling the nasty illness that had kept her from taking the kids to the airport herself, she desperately needed answers now. Had she taken the kids, she would have seen the flash explosion herself on the way home.

For now, based on Mikel's response, she only knew the plane carrying her children had gone down, but she didn't know any other details. As a career aviator, she repeated a lifetime of pilot mantras: *A downed plane could be an emergency landing because of a catastrophic mechanical failure. Don't assume anything until you know the facts. Sometimes small planes crash and all aboard walk away uninjured.* When Eva Morgan arrived, the two friends embraced in a blur of tears.

AT 8:39 p.m., helicopter pilot Banning returned to the flaming crash site and inserted a team of two search-and-rescue volunteers, who would spend the night there to secure the area from hikers entering from the east. As Banning lifted off, volunteers Pat O'Connell, a retired firefighter, and Rick Carpenter were left alone near the scene of devastation. Their assignment was to protect and preserve the scene and evidence. The intensity of the flames and smoke had lessened considerably since Russ Dodge first walked the area, but there were still smaller spot fires burning everywhere. The two volunteers set down their packs and moved carefully around the edges of the debris field to make an assessment.

Given that they knew there were six passengers aboard the airplane, and the various human remains Dodge had already reported, the chances that anyone was still alive were essentially zero. But the greatest fear at such an event was that by some miracle someone had been ejected into the black night and was lying unconscious down a dark slope or beneath twisted wreckage. Perhaps in the first sweep of the area by Dodge, when the inferno raged at its peak, just such a survivor had remained hidden from view or out of earshot. With the fire and smoke now much less intense, the two volunteers could make a closer inspection of the scene.

"Our fear at that time was to have someone still alive in the area," said Sergeant Messing. But, sadly, that fear was quickly proved unfounded.

"I've been to a lot of industrial accidents and car crashes in twenty-four years on the fire department," said O'Connell. "This was unlike anything I'd seen before. It was almost surreal, like it shouldn't be there.... You didn't see a lot of plane parts. The plane had pretty much disintegrated."

O'Connell and Carpenter soon made several macabre discoveries of various human remains, and used the radio to communicate their findings back to the command post. O'Connell found a fragmented human remain, which was a small torso with an intact arm and hand. Looking closely, he said he believed it was that of a child, due to the small hand size. Said O'Connell, "We knew this had been over right away and there were no survivors."

After the initial assessment, and without seeing any hopeful signs of life, they carefully retraced their steps, gathered their packs, and moved downhill about fifty yards away to set up a camp, which was just bedrolls and sleeping bags. Any remaining fire and burn-off would travel uphill, so they were safe here. Camping at the top of a mountain, however, meant full exposure to the elements. It would be a cold and windy night with little sleep.

After inserting the two-man team, Banning returned to the command post and advised that they were not going to be able to insert any more teams due to the fire and the amount of unburned fuel still on the ground. Banning and Dodge flew west to return to the fire station.

"We soon knew who was on that plane and what type of plane it was," said Sheriff Babeu, which meant he knew what needed to be done next: go notify the mother. Because of the gravity of the situation, Babeu wanted to personally deliver the news.

Around 9 p.m., Sheriff Babeu, Detective Leonard, Lieutenant Scott Elliott, and Chaplain Gary Croll made the short drive to Karen Perry's house in nearby Gold Canyon. Before knocking, the assembled group could see that Karen's friends had already taped paper over the two sidelights, on each side of the front door, to keep the media from peering inside.

"She was expecting us," Babeu said, in reference to the brief and cryptic conversation Karen had had with Mikel Hardy. Babeu had actually once met Logan Perry, Karen's middle child, at a public safety community event held at a local grocery store. The sheriff and young boy had shaken hands and laughed as Logan said something funny as he always did. That was the moment when the idea of becoming a sheriff was solidified inside Logan. To be here now, for Babeu, was almost incomprehensible.

The group of four walked solemnly into her living room, where another small group of friends and supporters had gathered. Babeu tried to be as compassionate as possible in sharing what they knew, but he also wanted to be clear and direct to dispel any false hopes. They had just spoken with individuals who were up at the crash site, he said. There had been a massive explosion and, considering the manner of impact, there were almost certainly no survivors. He expressed his condolences. Karen will forever remember the gentle and kind way he spoke to her.

They were looking for survivors.

Karen sat in stunned silence, latched onto that possibility, and didn't hear much else of what he said. *But we believe that almost certainly there are no survivors.*

"She was in disbelief," Babeu said. "She was amazing to be able to even process the information and ask questions, but clearly she was in disbelief. Anything that was difficult for us that night paled in comparison to the inconsolable pain of the information being shared about her three children, their father, and the other two aboard that airplane."

Phone calls started coming from Karen's wide network of airline friends around the country and world, but she was in an unworldly state, unable to speak or process what was happening. Her children were never coming home.

As her own state of shock entrenched itself, Karen was actually more concerned about her friend Eva Morgan's pain and hurt. Karen knew what a tremendous loss this all was for Eva, too. The constant and insane chaos that had always been Karen Perry's household—three kids and three dogs going in six different directions, each at full volume—was now this eerily quiet confine of painful loss and grieving.

BACK at the mountain, the PCSO search-and-rescue posse and the three hikers arrived at the incident command post. One of the hikers had an ankle injury, and they were all emotionally shaken by their proximity to the violent crash. Deputies called the Apache Junction Fire District to evaluate the injured hiker. Then the three hikers met with Detective Leonard to describe what they'd seen and heard.

Deputy McGinnis and Deputy Love, meanwhile, were making plans to secure the crash scene for the night. There were already two PCSO search-and-rescue posse volunteers, Team 1, at the crash site. Pat O'Connell and Rick Carpenter had been dropped off at 8:39 p.m. Love directed Team 2—comprising four PCSO search-and-rescue posse volunteers—to hike up to the Waterfall in Siphon Draw, where they would remain in position until the following morning to keep anyone from accessing the crash scene. The team set out just before 10 p.m.

With temperatures dipping into the thirties under the clear black sky, it would be a cold, uncomfortable, and windy night in the canyon for the unpaid volunteers. Love directed a third group, Team 3, to establish camp at the entrance of No Name canyon, which was one canyon to the south of Siphon Draw. That team, too, hunkered down in the cold darkness until Thanksgiving morning.

Atop the mountain, Rick Carpenter and Pat O'Connell sat, talked, and processed the violent scene. There was little they could do except discuss initial ideas on how to advise deputies to tackle rope-setting in the morning. Throughout the night they checked in periodically by radio as a safety precaution.

Farther down the mountain, the four-person Team 2, led by Tom Felix, was on its way up the long trail to Siphon Draw in complete blackness. They would hike up into the canyon to their destination at the Waterfall. With Team 1 scouring the crash site for any possible survivors, once Team 2 and Team 3 had hiked up to their assigned location assignments to secure the crash site, there would be nothing more anyone could do until first light on Thanksgiving Day. Deputy Love, too, would remain below at the incident command post throughout the night. In the relative still of the mobile command van, he was formulating a game plan for the morning, including all personnel assignments.

"No sleep is pretty standard sometimes," he said. "You can't let it bother you at that point. It's your job, and you have to go into business mode."

BEFORE her world had been obliterated, Karen had made plans for a friend to visit over the long Thanksgiving weekend. Around 10 p.m., she announced to the assembled friends and law enforcement officials that she had to leave to go pick up her friend at the airport. Her statement highlighted to everyone in the room her intense state of shock. Instead of Karen, a uniformed Pinal County Sheriff's deputy met her friend in the airport Jetway to bring him to her house.

By 11 p.m., the planning and preparation at incident command had officially transitioned from rescue to recovery. All efforts were focused on starting the full recovery and investigation the next morning. That meant completing many command forms to requisition resources and equipment for Thanksgiving Day. They needed a helicopter and pilot to ferry personnel back and forth to the crash site. They would have to make contact and coordinate all their efforts in the coming days with investigators from the National Transportation Safety Board and the Federal Aviation Administration. They also had to coordinate with the medical examiner's office for the six fatalities.

The plan for the morning was to helicopter in a rope-certified team to set safety lines. Like Sherpas sent up Mount Everest ahead of climbers, they would navigate the precariously sloped crash site and install fixed ropes so all subsequent personnel at the scene could be attached to the safety line with carabiners.

By 1 a.m., it was officially Thanksgiving Day 2011. After an intense buzz of activity for hours, the command post was now quiet, with only Deputy Love and Sergeant Messing still there. Any notion of a traditional holiday weekend had long been wiped away, which was nothing new for a sergeant with eighteen years of law enforcement service. The younger Deputy Love, too, knew the drill.

With the three separate teams camped on the mountain, there was nothing more to do. Carpenter and O'Connell were huddled in their sleeping bags on the steep slope of granite as the fires began to wane and smolder.

"It was rough," Messing said. "It was not fun."

Most of the short grasses had burned away, but the scrubby desert trees and various pieces of Styrofoam and wiring were still glowing, visible down at the command post. Throughout the night, as the moisture came up and transpired into the darkness, the fires faded altogether into a warm smolder. Messing said good-bye and climbed in his truck for the ninety-minute drive home. He would be back at the command post before 7 a.m.

At home, Karen was still whirling in a disconnected freefall. Other than parts of the upcoming memorial service for her children and some other brief flashes, she would have few memories or recollections of the remainder of 2011 and much of 2012.

Back at her own house, but deeply distraught, Eva Morgan could not sleep that night. She had lost her close friend and coworker Shawn Perry, a man she admired in many ways, and especially for the way he loved his children. She had also lost Morgan, Logan, and Luke, her three "adopted" children who had become a special part of her own family. Her three sons, too, would be crushed, as they had all eagerly taken on the role of protective big brother to each of Karen's kids.

It was an agonizing night.

In the cool dawn of Thanksgiving morning, Eva Morgan watched from her house near the mountain as the lights of a helicopter circled the crash scene near the peak.

TWENTY

Light of Thanksgiving Day

THE TEMPERATURE WAS IN THE THIRTIES on November 24, 2011, and dawn illuminated a handful of sympathy cards in envelopes on the doorstep of Karen Perry's house in Gold Canyon. From there, the top of Superstition Mountain became visible as it emerged from the disappearing darkness, a cold light penetrating the silent crash scene. To see everything now in eerie starkness would confirm the earliest reports: no one could have survived this crash.

The crash site was at 4,650 feet, oriented west to east, on the northwest-sloped area that tilted a steep forty-five degrees downhill and then dropped off into the canyon. The aircraft had been traveling at 230 miles an hour when it hit the mountain. After impact, the wreckage traveled up a sixty-degree slope for seventy-five feet, where the wings and aft portion of the engines now lay in crumpled disarray. Thirty-five feet up the slope was the vertical rock face, rising another 150 feet. Investigators would later find wreckage up and over the 150-foot vertical rise, as far as four hundred feet away, which had been catapulted such a distance by the second fireball after impact. Those vertical rock formations, called hoodoos, were soot-blackened and charred all the way to the top. Where the violent explosion and burning jet fuel had unfurled some twelve hours earlier, the powdered formation now sat silent.

The sloped area was primarily rock, interlaced with cracks, patches of soil, boulders, scrub trees, low cactus, and other vegetation. Scattered up the steep slope was a debris field of what used to be an airplane. The large swath of scattershot measured about 150 feet by about 80 feet. Up near the top, a significant amount of debris clustered near the base of the vertical face. The force of the impact had even lodged some debris into crevasses within the immovable face. Everything in the blast zone was fire-damaged, soot-covered, or scorched. The burned-out swath of debris was still smoldering in places.

In some aviation crashes, the airplane remains relatively intact. Here, however, the airplane was highly fragmented, similar to throwing a wine glass against a boulder. The largest wreckage section was a portion of an inboard wing box with one engine still attached. In other crashes, too, the pilots and victims could be more or less intact and even identifiable. What awaited investigators and others here, however, was an entirely different and macabre scene that would take days to sift through and years to process emotionally.

By 6 a.m., Sergeant Brian Messing from the Pinal County Sheriff's Office had returned to the command post and stepped into the early morning chill. Deputy Jeff Love assumed the role of incident commander. Others began to arrive and mingle to discuss and plan for the day. ID Technician Jennie Randall met with Detective Leonard and Sergeant Messing. Randall would be transported to the crash site via helicopter to assist with documenting and recovering human remains. Deputies Brian McGinnis and Scott Abernathy were also assigned to the crash scene to assist detectives in locating and marking human remains for later collection. Detective Brian Hillman would be assisting with evidence collection. Although the probability of finding any survivors was almost certainly zero, they would look and listen for any such miracle. A helicopter operated by a Maricopa

County Sheriff's Office pilot waited in the landing zone to ferry personnel back and forth to the mountaintop.

Still needing to guard the scene, various other teams took to the mountain to block trails and keep the curious away. Clarissa Chapman led a three-person team to the Jacobs Creek Cut trail. Kelly Schroder led a two-person team up to Siphon Draw Canyon to the Crying Dinosaur. Tom Felix led a three-person team to Siphon Draw Canyon to station at the mouth of the canyon. These teams would all remain overnight to keep any hikers from approaching the crash location.

Abernathy and McGinnis were on the first flight up as part of the rope team to set safety lines for the day's work. To see the debris field, a wide swath of devastation that led up to the cliff face blackened by the resultant fireball, was immediately sobering in the early morning light. The pilot landed on Flat Iron.

The search-and-rescue volunteers Carpenter and O'Connell had already surveyed the crash scene again, with morning light, and had been radioing what technical gear, ropes, and harnesses the deputies should bring. News helicopters were flying overhead, too.

"The people who came up in the morning should be commended for what they had to do," O'Connell said. "They experienced a lot of emotional strain. I've seen a lot in my time in the fire department, but nothing like this…. It was a terrible tragedy. There's no question."

After the quick debriefing, Abernathy and McGinnis hiked to the crash site. The area was still a hot smolder with small, intermittent brush fires crackling. The smell that hung in the air was a sickening mix of burnt fuel and human remains.

"It was a horrendous plane crash," said McGinnis, who had been a PCSO deputy for five years. Setting the safety lines was critical because areas of the debris field were slick from all the fuel on the rocks. Directly below the site, about forty yards down the steep gradient, was a sheer drop-off of three hundred feet.

Carefully tiptoeing around the scattered debris and steep terrain, it took the duo about an hour to set the safety lines. As Abernathy started to work, he saw a cross section of a human torso. McGinnis, too, was encountering the same level of carnage. They each had to mentally compartmentalize what they'd just seen and put it aside to do this job, which was to rig lines so the investigation and evidence collection could begin in earnest. Only days later, alone and away from the scene, would they and their peers have the luxury of time and space to open the emotional box and access the impact of seeing such horror.

With the safety lines set, other personnel stepped from the helicopter and made their way over to the crash site. Sergeant Messing, detectives Leonard and Hillman, and ID Technician Randall joined the deputies and two volunteers. Already, Sergeant Messing could see the volunteers were having difficulty with the extreme nature of this scene. Indeed, for Messing, after eighteen years of search and rescue, this was the worst scene he had ever encountered. What he had seen in the past had led him to expect to find relatively intact burned bodies. But instead, what they were each dealing with was a horrifying collection of human mush and fragmentation. When he went to move a charred seat he realized it was actually a lower leg. Overhead, Daniel Lopez and Lieutenant Scott Elliott conducted aerial photography of the crash site until just before 10 a.m.

On the ground, they worked in teams with a finder and photographer. They systematically photographed each find of human remains and noted a GPS reading to mark the exact location. Detective Hillman was in charge of the recovery and documentation efforts. Detective Leonard was the overall case agent, tasked with family communication and follow-up interviews as necessary.

And then, as carefully as possible, investigators placed each find in a body bag. Eventually they carried all the evidence back to Flat Iron and loaded it on the helicopter for transport back to the command post. From there Pinal County Medical Examiner's Office personnel were next in the chain of custody. Eventually they coordinated the custody transfer to the Pima County Forensic Science Center in Tucson, where personnel would be performing the autopsies and subsequent identification of the human remains. By 11 a.m. the FAA investigator was atop the mountain. Sheriff Babeu, too, went up to Flat Iron that Thanksgiving Day and stepped into what he saw as a macabre juxtaposition.

"It was very surreal," he said of the day. "I was shocked by the contrast of this unimaginable tragedy surrounded by natural beauty."

Sergeant Messing briefed Babeu on their progress, which was slow, difficult, and would take days to complete. They had made a key evidentiary discovery:

a perfectly level impact strike across the rock face below the highest peak. The horizontal strike etched in stone by the airplane wings indicated the pilot had never made any evasive maneuver. If he had seen the mountain, he would have turned in those last seconds.

One of the oddest and eeriest elements of the crash scene investigation was the absolute quiet. When cops gathered to do anything, even work a suicide, homicide, or grisly car crash scene, there was almost always conviviality and laughter. Dark humor interjected light into their sometimes difficult work and offset the trauma first responders encountered daily. *Just another dead body, just another normal day at work. Are you going to eat those fries?* Working inside this debris field, however, was altogether different, and was conducted under an uncommon solemnity. Abernathy found a child's shoe with the foot still inside, the leg severed cleanly above the ankle. The skin was colored gray in a way that imprinted immediately. Abernathy did not know he would never be able to erase that awful color from his mind. There were black charred arms and legs scattered as though a giant being had tossed a handful of curled matches. There was the gentle scrape of shovels and other fine tools to collect what they could of human remains from rock faces and crevices. Everywhere they tiptoed, in and around the debris field, they could not escape the silent roar of death. They worked steadily, and they breathed the stench of finality that arose near their boots and steadily pulsed skyward. They moved with an unspoken sense of reverence and respect for everything their gloved hands touched. They were the living, walking holy ground.

Without need of being so instructed, there was no laughter or joking. Instead, people barely spoke other than to communicate the work they were doing. The only consistent sounds were the coming and going chop of helicopter rotors, shutter clicks of cameras, and the scrabble of scraping rocks as personnel moved carefully around the wreckage. Other than that, they collectively worked until late that afternoon in almost total silence.

"We try to forget about it or deal with it in different ways," said Sergeant Messing. "You keep it bottled up and try not to deal with it…. I never want to do it again."

"You'll never get the images out of your head," said Abernathy, now an officer with the Phoenix Police Department.

Finally, after 4 p.m., with the winter light fading, the helicopter shuttled everyone back off the mountain. They gathered at the command post and debriefed. Everyone was to report early the next morning, by 7 a.m., for another day of the same. No one complained of the lost holiday or the almost unbearable repeat that awaited. They each knew what they had to do.

Meanwhile, throughout the day, local church volunteers had banded together, shopped, cooked, prepared, packaged, and delivered an impressive Thanksgiving dinner that awaited the law enforcement officers and volunteers. There were lukewarm bowls of mashed potatoes and stuffing, and thick slices of turkey. There was thick gravy waiting to be ladled, rolls to be buttered, and cranberry discs evenly sliced. It was all a generous and time-consuming gesture, but the day's horrible tenor had collectively tamped any desire to eat.

"I wasn't hungry at that point," said Love, who had worked his regular shift Wednesday, stayed up all night at the incident command post, and worked all day on Thanksgiving without a break. "I was just tired."

"Working that scene affected everyone in different ways," said Messing. "There's no one it didn't affect."

Said Abernathy, "That was the worst day of my law enforcement career."

ON Friday, November 25, 2011, low clouds descended onto the mountain and delayed any helicopter flights and personnel insertions until around 11 a.m. Then began a grim repeat of Thanksgiving Day: three teams inserted at the crash location to continue documenting and collecting human remains. The full complement of investigators was on scene, including Michael Huhn from the National Transportation Safety Board (NTSB) and two from the Federal Aviation Administration (FAA), Leon Kelley and Jill Schenewark.

Command staff from the Pinal County Sheriff's Office issued a new order: only certified personnel and federal investigators would be allowed near the scene. The gruesome reality of the work on Thanksgiving Day had proved too disturbing for the valiant volunteers. This was a job for professionals only, who were being paid and had no choice but to persevere through the worst sort of horror imaginable. Said Abernathy, "It screwed up a lot of people's minds." Instead, the volunteers continued to hike up the mountain to the forest boundary fence line and remain in place throughout the day as trail blockers to reroute hikers.

Up in the debris field, the sworn deputies and detectives continued to put body parts into body bags and airplane parts into separate, designated bags for transport. The NTSB and FAA investigators provided guidance about what they needed for their investigations. It was another solemn day of difficult work atop the mountain in the chilly altitude of November. The horrible and unmistakable smell lingered, too, and lessened only when the cool breeze stirred the air.

They found a console from the aircraft and made other, more disturbing, discoveries. High atop one of the spidery rock fingers, in an area accessible only by rock climbers, was a cranial skull cap resting on top of the cliff. Based on its size and location, it had to be from one of the two males sitting in the front seats of the airplane. From there, beyond the cliff and the next canyon, four hundred feet away, was an adult male torso. The minute-by-minute collective grind of such gruesome discoveries made for another nightmarish and emotionally devastating day. As the light started to fade in late afternoon, the helicopter plucked everyone off the mountaintop, group by group, and left the graveyard scene under darkness at 7 p.m. The breeze whistled through the clumps of wreckage as a narrow hawk landed on a spidery branch of the lone tree that had somehow withstood the blast and sat unscathed in the field of black desolation. The hawk's head pivoted right and left, while the cloying odor continued to emanate toward the eventual cold of outer space.

BY day three of the recovery and investigative efforts, Saturday, November 26, the deputies and detectives were, thankfully, mostly picking through airplane parts and wreckage. By 3:30 p.m. that afternoon they were back at the command post and cleared the area half an hour later. The Pinal County Sheriff's Office officially turned any further investigation of the crash site over to the FAA and NTSB investigators, the Medical Examiner's Office, and their own PCSO homicide division because every unusual death has to be investigated.

"This one is going to stand out in my mind," said Brian McGinnis. "Someone has to bring them home to their family."

"You really cherish what you have a lot more, as far as your kids, and how quick everything can be taken away," said Love, father of three.

"We were done, thankfully," said Sergeant Brian Messing. "On major scenes you try to desensitize yourself. It was one of those scenes where you just tried to do your job. We'll talk about it once in a while, but it's something you don't ever want to deal with again. Every one of us has kids."

TWENTY-ONE

Aftermath

KAREN PERRY WALKED DOWN THE AISLE of a Boeing 777, each hand aloft deftly skimming the hard plastic of closed luggage containers, the aircraft completely empty, no pilots, no passengers, not a single goat or horse or chicken this time, thank God! She noticed the dull roar of altitude was especially loud. Hmmm ... better check that out on our layover. Kona. Sydney. Hawai'i and Australia now joined by that beautiful walking bridge the kids loved to run along above the watery light. Enveloped by the effervescence of normality once again in the cold wonder of outer space. Oooh, I like that: the cold wonder of outer space. Wait, that's not right. Sir, we cannot push back, and now she sees them seated side by side in the last row: Morgan, Logan, and Luke. My sweet babies! Oh my God, how worried you made Mommy! My sweet babies are OK. Don't you ever do that again to Mommy, never ever ever! Karen? Karen? You need to eat something. Just try... *Silent, slack faces.*

These children are <u>never</u> silent LOL. The colors are just, wow. Buzzing purple tinge around Morgan's mouth. White neon for Logan's face. Logi Bear how do you even do that? Look at your brother Luke: He's electric blue, a brilliant unnatural flavor so vivid it's like that thick cream-cheese cake frosting you love; oh, Luke would love that color. They were able to estimate the size of the aircraft, which eliminated many other more dire scenarios, and they had determined, sadly, there were no survivors. *I'm just so happy it's not true. Ma'am, if you don't turn it off ... what is it, sweetheart, tell Mommy. Morgan opens her mouth to speak: a powerful beam of light fills Karen with a sense of awe and wonder and splendor, and then Logan begins spinning, hovering, spinning faster and faster like the Tasmanian Devil, laughing and laughing and then gathering up his little brother Luke and then Morgan, and they spin into a great ball of lighted energy so fierce Karen has to shield her eyes.* Karen? Are you OK, sweetheart? *Fish red shirt! FISH RED SHIRT!* We are just so sorry for your loss. If there's anything we can do, absolutely anything, just let us know. *Today is a beautiful day, Mommy. I should do more. I should be with them on holidays. i changed my mind i'd like to go to safford to be with them for thanksgiving i don't know what i was thinking!* Karen, dear, I'm so sorry they're gone your kids are gone *where are my car keys i need to go to safford it's thanksgiving i miss them terribly who's coming i'll drive we can get logan his snack on the way make sure to pack morgan's meds and that pair of pants she loves because i don't want to deal with a meltdown right now has anyone seen my keys how strange where are my keys.* A massive explosion and secondary blast ripped open the night and bled white-hot orange into the crystal sky. *Morgan, Mommy is tired: I don't want to play this game right now. Come out here now. Logan, Luke, you too!* Soot-blackened rock. No survivors. *November 23, 2011. Thank you, yes, I'm hanging in there. Thank you so much this looks delicious. I just wish they could all taste those colors right now. I'll need to get that recipe.*

KAREN Perry's state of shock was so deep, comprehensive, and severe that she had been transported to living alone in a fevered dream state. That topsy-turvy blackness would inkblot almost all memories of late 2011 and much of 2012. She did not know when she was awake or asleep, or how to discern the difference between the two states. It all blurred together: she was a carved-out shell floating through some strange reality that did not allow her to pinpoint any sort of anchoring reference. The weight of the pain pushing down on her was a suffocating force she could not evade. It felt like cement had been poured over her body and solidified.

Her cadre of friends from Delta Air Lines, her fellow flight attendants, rushed to be by her side and marshal her through this unimaginably dark void. Eva Morgan was a steady presence. Vickie Longi came from Los Angeles, as did four more flight attendants from Karen's base there: Debbie Bunch, her field service manager, and peers Mimi Rawlinson-Caijoy, Trinh Than, and Brenda Webber. Longi had gotten the call on Thanksgiving from a mutual friend and flight attendant.

"Have you watched the news?" the friend asked. "Are you sitting down? Karen's kids were in an accident."

"I didn't know what to do," Longi said. "I was numb." It was a reaction common to everyone, and happening throughout Delta Air Lines, the wider aviation community, and everywhere the news surfaced: numbness, shock, and devastation, followed by an overwhelming urge to somehow help.

Bunch, who started with Delta Air Lines July 4, 1989, and supervised 250 people at the Los Angeles base, including Karen, immediately called Karen to ask how she could help. Bunch's supervisor said the company would pay for hotel rooms in Phoenix for the five flight attendants going to support Karen.

"Our Delta Air Lines leadership was phenomenal," said Bunch. "They gave me carte blanche for anything and everything Karen needed. I couldn't have been more proud of the company we worked for."

Once in Arizona, the women could see Karen was conscious and moving through her house, but her mind wasn't fully registering time, space, and events. On Facebook, there was an enormous outpouring of support from flight attendants, pilots, and friends around the world. But Karen was trapped in some blurry netherworld inaccessible to anyone else. She definitely needed friends around her, which is why Bunch ended up staying two weeks in Phoenix.

Just days after her three children perished, a brilliant rainbow appeared on the mountain, visible from Karen's house. It was unlike any she had ever seen, with the arch going straight through the crash site. In her grief, Karen took solace in the beauty. And then, almost immediately, she and her friends started noticing other odd markers without rational explanations.

Her kids had always loved playing Angry Birds. Now, repeatedly, the Angry Birds application would open on her phone without warning, including versions of the game she had never downloaded. She started noticing lights flickering from time to time, especially when she was talking about Morgan, Logan, and Luke.

Logan used to call Karen's friend Eva Morgan almost daily. Just days after his death Eva Morgan started receiving repeated calls from a Tucson number, but there was only silence on the line. When she called the number it turned out to be a hospital in Tucson. The person who answered the phone said that outbound calls from that particular number were not possible. The remains of Logan, his two siblings, their father, and the other two men who died in the plane crash were at the Medical Examiner's Office in Tucson.

Karen also later learned that on Wednesday, November 23, 2011, the day of the crash, Logan walked up to the school secretary and said, "I just wanted to say good-bye. Today is my last day, and I'm not coming back."

Karen's own ongoing mantra, when things were most difficult with three young children, later proved troubling: don't wish it all away. It will be over before you know it.

Many might chalk up the various mysterious events to coincidence, but for Karen there were too many. Her friend Eva Morgan, too, was experiencing much of the same.

While helping plan the memorial service, Eva was having trouble finding the right passage from scripture. Feeling stuck, she offered to run one of the many errands that were arising while being posted at Karen's house. But when she got in her Jeep, it wouldn't start. She let out a sigh and looked at her Bible sitting on the passenger seat. She picked it up, opened to a random passage, and read Psalm 43.3:

> *Send forth your light, your truth. Let them guide me. Let them*
> *bring me to your holy mountains to the place where you dwell.*

Bunch helped complete paperwork for a Delta Care Fund, which provided grants to employees in need. Karen received the full allotment of $4,700 to help with expenses. Meanwhile Delta employees around the world started donating their vacation time, which eventually accrued more than one year of paid time off for Karen. Inside the house, her flight attendant friends were helping plan the memorial service for the children, fielding endless phone calls, sorting mail, planning and picking up meals, and keeping the household running. Leanne Peters, a friend Karen knew through church, was at Karen's house day and night, too, to help. Collectively, they all attended Shawn Perry's memorial service with Karen.

At some point during the flurry of activity, Longi had an inspiration and announced it: "We need to get a jet for people to attend the memorial service for Karen's kids." That is, order up a full-size Delta jet and take it out of active service for a couple days to ferry Karen Perry's coworkers from Los Angeles to Phoenix. The idea, while heartfelt and noble, was immediately met with a chorus of rejections by flight attendants who knew the way airlines operated. The sheer cost, logistics, and bureaucratic labyrinth would kill any possibility of the idea becoming reality. Even more important was the historic precedent: nothing of the sort had ever been done at the airline in its ninety-year history. Even Karen, in her detached sort of state, simply offered, "Vickie, that will never happen."

Said Bunch, "My first reaction was there was no way this was going to happen."

Despite the unanimous vote against, Longi quietly went to work and started making phone calls. As the impossible request worked its way up the chain of command, Bobbie VanSchoonhoven, base director of LAX in-flight service at the time, eventually took the baton and ran with it. Such an expensive logistical feat required multiple levels of consent by Delta Air Lines' senior leadership. Unbelievable as it was to everyone involved, the wild brainstorm continued to clear hurdles and finally made it all the way up the chain to the desk of the final arbiter, Richard Anderson, who had been chief executive officer at the almost thirty-six-billion-dollar company since September 2007. Soon thereafter VanSchoonhoven called Bunch and asked, "Are you alone?"

Bunch stepped away from the fray for privacy. "What's happening?"

"I think they're going to charter a plane," VanSchoonhoven said.

Although it had never been done in history, Karen's tragedy had touched a nerve—losing her entire family the night before Thanksgiving—and made the impossible possible.

"The LA base is a very close group of 1,100 flight attendants," said Bunch. "We are very caring and supportive of one another."

For the first time ever, executives at Delta Air Lines ordered a special charter flight for Los Angeles–based employees to fly to Phoenix with one purpose: support fellow employee Karen Perry by attending the memorial service for her three children. A full flight crew donated their time to work the special charter, including pilot, copilot, and flight attendants. Other flight attendants from throughout Delta came to cover their peers' trips so they could attend the memorial near Phoenix. It was an enormous outpouring of love and support for one of their own, and Karen was overwhelmed.

She said to her supervisor, "How am I going to ever pay people back?"

Bunch smiled and said, "You don't need to pay anyone back, Karen."

When the Boeing 757 landed December 3, 2011, at Sky Harbor International Airport, 150 of Karen's coworkers walked across the tarmac onto awaiting buses for the forty-five-minute drive to Gold Canyon.

"That was a historical event in the airline industry," Karen said. "It had never happened and probably never will happen again."

Karen herself was shuttled to the memorial service in a black limousine trailing a Pinal County Sheriff's Office escort of vehicles with lights flashing. When they arrived at Gold Canyon Methodist Church, Karen was stunned to see her friends, known and unknown—150 flight attendants lined up in full uniform, two lines positioned on each side of the long stairway.

"We have such good people at our LA base," she said. "The support was overwhelming."

The blips and flashes from the memorial service, which dot Karen's memory, include the towering Christmas tree for people to drop off donated toys. There was a sea of faces and people speaking and then … the black void returns.

Her employer, Delta Air Lines, took Karen off the schedule for a full year at full pay, which was only made possible by her peers rallying and donating all that vacation time to the cause. Although she would be able to process it only later, Karen's loss was producing profound ripple effects.

"People were realigning their priorities," she said. "Things like this wake people up. Life truly is short. We don't know how long we have our loved ones."

"It changed me completely," said Longi. "Now I live one day at a time and do the best I can, because you don't know what tomorrow will bring."

IN the week after the crash, the two assigned detectives from the Pinal County Sheriff's Office did their due diligence. Although nothing suggested immediately that the six deaths were anything other than a horrible and tragic airplane crash, every unusual death had to be investigated. Their mission was to conduct the investigation quickly and quietly to officially dispel any potential misinformation about the possible cause of the incident. With that, detectives Hillman and Leonard interviewed people who were working at the departure airport on November 23, 2011. They also talked to officials from Ponderosa Aviation, which owned the aircraft that crashed and which had lost two owners of the company and a third employee. However, during what was supposed to be a cursory and routine investigation, some new facts came to light and, all of a sudden, detectives were considering an unimaginable possibility.

Rather than a tragic accident caused by pilot error, was something much more ominous afoot the night of November 23, 2011? More specifically, had the plane crash been a deliberate act?

TWENTY-TWO

Death Investigation

DESPITE WHAT POPULAR FILMS AND NOVELS PORTRAY, conducting any investigation is quiet, slow, tedious, and largely administrative work. It is less gunfights and car chases and more riding a desk. Rather than trolling alleys and arranging clandestine meet-ups with shady informants in neon-infused topless bars, the workday of a detective is spent on the telephone, leaving voice messages, requesting and checking documentation of every kind, and endlessly following up to steadily piece together a clear picture and chronology of what has happened. Additionally, detectives have to create an accurate portrait of both the victims and anyone involved who may rise to the level of suspect. By Friday, November 25, 2011, less than forty-eight hours after the crash, the investigation into any related malfeasance was already well under way by two Pinal County Sheriff's Office homicide detectives.

Detective Brian Hillman would remain on and near the crash site to lead recovery and documentation efforts. Meanwhile, case agent Detective E. Scott Leonard had begun casting the wider net of the methodical investigative process. That morning he called Troy Perry, the brother of the deceased Shawn Perry, who lived in Virginia. Detective Leonard had to, as delicately as possible, provide the grim facts: there were no survivors. And, he said, all the victims' bodies were fragmented, which would require the expertise of forensic anthropology professionals to accurately identify remains. Delivering this sort of unpleasant news was part of the job. The detective asked Perry if he had any reason to believe that this plane crash was anything other than an accident, to which the brother of the deceased emphatically replied, "No."

Later that day, the detective, together with Sheriff Babeu and Detective Sergeant Philip LeBlanc, met with Karen Perry, who was lost in her netherworld. As the trio sat with her at her home, they relayed what their peers were confirming atop the mountain: no survivors, and fragmented remains only. There would be no traditional burial for Morgan, Logan, Luke, or the other three, because their bodies were so badly disintegrated. Even more grimly, they had to ask Karen how she wanted them to advise staff at Pima County Forensic Center to manage small pieces of recovered bone and flesh. She asked that the staff only identify large remains of her children, Morgan, Logan, and Luke, and humanely dispose of the smaller, unidentified trace pieces.

Detective Leonard was able to speak with Eva Morgan, who told him that she had known Karen, Shawn, and the children for the last five years. Eva said that over those years she and Karen, and their respective children, had all become very close. Delicately, Detective Leonard asked her about Shawn Perry and his relationship with his children. Unequivocally, Eva Morgan said that Shawn loved the children intensely, and they loved him. Eva said that if Karen had been on the plane instead of Shawn, Shawn would not have been able to move forward emotionally. The detective had to ask the next question, which was never easy: *Did she have any reason to believe that this plane crash was anything other than an accident?*

"No, oh my God, never, no," Eva Morgan said just as emphatically as Troy

Perry. For Detective Leonard, early in the investigation, nothing ominous had emerged.

The next day, November 26, 2011, Babeu, LeBlanc, and Leonard met with the family of Joseph Hardwick, 22, the avionics technician and mechanic who had been sitting in the right-front seat of the airplane. The group, including Russell and Jeanie Hardwick, Joseph's parents, and his brother John Hardwick, met at the Hardwicks' house in St. David, a tiny town of less than two thousand people in the southeastern corner of Arizona. Detective Leonard had to repeat the sad and grim news.

Leonard asked John Hardwick who in the family was the most familiar with Ponderosa Aviation. John said he was acquainted with Shawn Perry and Russel Hardy, the pilot that night, and had been to Ponderosa Aviation before. Detective Leonard asked again: *Did John or anyone in the family have any concern that the plane crash was anything other than an accident?*

"No," John said. "They were all friends."

By Sunday, November 27, 2011, Pinal County Sheriff's Office personnel had cleared the crash site, leaving only investigators from the FAA and NTSB. Detective Leonard continued the investigation that day with another scheduled meeting with the Hardy family. Once again, Babeu and LeBlanc accompanied Leonard to share difficult news and ask the troubling question: *Could this crash have been a planned and deliberate event?*

The law enforcement trio drove to Thatcher, another small town of a few thousand centered in the Upper Gila River Valley in eastern Arizona, in Graham County. In attendance were Gary and Ida Hardy, parents of the deceased pilot Russel, and his now widow, Joanna Hardy. When Detective Leonard posed the question about intent, Mikel Hardy, brother of Russel, replied, "No, no way—they were friends."

As the new week unfolded on Monday, November 28, 2011, Detective Leonard had two leads regarding witnesses to the plane crash five days prior. Unfortunately, when he later followed up, the witness accounts only corroborated known facts rather than turning up anything new or particularly useful.

Leonard called the Pinal County Medical Examiner's Office and spoke to

Beth Calhoun to let her know he was on the way to their office in Florence to inspect the additional human remains recovered on November 25 and November 26 by Detective Hillman.

At the facility, Leonard watched as the remains were removed from cold storage. The remains were in individually marked paper bags, which were all placed inside a child-size body bag. He visually inspected each bag and observed that the remains were consistent with what he had recovered on Thanksgiving Day. In one of the bags he noted a set of keys. In another, a skull fragment with a metal staple attached. The staple was important because it was from one of Morgan's surgeries and confirmed her identity. Likewise, identifying the various fragmented pieces ruled out conclusively that there was anyone aboard the airplane other than the six known passengers. Upon completion, Leonard asked that the remains be resealed and placed back in cold storage to await delivery to the Pima County Forensic Science Center, where staff would conduct the forensic identification.

On Tuesday, November 29, 2011, just after 9 a.m., Leonard received an email from Detective Sergeant LeBlanc with attachments from Michael Huhn, NTSB safety investigator, including a record of a conversation dated November 24, 2011, and a written statement from line service person Joe Coffey with the same date. Coffey worked for Falcon Executive Aviation at Falcon Field Airport (FFZ) and had overseen the arrival and departure of the flight that night. Through his job, Coffey had become familiar with Morgan, Logan, Luke, and their father Shawn Perry. Leonard reviewed the conversation and subsequent written statement, neither of which indicated any mechanical trouble or suspicious actions on the part of any plane occupant. Coffey said he saw Shawn Perry get into the back of the aircraft with his children.

Leonard left three voicemail messages with Coffey, Michael Huhn (FAA safety inspector), and Leon Kelley. When he spoke to Kelley, the FAA investigator told the detective that the aircraft had ascended to 4,500 feet and taken a flight path toward Safford with no height deviation as far as they could tell. Kelley said the aircraft was restricted from "bravo airspace," which began at 5,000 feet. Kelley told the detective that to get answers about pilot licensing and medical clearance he should talk to Jill Schenewark with the FAA. The uneventful investigation was about to take a surprising turn.

At approximately 2:15 that afternoon, Leonard got a phone call from Detective Sergeant LeBlanc, who asked that Leonard meet them at Karen Perry's residence because new information had come to light. Just as Leonard ended the phone call, Elias Johnson, the PCSO public information officer (PIO), walked up to Leonard's desk.

"Did you hear?" Johnson asked.

"Hear what? I just hung up with LeBlanc," Leonard said. "What's going on?"

Johnson said the media was asking questions about three incidents in 2010 involving the Pinal County Sheriff's Office and Karen and Shawn Perry. Johnson had printed three PCSO reports from 2010, for separate incidents occurring September 21, October 2, and November 1. This was during the time that Karen and Shawn had split and were enduring a bitter divorce. The media had dug this up and was now, in the race for ratings, asking whether the plane crash might have been an intentional plot. Leonard needed to read all three reports before going to talk to Karen Perry again.

In the absence of any context or explanation by Shawn or Karen Perry, the report narratives in isolation made serious allegations: child abuse, violation of court orders, and welfare checkups. Without knowing Shawn or Karen, investigating detectives had to consider the possibility that the plane crash may have been caused intentionally, as the final act in a bitter divorce and feud.

After 3 p.m. that same afternoon, Detective Leonard arrived at Karen Perry's residence in Gold Canyon. Already there from the Pinal County Sheriff's Office were Sheriff Babeu, Director of Administration Tim Gaffney, and PIO Johnson. They were seated in the backyard with Karen and a friend. Detective Sergeant Phil LeBlanc arrived a few minutes later.

When Leonard arrived, the group was already discussing whether Karen Perry was inclined to make a statement to the media. In the vacuum of information, with a lack of any official statement thus far, the media was digging through public records and finding Karen and Shawn's past involvements with the Pinal County Sheriff's Office. From there, they were reaching their own conclusions based on reports generated more than a year before. It hadn't even been one week since Karen had lost all three of her children, and now she was trying to process how any of what the media were uncovering was relevant.

Sergeant LeBlanc began asking Karen questions about her ex-husband, who had been a licensed pilot but had voluntarily given up the medical certification for that license. Karen said that without the certification Shawn could not pilot an aircraft by himself, but could do so with another licensed pilot on board who had a medical certification. Yes, she said, the divorce had been difficult and bitter, and they had each had to process and deal with the emotions as best they could. The detectives carefully delved into the relationship and breakup between Karen and Shawn before bringing up the three specific incident reports from 2010.

The first, the child abuse allegation against Karen in September 2010, turned out to be a misunderstanding that was dismissed without charges. The whole mess began early the morning of September 21 with Karen, as usual, frantically trying to get all three children loaded into the car and off to school. Chaos ensued when their two dogs joined the melee, jumped inside the car, spilled hot coffee, and scratched up Morgan's legs. After the pandemonium, Karen got the dogs back in the house and put ice packs on Morgan's legs, which were visibly burned from the coffee and scratched from the dogs' toenails. Karen told the teacher at drop-off what had happened, but the teacher suspected foul play and contacted the sheriff's office. As a devoted father, Shawn Perry was concerned when he learned of the allegation, which eventually led to the next documented incident in October 2010.

With the back and forth of a bitter divorce in full swing, Karen had filed an order of protection against Shawn Perry. Shawn contacted Karen about the incident, but even making a phone call was officially a violation of the court's directive. Karen later realized that the intent of filing the order of protection— to provide some safe time and space for the kids between the two estranged adults—made the larger goal of co-parenting impossible.

The last documented incident, on November 1, was the misunderstanding when Karen had come off the all-nighter, completely exhausted. When she had fallen asleep in a near-coma state and Shawn had been unable to reach her, he called the sheriff's office to go check on her and the kids. Upon closer inspection, these were nothing but incidents of two good people who loved their children dearly and were trying to do best by them at every turn. That their personal struggles had become public knowledge was unfortunate, but nothing more. However, in the feeding frenzy the media trampled grace, dignity, respect, and privacy—for both the grieving mother and deceased father—and went straight for the sensationalized sound bite: *Plane crash may have been intentional!*

With that, Sergeant LeBlanc had to ask the question, to which Karen said, *No, no, no.* Detective Leonard, uncomfortable with the line of questioning, interrupted and wanted to clarify things for the record: *Had Shawn ever threatened to harm the children?* Of course he had not. *Did she have any reason to believe he wanted to hurt the children?* Absolutely not. *Ultimately, didn't Shawn want custody of the children?* Of course, yes, Morgan, Logan, and Luke were Shawn's entire world.

Shortly thereafter the meeting disbanded, and everyone left the residence. As Detective Leonard drove, he mentally worked through the totality of the case and what they had learned. Specifically, they had been able to establish that Shawn Perry did not assume either pilot seat; rather, Coffey saw him as the last to board the airplane by entering the back seating area with his children. Coffey's account to the FAA and NTSB safety investigators squared with Falcon Field security video footage. Additionally, Leon Kelley of the FAA had said the plane ascended to 4,500 feet and flew straight with no notable deviation in altitude or direction. Any sort of dark plot hatched during the short flight, and any ensuing struggle, would have certainly caused a more erratic flight path. But Leonard himself had seen the evidence atop the mountain in the cool morning chill on Thanksgiving Day, the perfectly level wing strike across the rock face. That airplane had flown straight into the mountain on a dead-straight run, as though the pilot did not know it was there.

Leonard was likewise not swayed by any of the three 2010 incident reports, which were more than a year old and had all originated within months of the particularly difficult time for Karen and Shawn. How many divorcing couples went through similar gyrations and emotional ups and downs without ever involving law enforcement? Further, the only verifiable evidence was that by all accounts Shawn Perry was nothing but a loving father who wanted to be with his children as much as possible: he had sought sole custody. Through what the detective had learned, these were two dedicated parents with two special needs children going through a crummy divorce. Leonard continued his investigation, but he was not going to dignify the firestorm the media were trying to create.

ON November 30, 2011, just after noon, Leonard and detectives Todd Nelson and Brian Hillman arrived at Falcon Field Airport (FFZ) to speak with line service person Joe Coffey, who worked for AV Fuel. He was the last person to interact with the three adults and three children before takeoff on November 23, 2011. He'd already been interviewed by the NTSB investigator on Thanksgiving, and the detectives had already reviewed those transcripts. They did glean some new information, however, which was that every two weeks the children took a flight from Mesa to Safford with their father Shawn Perry. Coffey confirmed that he had observed three adults arrive inbound to FFZ and the same three adults, plus three children, depart outbound from FFZ. Coffey was able to point out Shawn and each child by name during the security video playback. Leonard asked whether Coffey had ever seen any problems between Shawn and the children, and he replied that Morgan sometimes did not want to get on the plane, but he'd never witnessed her father force her or become angry.

Leonard watched the video footage with rapt attention, a grim silent film now of life's final hour. At approximately 5:31 p.m., Morgan, Logan, Luke, and their nanny Jalessa arrived at the pedestrian gate of Falcon Field Airport (FFZ). At 5:36 p.m., the foursome entered the AV Fuel office. Four minutes later, the children left with Coffey, who escorted them to a preboarding area.

At 5:46 p.m., the airplane arrived and stopped on the jet ramp. The engines shut down and the propellers stopped spinning. For Leonard, Coffey pointed out Shawn Perry and Joe Hardwick exiting the aircraft. Shawn Perry spun the aircraft propellers with Joe Hardwick in attendance. Coffey explained to Leonard that, on this particular aircraft, each propeller must be spun by hand approximately fifteen times.

In the video, Leonard watched an occupant in the right-front pilot seat moving around with a flashlight: that was Russel Hardy, who remained on the aircraft during the short stop. At approximately 5:50 p.m., Shawn Perry walked away from the aircraft toward the children. Shawn held his daughter's hand as they walked back to the aircraft. One minute later, Shawn Perry removed the wheel chocks. Joe Hardwick boarded and took the right-front pilot seat. The children climbed in after Hardwick. Shawn Perry was the last to board.

While there at AV Fuel, Detective Leonard interviewed Paul Lessaongang, owner of AV Fuel and Falcon Executive Aviation. He had known Karen and Shawn for some twenty years each, since well before they married. He had high regard for Karen and Shawn alike as very good pilots. He said that Russel Hardy was an excellent pilot, too, and had made this trip before. When Leonard posed the dark question, Lessaongang said, "Never. Never in a million years. I would let my own kids fly with them."

A week after the crash, a letter from the White House arrived in Karen's mailbox, but in her state she could not fully process such a communiqué from the leader of the free world and his wife:

> We are saddened to learn of your loss. And we extend our
> deepest sympathies to you. May you find solace in your cherished
> memories and comfort in the presence of family and friends. Our
> thoughts and prayers are with you at this difficult time.
>
> Sincerely, Barack and Michelle Obama

As a gesture of support a local company, Holiday Magic, had created three lamp sculptures with wooden wreaths and the three children's names inscribed on placards. The company placed them, each standing five feet tall, near Karen's front door and also strung holiday lights on her house. When she awoke and was marshaled outside by a friend to see the generous gift, it brought a smile to her face. She was so touched by the act of kindness and, yet, it was a disconnected smile. Karen had an abiding sense that something was wrong about all this—

except she could not access the source of her concern. Everything, in fact, felt just beyond her reach. She needed some time to think about it and wondered how she might grasp something tangible that might provide understanding. She went inside and closed the front door without looking at the lighted lanterns again. She had just one second ago been thinking about something important but now it had completely escaped her, and she was immensely frustrated.

"I need to go write that down," she said to someone standing near her. Karen managed another smile and did not let on that whatever she had just said had once again escaped her. *Write what down?*

Every thought was sand pouring through her fingers, and the harder she tried to cup her fingers or grasp something, the faster the sand flowed. Then she wanted to cry, but no tears came, and she just felt exhausted again. People were talking to her again; people were always talking to her and presenting warm, rectangular casserole dishes covered with foil, and not once can she recall eating any of it! *Is that wrong? Where are all those rectangular dishes piling up, because there must be enough of them to fill the garage.* Has she been eating? *Have I been eating?* She could see mouths moving and concerned faces. She felt gentle touches at her elbow trying to move her this way or that. *Why does everyone always want me to sit down? Stop already with the sitting down. Who has time with three children to ever sit down?*

Now all she wanted to do was crawl back in bed and go to sleep forever. That blank slate, at least, momentarily stopped the confusion and questions and endless agitation. Or at least it had, but now there was no discernible line between sleep, whatever that was, and being awake, whatever that was. *Wait, am I awake now or this a dream? Because the sleeping is even worse, with all the weird dreams. Numb. Is there a way to just stay numb and stop thinking? Sure there's a way: go be with Morgan, Logan, and Luke. Sweet babies. That's the only way you get peace. But how? With all these people everywhere all the time asking me to sit down and handing me casserole dishes and looking so sad and forlorn. Who has time to eat seven hundred casseroles? Is there some way we could freeze those, because that will feed Morgan, Logan, and Luke until they head off to college. OK, that's never going to happen and you know it: Morgan will live with you for the rest of your life. She will never be fully independent. That's just a given, and that's OK.*

Luke, too, will probably never succeed in that sort of academic environment, but he will find his way, absolutely he will. He's so bright.

Now, Logi Bear will go to college—he has the intelligence and demeanor, and his personality, oh my God, he will be the most popular kid on campus! But as far as going to be with them NOW... really, Karen? You know there's no way you could do that. But if you could just somehow fall asleep and have it happen naturally, use some special prayer or force of will to be transported to them. Well, then that would be a beautiful thing. Everything would be OK again. A mother is supposed to be <u>with</u> her children always, always, always. Yes, please God just take me now because that is the one and only place I want to be.

AS November turned to December, Detective Leonard moved through myriad details. He spoke with Jill Schenewark from the FAA and emailed contact information for the three hikers on the mountain the night of the plane crash. Leonard had more witness accounts to follow up, but nothing useful turned up. Then he was away for training. When he returned by mid-December 2011, the death investigation was wrapping up. As the final part of his investigation, Detective Leonard sat down and wrote his findings:

> *Case Agent Opinion: Through the course of the investigation I found no evidence which would lead me to conclude that this was anything other than a tragic accident. Nothing in the adult victims' history indicated that they were anything other than good friends and co-workers. No malice or indifference to life was ever observed in prior behavior either in report form or by the people who knew them best. Law enforcement involvements between Shawn and Karen were results of their divorce and not specific to threats against the children.*

> *All recovered remains I have been notified of, have been transported to the Pima County Forensic Science Center (PCFSC) for identification, their status is pending at this time. The Pinal County Medical Examiner's Office (PCMEO) has been given*

medical and family contact information for the victims; they will
coordinate with the PCFSC. The cause of the plane accident will
be determined by the NTSB. Incident closure will follow when
the remains are identified and receipt of the forensic report(s).

The thorough investigation corroborated the original hypothesis, which meant there was no criminal wrongdoing or charges to be filed. Case closed. However, even before December 2011 ended, Sheriff Paul Babeu called Karen Perry about another possibility: a civil case. In that case, there might be a clear villain whose gross negligence might have contributed to the plane crash. And the sheriff knew someone who might be able to help in going after just such a defendant legally.

During the initial investigation, when Detective Leonard spoke to Leon Kelley of the FAA, Kelley had told the detective that the aircraft ascended to 4,500 feet on November 23, 2011, and took a flight path toward Safford with no notable height deviation as noted by radar. Kelley also said the aircraft was restricted from "bravo airspace," which began at 5,000 feet. Without a wider aviation context, nothing in that statement had any particular relevance for Leonard beyond the basic facts.

However, back in 2006, the FAA had lowered the controlled class B airspace ceiling near Superstition Mountain from the previous level of 8,000 feet to 5,000 feet, the "bravo airspace" mentioned by Kelley. The reason for the change, ostensibly, was to clear the busy inbound and outbound commercial flight paths surrounding the airport. Picture a glass ceiling in the sky at 8,000 feet. Prior to 2006, all small aircraft could freely fly up to 8,000 feet without restriction and without needing to request special permission. But after 2006, pilots in all but the largest commercial jets were squeezed down to 5,000 feet and below, meaning a small-aircraft pilot could not go any higher without requesting special clearance from air traffic controllers. There was a big problem, however, with this change in the airspace ceiling, because the inbound and outbound paths to the desert floor of Sky Harbor International Airport were surrounded by craggy mountain peaks that rose *above* the new ceiling.

Therefore, on the night of November 23, 2011, as Russel Hardy deftly piloted the Rockwell Commander 690 aircraft out of Falcon Field Airport (FFZ) in Mesa, Arizona, and turned east as instructed, he was legally required by FAA regulations to stay below 5,000 feet if he hadn't requested special clearance to ascend higher. Prior to 2006 he could have gone up to 8,000 feet without issue and without needing special clearance. There was, however, an ominous and lethal issue with this redesigned airspace: the top of Superstition Mountain, only minutes ahead of their aircraft as they sped unknowingly into the pitch-black darkness, rose 5,057 feet above sea level. How can a pilot stay below 5,000 feet, as required by the new airspace design, and clear rock fingers reaching above that line? There were only two answers: go around or request clearance to go over. Simply flying over on one's own accord would violate FAA regulations.

The lunacy of this dangerous situation had already landed the issue in court, with the Aircraft Owners and Pilots Association bringing suit against the FAA. The AOPA claimed in a lawsuit that the FAA neglected to follow its own rules for creating and modifying airspace and alleged the FAA had neither adequately addressed the airspace compression caused by the redesign—squeezing more small aircraft into a tighter space—nor provided proof that the modifications were even needed. The US Court of Appeals heard arguments from both sides but, in the end, sided with the FAA. To those in the AOPA, it only seemed a matter of time before the redesigned airspace invited disaster.

Barely a month after she had lost her three children, Karen Perry faced a disturbing new possibility: Was the crash entirely avoidable and directly caused by a bureaucratic blunder still unresolved after three years in court? Karen was reeling emotionally, but she was clear on one point: her children were gone, and she wanted answers about how and why the crash had happened.

Accountability was on its way to her in the form of a 66-year-old legal raconteur she had not yet met. This lithe and shrewd practitioner had spent four decades in the Phoenix metropolitan area as a sort of modern-day Robin Hood, a trial lawyer with a bent for taking on big industry on behalf of people with little, if any, recourse against such power. And there was no more all-powerful target than the US government itself, in the form of the Federal Aviation Administration.

Twenty-Three

A Civil Case

IN THE NATURAL WORLD GOVERNED BY TIME, space, and physics, Karen Perry had lost her three children in the mere flash of a few violent seconds. However, understanding exactly what had happened and why, and finding some accountability for her loss, would play out on the entirely different and agonizingly slow timeline of a civil action under US law.

That tedious process began for Karen at her home at 7499 East Cliff Rose Trail in Gold Canyon, where she had lived since December 2004, and where she had paced frantically a month earlier on the night of November 23, 2011. The constant swirl of friends and supporters in those early weeks had given way to longer stretches of being alone in the disturbing calm and quiet of a house absent children. Karen was breathing and functioning but still solidly lost in the inkblot of grief that erased all memories of what was transpiring around her.

Seated with her now was Patrick J. McGroder, of the Gallagher & Kennedy law firm forty-three miles due west, and his son, with the same name and "IV" to designate his place in the proud family lineage. The son would later leave the world of personal-injury and wrongful-death cases to join the Maricopa County public defender's office, which is exactly how his father had started his legal career in 1970 in Phoenix, representing those who could not afford to hire their own private attorneys. The father, Patrick McGroder, had steadily migrated west from his hometown of Buffalo, first with a stop at Notre Dame in South Bend, Indiana, for his undergraduate studies, then to Tucson for law school at University of Arizona, and finally settling in Phoenix for life and career.

By 2011, the senior McGroder had been in the legal trenches for more than forty years and had carved out the trial lawyer's measure of justice through large settlements paid to his clients who had suffered at the hands of big government and big business. Karen Perry's case, with three young children gone forever, was especially disturbing to the lawyer who was also a father of three, including his lawyer son and two daughters. One of those daughters, Caroline McGroder, had also followed in her father's footsteps and was a practicing attorney at the same firm.

Little more than one month after the crash, there were few certainties. The lawyer and his putative client knew the end result of what had happened, but not the "how" and "why." Why did an experienced pilot, one so familiar with the short route, fly the airplane straight into a mountain? Something had gone horribly wrong, and Karen needed answers.

"I was struck by her epic and unfathomable loss," Patrick McGroder recalled. "I felt almost hopeless and helpless as to how I might be able to help her, as a human being and a lawyer."

During their first meeting, the lawyer inwardly acknowledged that he was unsure whether he could deal with the same tragedy of losing all his children. The proportion of Karen Perry's loss and grief was completely overwhelming even to someone whose cases revolved around serious medical malpractice, devastating personal injury, and death. The lawyer steeled himself emotionally and put forth the legal issues regarding the crash and various possibilities for determining causation. In Arizona, every case of negligence was decided under comparative negligence, which meant that whatever person or entity had contributed to the deaths could be held liable by their percentage of causation.

"When you start a case you have to cast a very wide net in looking at what happened," said McGroder. In this case, he would begin by hiring aviation and forensic experts to investigate every aspect of each of the parties involved, to see what had happened. At the top of the list were Ponderosa Aviation and the deceased pilot, as well as the Federal Aviation Administration (FAA), which controlled the airspace and employed the air traffic controllers.

The lawyer and his client were already aware of the airspace issue created by the line in the sky at 5,000 feet, which was *below* the peak of Superstition Mountain. That would be one foothold for the plaintiff's legal theory later posited by McGroder. Along with pilot error, the inevitability of a crash had been compounded by the revised parameters of the class B airspace, which pointed back to the US government and its FAA. In fact, McGroder had hard evidence directly from the FAA itself that might have bolstered this legal theory. Dated December 7, 2011, the FAA accident/incident report included, in part:

> *Given the visual flight rules under which the aircraft was operating, the aircraft had to maintain altitude below class B airspace until approximately 1.1 kilometer before the impact point. Traveling at approximately 200 knots, the pilot had very little time to establish a rate of climb sufficient to avoid the rapidly rising terrain. The airspace involved is the portion of the class B airspace adjacent to the accident site... where the class B airspace is restricted from 5,000 feet MSL (mean sea level) to 9,000 feet MSL.*

However egregious that might have seemed, McGroder had a strong sense the airspace design was a legal black hole. There was no legal precedent to instill any sense of hope that they would be able to successfully win a civil action against the FAA. But they would try nonetheless. Karen told her new lawyer that the NTSB almost always ruled the cause as pilot error. Whatever the eventual outcome, they both knew this process would be anything but expeditious, and

Karen knew to temper her expectations for what would be a long and difficult legal battle. Step one, then, was standard in aviation crash litigation: first file a lawsuit against the operator, Ponderosa Aviation, for its culpability in the crash.

They concluded their meeting, and the senior McGroder hugged Karen and held her; the slow tick of the litigation clock had started. It would take another two full years for the National Transportation Safety Board to release its official probable cause report, in December 2013.

During the meeting, McGroder was the consummate professional. From that point forward he would be Karen Perry's voice, her knowledge base, and her advocate. Inwardly, for him, there had been the overriding sense of a lack of air in the room as they talked. Later when he was alone and away from his client and son, McGroder broke down and allowed the tears to flow.

IN January 2012, the NTSB issued its preliminary report, which was little more than a summary of the event facts and not of much use legally. Karen was still lost in her reverie of grief and altered state of consciousness. The story of her loss was generating widespread local and national media attention, so as she slowly started venturing back into the world she was no longer a completely anonymous and harried mother of three. At the gas station where she had regularly stopped with her three kids in the car, she knew the attendant as Vinder from India. He came out and tearfully pointed to the mountain, where the blackened crash site was visible against the cobalt backdrop.

"That cute little boy," he said, referring to the endlessly charming Logan Perry, "he was your son?"

"Yes," Karen said, nodding and holding back her own tears.

She was overwhelmed again with the sense of how different everything would be from now on, even stopping to get gas. Normalcy had been obliterated, but it was about to get worse. By early 2012, Karen's post-divorce financial woes became national news.

When Karen and Shawn split in October 2009, he had moved out of the house, which left her with a $3,300 monthly mortgage payment she could not afford on her flight attendant salary. The only reason she attempted to stay was that she did not want to uproot the kids even further. Her two special needs children, Morgan and Luke, were extremely sensitive to change, and they were already adjusting to a divorce. In hindsight it was only a matter of time before she would be forced out by foreclosure, but no one could have predicted all that would transpire on the night of November 23, 2011.

In early December, barely two weeks after losing her three children, Karen called her real estate agent, Nicole Hamming, a friend of twenty years. Karen knew she was at risk of losing the house and asked Hamming what she should do. When Hamming pulled the property tax records she discovered a foreclosure date looming just two weeks away, which had been set on the property by mortgage holder Ocwen. Hamming arranged an appointment for Karen to meet with attorney Scott Drucker at Mack, Drucker, and Watson, to avoid foreclosure and negotiate a short sale.

"My goal was to give Karen time in her property to properly mourn the loss of her kids," said Hamming. Depending on how the short sale process proceeded, Karen would likely have at least three months in the house and maybe as long as a year. But as the story of Karen's tragic loss was regularly splashed across local and national news, the short sale option became problematic; the property had become stigmatized by the news coverage.

Meanwhile, anonymous citizens were contacting Hamming and offering to help any way they could. Some offered Karen a place to live temporarily. Others offered to buy the property and rent it back to Karen so she wouldn't be uprooted at the worst time of her life. Freddie Mac officials, however, would not allow the rent-back option. That solution violated the "arm's length transaction" policy on short sales, which had been established to prevent fraud. Ousted homeowners, in other words, were not permitted to stay in their foreclosed properties, regardless of extenuating circumstances. On short sales, the federally backed mortgage holder required that buyer and seller have no connection when a property sold for less than the amount owed. The rule had originated in September 2010, when borrowers were using straw buyers, who then returned the same property to the distressed borrower at a greatly reduced price.

Unfazed, Hamming contacted Arizona Senator John McCain's office to see if there was anything he could do to wield some influence to help Karen stay in her home, where Morgan's, Logan's, and Luke's bedrooms remained untouched since the night they had died. The senator was not able to help. In the end, Hamming had at least helped delay the inevitable for a few months.

On March 6, Karen got the call from a bank representative: she had nine days to vacate the home. The previous December, Karen had donated all the Christmas presents she had purchased for her children to the W. Steven Martin 911 Toy Drive, which works with Phoenix-area law enforcement agencies to reach at-risk families. Martin, expecting media coverage, called his lifelong friend Carole Bartholomeaux and asked her to coordinate all the press activities. After Karen and Bartholomeaux met for the first time, Carole realized that Karen needed more help due to the widespread media interest in her story. For the next two years Bartholomeaux worked pro bono, coordinating media contacts for Karen and generating millions of dollars in coverage.

One of Bartholomeaux's contacts, Laurie Roberts of the *Arizona Republic,* published a March 9 editorial under the headline "Would it have killed the real-estate world to give Karen Perry a break?" On March 13, Gretchen Carlson invited Karen to appear on camera on a national Fox News morning show. Her other guest was well-known attorney Bob Massi, a personal injury lawyer with expertise in real estate and business law who made a career of taking up the plight of the underdog.

"This is an exception to the rule," Bob Massi said on air in reference to allowing Karen to rent the house back. "It is sickening. … Unfortunately, legally, there's nothing that can be done."

Similarly, through Bartholomeaux's mission to get justice for Karen and her children, additional national media came calling. Karen's story and plight next appeared on the national *Inside Edition*. In the end, however, the short sale went through and forced the grieving mother to leave the house.

Simultaneously, Karen had to renew her flight instructor certificate. Given what she was enduring, it might have made sense to skip it, except that if she missed the deadline and her certification lapsed, she'd lose her rating and have to start over. In an odd twist, the two-day ground school training at Salt Lake

City International (SLC) offered a silver lining. While Karen was away for those two days doing her training, her friends took on the task she would have found impossible, which was cleaning out the children's rooms and moving everything into storage until she found a new place to live.

"It was horrible packing up her kids' rooms," Hamming recalled. "I wanted to make sure Karen was taken care of and was fully engaged with making sure she was OK."

A local moving company, Clean Restoration, donated boxes and packing paper and promised a truck and two movers at no charge when everything was ready to go. Concurrently, staff and volunteers at the international nonprofit women's organization Soroptimist went to work and contacted Canyon Rose Storage, which donated one year of free storage for all Karen's belongings. The one-year commitment later turned into two full years at no charge.

When Karen came back from Salt Lake City and looked in the kids' rooms, they were empty. All that remained was the carpet and individualized colors on the walls that each of the children had chosen. Karen remembered distinctly how their father Shawn had painstakingly and lovingly painted each room. The children's rooms also had special ceiling fans that matched their own personalities and the themes of each space. Everything else was gone. Karen broke down and cried. She still had the task of packing the rest of the house, with numerous friends helping. Once everything was packed, the movers arrived to pack the truck.

By now, Bartholomeaux was sending out news releases weekly. She had worked with David Spade, the actor and comedian, on another client project and knew of the actor's ties to Arizona. When Karen's story reached Spade, he wrote a personal letter and sent it to Karen with a $10,000 check, which was how she paid her rent at a small house less than a mile from where she had lived with her children. She continued living her life, as always, under the steady presence of the mountain. Karen called and spoke to Spade's assistant and asked that she tell him how much the gesture meant; Karen was never able to thank him directly.

ALTHOUGH she didn't openly share her emotional darkness, by March 2012

Karen had found an unlikely confidante who was helping keep her out of the abyss. Ashley Davis Bush is a licensed psychotherapist and grief counselor in private practice in Epping, New Hampshire. She has published six books, including *Transcending Loss*. In her practice and writing she focuses on, among other things, coping with loss and navigating transitions. As a parent herself, Bush had seen online coverage of the plane crash the night it happened, November 23, 2011, and felt horrified and sickened for a mother she had never met. After following the story online for a few days, she felt a connection with Karen Perry.

Maybe because they each had three children, or the extraordinary circumstances, or the horror of losing all of one's children simultaneously in a single furious mishap, she felt compelled to do something, and she sent a copy of *Transcending Loss* to Karen Perry, who read it and emailed the author. From there they began to meet regularly via online video conference. Bush was not trolling for new clients; she just genuinely wanted to help Karen and did the initial sessions pro bono.

"I really do believe that death is not the end," she said. While she didn't push that spiritual view on her new client as some sort of evangelist, she helped her see new possibilities.

"It's important to continue to talk to someone you love who's no longer here," she said. Along with that, she suggested that Karen remain open to perceiving signs that her children's presence was still with her. Said Bush, "When you start to open yourself to that possibility, you start to see more evidence and be comforted by it."

Indeed, Karen was already experiencing odd markers. In the spring of 2012 Karen had planned a trip with two friends to southern Arizona, just for a change of scenery and perspective. With her car in the garage, they were packed up and ready to go. As Karen went back into the house to retrieve a forgotten item, the electric-powered garage door mysteriously closed. Her friends standing in the driveway remarked that the door had closed, but that neither they nor Karen had pressed the button.

Later on that same road trip, Karen was taking photographs with her camera. When she handed the camera to her friend the shutter started clicking repeatedly.

Karen laughed and told her to stop.

"I'm not doing it!" the friend said, removing her hand entirely from the camera that continued to operate on its own. *That little devil Luke*, Karen thought, *he always loved to nab my camera and take lots of photos.*

The most continual and interesting of all signs, however, was a little farm toy that made all the barnyard sounds, which the kids had enjoyed immensely. After the children died, the farm toy continued to make the horse whinny sound. The first time this had happened was about a week after their death when Karen had a full house of friends and supporters. Karen would not have trusted her own shattered state of mind, but here were at least three others who heard the horse whinny even though no one was touching the toy. After that first instance, there were many other occasions when the horse whinny started again on its own, which had never once happened prior to the children's departure.

Karen started counting how many times it made the whinny sound. The longest was a stretch in the middle of the night when Karen stopped counting at one hundred times in a row. Most would simply dismiss the horse whinny with common explanations: the batteries were dying, the wiring was faulty, or the toy was simply broken. But as Karen lay alone in the darkness, she could only wonder what her babies were trying to tell her. It did not matter to her if people thought she was crazy; a grieving mother owed no explanation or rationalization to anyone for whatever she needed to feel, think, do, or believe to process the unthinkable.

For Karen, each subsequent horse whinny carried a greater sense of urgency, which is when it hit her: *We are all right, Mommy, and we are with you. We are all right, and we are with you. We are all right, and we are with you.* Over and over and over again. Karen cried and talked aloud in the darkness to tell them that she loved them dearly and missed them so much, and how it meant everything to her that they were giving her so many signs.

The last time Karen heard the horse whinny was about ten months after they died, in the fall of 2012. The little farm toy gave her three, final distinct whinny sounds, the meaning of which she did not miss: one last good-bye from each of them. Although to this day she keeps the farm toy nearby, in her closet, it has remained silent.

TWENTY-FOUR

3 Wings of Life

SIX MONTHS AFTER HER THREE CHILDREN DIED, the huge hole in Karen Perry's life felt just as gaping. She was still subsisting in that disoriented, altered state: awake, but not fully conscious. Alive, but not really living. Trying to stay busy, but without any real purpose. The gracious supply of donated vacation time by her coworkers meant she did not have to worry about the stress of work, but at the same time she needed something to start at least inching her way back. Flying had been the constant thread in her life for three decades.

"I wanted to get back in the game of living again," Karen said. In May 2012 she did just that by returning to work as a flight attendant for Delta Air Lines, albeit on a very limited basis. She started with two trips that month, more as diversion than anything else. She put on her uniform, went to the airport, and went through the motions, but she was still numb. Her first trip was back to

Kona, one of the magical stops on her journey through places. She had spent years there in her teens and twenties during the 1970s and 1980s. She married Shawn Perry there in 2001, then returned with her one-and-a-half-year-old daughter Morgan in 2003, the month before Logan was born. Kona was her last working destination two days before the crash, in November 2011, and now her first destination after everything that had happened. But she was numb to the magic the place had once offered. It was still almost impossible to imagine fully rejoining the living.

That month, on a six-day trip with a layover in Tokyo, her coworkers were doing everything they could to help Karen acclimate to the world. One rule was to keep Karen from isolating in her hotel room; she agreed that all that waited there was brooding and a dark spiral to depression. Karen had no interest in socializing, but she also had a sense of her children saying, *Mother, get up and go down to the lounge!* Oddly, they even told her right where to sit in the sports bar at this unofficial Delta hub, a Radisson property in Tokyo. It was the last place on earth she wanted to be, but there really was not any place she wanted to be except back with her kids, a reoccurring longing she could not shake.

At the bar, she took a seat next to a man she didn't know. Other friends arrived, a crew from Honolulu, and conversations ensued. At some point, she exchanged small talk with the man next to her. He appeared older than she, with silvered hair, a soothing voice, and friendly eyes. At least, as it turned out, they could talk aviation.

GORDON Barnard was born in 1953 in Inglewood, California, and grew up in Ladera Heights near Marina del Rey. His father had a thirty-nine-year career as a pilot with United Airlines, which set the career template for the son.

"I was brought up in the culture," Barnard recalled.

In 1970, when he was a junior in high school, Barnard's father paid his son's way to get his private pilot license at Torrance Airport (TOA). From there Barnard earned a bachelor's degree in business administration from University of the Pacific in Stockton.

"My idea was to get through college and get a degree, because all the major airlines required a degree," he said.

After college and a short stint as a metal salesman for Milligan-Spika, at age 24 Barnard moved to Vero Beach, Florida, to work as an instructor at Flight Safety International. When he was 26, he became a copilot for Chautauqua Airlines in Jamestown, New York, which is still an operating regional company. He worked at two smaller airlines, Imperial Airlines and Orion Air, before Northwest Airlines hired him in 1983, based out of Minneapolis, Minnesota.

It was there that he began a three-decade career flying Boeing aircraft (727, 747-200, 747-400) and the Airbus A330, with a captain rating on all four airplanes. In 2005, a company merger with Delta Air Lines meant he was employed by the same airline as the flight attendant he would meet seven years later in a Tokyo hotel bar. By then, he had amassed more than 10,000 hours as a captain and 25,000 total flight hours going back to 1970.

THE conversation flowed easily that night in 2012. Karen mentioned that she lived in Phoenix.

"Really?" Barnard said.

It certainly was not odd to run into a coworker at this particular hotel, because it was regularly overrun with Delta flight crews on layover. During his career, Barnard had spent more than five hundred nights at the hotel. But meeting a peer from Phoenix, where Delta had no base, was unusual. Being from the same sprawling metropolitan area, he asked her to narrow things.

"I live in Gold Canyon," she said. Almost immediately, she watched the color drain from his face. Then she knew he was putting it all together.

"Are you who I think you are?" he said.

"Yes."

The man she had just met got tears in his eyes and said, "I don't know what to say to you."

"Don't say anything," Karen said. "Just give me a hug."

From that moment, the conversation no longer flowed freely. The air between them filled with heavy sadness, the grief she had tried to outrun by flying halfway around the world only to meet someone who had been watching her face splashed across local news for six months. *Everywhere you go*, she thought, *there you are*.

"She told me the whole story and it was just horrifying," Barnard said. "This was a few months after it had happened."

Suddenly she felt exhausted again and had no energy to explain what it was like and how she was coping and all the rest. She just wanted to go back up to her room and go to sleep. Well, after a good cry then, yes, she would sleep. As a matter of courtesy she stayed on her barstool, but all she was thinking about was how quickly she could ditch this guy. But, oddly, they ended up talking long into the Tokyo night. What she had feared had become comforting and therapeutic: two pilots able to speak the same language and access the world of aviation from the same perspective. They exchanged email addresses, but Karen was not interested. Later she was surprised when he actually sent her an email, and they began corresponding. One month after they met he asked if she would like to go to dinner.

Dinner? she thought. *No, I don't want to go to dinner with you. My children are gone. How can I go to dinner? What a ridiculous idea.* He, at least, still had his two sons from a previous marriage that ended in 2002, two healthy, adult men he could call or see whenever he wanted. *Dinner? No way.* This new filter—*My children are gone*—would not be easily removed. It tinged everything, every experience, every thought of every moment of every day. There was an inherent duty and an honor to uphold as a grieving mother: *My children are gone.*

And then, for reasons she could not fathom, Karen accepted Gordon Barnard's dinner invitation. While they chatted briefly after he came to pick her up, she directed him to the couch while she sat across the room on a stool. Her state of mind would have been more pronounced only if she had built a brick wall between them and topped it with coils of barbed wire.

She knew she liked talking to him because they had aviation as a soothing common bond. That had been her world, her passion, her life, and career before the big surprise at 38: pregnant! But that was all she knew as far as dinner with a man she'd met in Tokyo: if this guy thought this was anything other than two pilots talking shop, well, sitting halfway across the room ought to do the trick. He didn't seem to mind, and he started coming over to go for walks with Karen and her dogs.

"It started very platonically," Barnard said. "I was trying to be a friend. She wasn't looking for a relationship, and I wasn't either. We had a lot of conversations about flying because we have that in common."

Almost unconsciously, the inner radar pulse of *My children are gone* from Karen kept romance at bay and allowed one of life's greatest pleasures when she least expected it: the blossoming of a friendship. Without even realizing it, Karen had taken another tiny step out of complete despair and hopelessness.

WITH the summer of 2012 approaching, Karen's lawyer Patrick McGroder called her and asked her to come to his office near central Phoenix. He had obtained footage of the air traffic controller's scope showing the trajectory of the aircraft that contained her children on the night of November 23, 2011.

Once there, Karen saw and learned a stunning truth: on the night of the crash, there had been a shift change in the Falcon Field (FFZ) control tower at precisely 6:30 p.m. The airplane had taken off at 6:25 p.m.; the crash occurred at 6:31 p.m. Technically speaking, the aircraft was just beyond the area of FAA air traffic controller responsibility by 6:30 p.m. as it sped east in the blackest of nights. So there was no official dereliction of duty even as the controllers rotated in a new crew. However, Karen was left to wonder, because any controller watching the radar scope at precisely 6:30 p.m. would have seen an airplane in peril on a trajectory directly toward a mountain. If so, that controller would have immediately issued a warning.

"That was another twist of fate," Karen said. "All those controllers know where the mountain is located. Meanwhile, because of all the radar vectors, the pilot probably had the false sense of security that the air traffic controllers were looking after him."

Indeed, in the minutes after takeoff the controllers had been issuing the pilot Russel Hardy radar vectors and a designated altitude just prior to the aircraft exiting their area and scope of responsibility. After that, only a few nautical miles separated the airplane from the immovable mountaintop looming in the darkness. Traveling 230 miles an hour, the Rockwell Commander would have covered that distance in less than a minute, timing that synchronized with the shift change and then the horrific crash.

Rewinding from there, if the incoming flight had not been late, then maybe Karen's children would still be alive, since the pilot would have been ahead of that ill-timed shift change. Even arriving five minutes earlier to pick up Morgan, Logan, and Luke—or minutes later, for that matter—might have spared six lives; someone in the tower might have spotted their imminent peril and issued a warning. The late arrival to pick up the children also changed the amount of air traffic they would encounter outbound, changing their course and the available daylight.

As an aviator herself Karen knew it was sheer madness to play such "What If?" games and to move around time, space, and events to rewrite a new outcome. But "What If?" has always been an inescapable part of the genetic code of motherhood, the hard wiring inherent in protecting helpless and innocent children. But there were more disturbing "What If?" scenarios headed her way.

On May 9, 2012, the local Phoenix Fox News Channel affiliate, KSAZ 10, aired a story by anchor John Hook. With two sons and a daughter himself, covering the story those first five months had proved emotionally wrenching.

"It was so cruel that it just affected me," Hook recalled. "It could have been any of us. When I would interview her I would get emotional and start crying at times. It became very personal for me. I wanted to make it right for her in some way."

As part of the story that aired, he and his cameraman created a reenactment of the ill-fated flight, showing three children boarding a small aircraft.

"Those are my kids in the reenactment," he said. "That drove it home even more."

During his investigation, Hook uncovered an apparent bombshell when he obtained an internal FAA memorandum dated January 20, 2012, less than two months after the crash. At first glance, the memorandum seemed to be the smoking gun the lawyer Patrick McGroder could point to as documentation of the very issue he had discussed with Karen Perry at their first meeting in December 2011. In part, the memorandum stated:

The airspace design with regard to obstacle (terrain)
clearance is not sufficient to ensure a margin of safety
necessary to preclude the possibility of an accident similar
to the one that occurred on November 23, 2011.

Hook agreed that the airspace was not well designed, with pilots flying too close to mountain peaks, and he went looking for answers. Remarkably, the internal memorandum included agreement by *four* different FAA investigators that the airspace design was a dangerous safety issue. Said Hook, "That, to me, carries some weight."

As he searched for answers, Hook said FAA employees at first flat-out denied that the memorandum existed at all. However, when they realized he already had a copy, they had to backtrack. Said Hook, "I had them dead to rights."

Or so it seemed. Like Karen's lawyer McGroder, similarly trying to breach the establishment's castle walls, Hook was about to discover the maddening difficulty of trying to wrench accountability from tight-lipped government officials. With the "smoking gun" memorandum in hand and a camera crew trailing, Hook went to each of the four FAA investigators' residences with hand-carried letters, but no one was willing to talk to the reporter, on camera or off.

"Going in I had this belief the FAA was mom and apple pie," said Hook. What he discovered instead was a bloated bureaucratic federal agency that was often making gross missteps. "It troubled me that they were so obstinate in not admitting there is a problem out there. I feel that the FAA had an assist in the crash with the design of the airspace."

Said Karen, "As pilots, we all knew the problems with the airspace, so I was furious."

Even more disturbing, Hook's sources privately told him that once the smoke cleared and enough time had passed, the FAA would likely quietly redesign the airspace to eliminate the issue at 5,000 feet. Doing so too quickly might be an indirect admission of culpability in the events of the night of November 23, 2011. Five years or more down the road, there would be less direct correlation to any specific crash and loss of life. Of course, in the interim, another pilot could suffer the same fate by staying below the 5,000-foot ceiling mandated without requesting special clearance.

"I could not believe the level of deception at the FAA," Hook said. "I've lost some faith in the FAA. I could not believe this agency and how they bunker themselves in. They answer to no one."

Likewise, on the legal front, the damning internal memorandum provided little ammunition for McGroder.

"Our problem was a legal impediment," said McGroder. He teamed up with Brian J. Alexander, a New York–based partner with the powerful aviation litigation firm Kriedler and Kriedler, to help work through the various air traffic control and airspace issues of the federal case. The lawyers carefully researched how the FAA had made their class B airspace determination, which certainly wasn't an arbitrary decision out of the blue, but rather a long and exhaustive process.

DURING the first year after Karen Perry's three children left this earth, the possibility of future hope and healing had slowly started to return. It happened unceremoniously, by invisible increments and without conscious realization, throughout 2012.

Karen's friend Eva Morgan had started helping a local Gold Canyon single mom who had five children, on her own after their father committed suicide. One of the kids had gone to school with Logan Perry. Eva did what she could to help with the three boys and two girls, ranging in age from an infant to 12, by babysitting and taking the kids for activities. At some point Karen tagged along for an outing, and then more and more. Soon she joined in regularly, and helped as they unofficially adopted a second family who had lost their trailer in a fire. They took the families food and helped with the many tasks related to raising children.

As summer wound down, Karen was also finding solace in her walks with her new friend Gordon Barnard. One day, as he was leaving her house and giving her their customary good-bye hug, he gave her a quick peck on the cheek and said, "Glad we can be friends." That's when it first hit Karen: *This guy is really nice.*

During the fall of that year, Karen went to Eva and said Eva had been right: they should formalize their helping efforts by applying for nonprofit status. Eva could only smile, nod, and give Karen a hug. It was Eva who had first suggested such an effort, years before, when they were juggling six kids and two busy careers between them. Except whenever Eva raised the subject, Karen looked at her as though she had a live raccoon on her head. When, exactly, did Karen Perry have time to operate a nonprofit, with her own three kids? The unfettered chaos that had been Karen's life left not one spare minute for a quiet bath alone, let alone starting a charity. Now, however, Karen had the time and space and, most important, the hard-won perspective of needing a new purpose.

She and Eva applied for a nonprofit charity status 501(c)(3), and established a board of directors. Initially their mission was to provide a place for grieving kids who had lost parents. Then they realized there were a number of national groups that covered that segment and demographic. So they decided to make it broader and just try to help local kids with whatever they needed: food, clothing, shelter, guidance, love, support, and activities. They started operating out of Gold Canyon Community Church, which had formerly been an elementary school so was already equipped with classrooms and a playground. Eva watched with admiration as her friend sprang into action.

"This was the beginning," she said. "It was all coming full circle as a place of hope and healing for kids."

Their longer-term vision was a fully staffed residential ranch for hope and healing, employing all manner of activities and modalities including horses for equine therapy. Of course there was the question of a name for their new venture.

They considered numerous possibilities. Since both had been flight attendants for more than three decades, and Karen a pilot as well, every name used the word "Wings." They eventually settled on 3 Wings of Life, which in January 2013 was officially incorporated as a nonprofit, with a 501(c)(3) designation pending.

On their first official day, they went to pick up two boys and ended up with a van full of kids clamoring to go along. As they spent time with the kids, they watched lives changing, whether through gardening, art, or some other project. What started with a few kids eventually grew to thirty kids coming every Wednesday from 4 p.m. to 6 p.m.

Meanwhile, Karen's earlier realization that Gordon Barnard was a nice guy proved prophetic when he accompanied Karen to San Francisco in December 2012, where Karen was scheduled for reconstructive breast surgery. Between the pre-op and the post-op recovery they were there for three weeks together. That same month, they bought a house together in Gold Canyon and moved in. Karen's friends, who had also been her protectors and confidantes during the most difficult year of her life, were understandably concerned. So were Gordon's two sons. Regardless, out of tragedy new possibilities were arising.

Time was a blur, but Karen had survived the first year without her children. Three missed birthdays, Mother's Day, each of the other holidays, and the first anniversary had all passed. To mark that one-year anniversary milestone date, there was a well-attended candlelight vigil at Gold Canyon Community Church on November 23, 2012. The next day Karen hiked to the top of the mountain with Eva Morgan and Gordon Barnard, marking the second time she had made the summit. This time they took a tent and spent the night. It was a long, cold night atop the mountain, and the trio was buffeted by strong winds that made sleep all but impossible. Even so, they were on sacred ground.

"It was so spiritual," Karen said. "The sunset was unbelievable from up there. It was magical. And cold and a little scary."

The first anniversary had come and gone and, almost unbelievably, she was still upright, living, and breathing. That, if nothing else, was an accomplishment. More importantly, she also had a new life partner and a new larger mission and purpose with 3 Wings of Life, which officially launched in 2013.

TWENTY-FIVE

The NTSB Report

IN JANUARY 2013, THE LAWYER PATRICK McGRODER recommended that Karen Perry settle her lawsuit with Ponderosa Aviation. Karen had driven to the Biltmore area of Phoenix and taken the elevator to the eighth-floor offices of Gallagher & Kennedy. She listened intently as they discussed their options. The grieving mother still did not have any clear answers about why the airplane had crashed and why her children had been taken from her. They knew about the airspace design issue and the air traffic controller shift change, but those were elements for a separate lawsuit against the Federal Aviation Administration. This case, against Ponderosa Aviation, was for the wrongful death of her three children.

"My kids were dead," she said. "I didn't care about the money. My children were innocent victims who had no choice or control over what happened. I just wanted some measure of accountability and closure."

Civil litigation is not hard science, but rather an imperfect art that almost never elicits absolute clarity or closure. In the end Karen agreed to settle the case, which avoided a long trial and potential appeals process that could drag on for years and years. The local media reported the settlement, but not the amount because it was confidential. Given what she had lost, the sum would not even allow her to give up her day job as a flight attendant.

"The issue was on collectability," said McGroder in reference to his recommendation to settle the case and move forward. More years of litigation, in his opinion, would accomplish little, if anything. "We were dealing with a family-owned company." As far as negligent causation, McGroder's exhaustive investigation had not turned up anything useful in the legal arena: "There seemed to be no evidence of a component defect or mechanical failure that caused this crash. We had a case of epic damages, but everything seemed to circle back to pilot error. We couldn't explain why an experienced pilot flew directly into the mountain. We're never going to know the answer to that question."

For the lawyer, the depths of the tragedy—Morgan, Logan, and Luke gone in a flash—resonated every time he picked up the Karen Perry case file. Legally, it was a perfect storm, where nothing came together on the negligence side except for the glare of pilot error. Said McGroder: "Sadly, Karen Perry is never going to get closure."

On the federal-case front against the FAA, the early prediction of a steep uphill climb proved accurate. In May 2013 the lawyers filed a twenty-million-dollar personal injury and wrongful death claim against the FAA. They referenced the actions of federal air traffic controllers regarding the final direction given to the pilot to turn right (east), which put the aircraft on a direct course for Superstition Mountain. The lawyers referenced the class B airspace issue in detail. From the addendum to the claim: *As a result, the right turn directed by Falcon Field air traffic control personnel placed the subject aircraft on a direct collision course for Superstition Mountain at an altitude below 5,000 feet.* Immediately after issuing that directive, the personnel conducted a position relief briefing between the controllers on duty. Meanwhile, no one mentioned that the aircraft had been vectored to the northeast before being approved for a right turn to the east, nor that the aircraft was heading right for Superstition Mountain. No one in the air traffic control tower caught the ominous blip. The claim then documented a long list of careless, negligent, and wrongful acts and/or omissions to act by the FAA air traffic controllers. In the end, however, the eight-figure claim was almost nothing more than a fruitless paperwork exercise. The usually powerful lawyers might as well have been shouting into the spinning turbines of a Boeing 747, where their voices were inconsequential.

MEANWHILE, Karen was inching her way back to a new normal, whatever that was meant to be. One Sunday a pastor invited Karen to speak at Our Savior's Lutheran Church in Gold Canyon. She read a narrative she had written about her life journey and the loss of her kids. Shortly thereafter, she posted the full text on Facebook. Within a week, the speech had more than ten thousand hits. Within two weeks there were thirty thousand hits.

"I was astonished by the response," she said. "I started thinking maybe this was a message that people wanted to hear."

She even had a passing thought that her story might be a good fit for the Oprah Winfrey Network, but realized that was a long shot and let go of the idea. Two weeks later, on April 11, 2013, to her astonishment a man named Ernest Martin left a comment on the Facebook page:

Hello Karen,

I'm writing from TBG Studios, a production company based out of New York. We are in the process of casting a new documentary TV series for the Oprah Winfrey Network.

As our team has been researching viable candidates, we came upon your story. This journalistic-style show focuses on stories of human resilience and extraordinary strength such as yours. We think that you have an inspiring story to tell that others could learn and benefit from.

I'm reaching out to see if this is something you would be interested in. If you'd like to know more about the series, please reach out to me via phone or email. I'd love the opportunity to speak with you.

Thank you,
Ernest

Soon Karen was on the phone with Martin doing a preliminary interview. Then she had a second call with producer Chad Ostrom, who was in New York, and then a third online video call with Ostrom and Jonas Elrod, director of *In Deep Shift*.

The show was a planned series of episodes featuring people who had suffered a breakdown of some sort, a breakthrough, and then an integration of healing and transformation. In addition to Karen, the production staff had assembled an eclectic group of people to feature, including an orthopedic spine surgeon who lived to share her near-death experience, a woman who revealed a brutally honest struggle with body image after her two-hundred-pound weight loss, comedian Maysoon Zayid's life with cerebral palsy, and a woman survivor of the 2012 Colorado movie theater massacre, whose boyfriend lost his life that fatal night by heroically saving hers.

"I had survived it and was moving forward," Karen said as she recollected the in-depth conversation with the show's director and producer. "And I told them about the mountain that's in my backyard."

The mountain. Ever-present and always powerful. The anchor and source of Karen's new place on the planet. It had always been there and always would be in her lifetime.

The timeline, cycles, and rhythms played out again, of her poem, her story, and larger narrative. The fragrant hub of Anaheim punctuated by the hospital smell and loss of a baby sister, an early perspective that launched a young girl on an unconscious journey to find immovable and impervious solidity. She was silently searching on those cool blasts, when the vibrating Ducati magnified every sense impression through lean angles and rare rain. The pulsing heat from the muffler reminded her that place *had* to supersede home; it just had to. And, then, the thunder roar of airplanes! A medium to transport and shape place into past, present, and future, a new ease and timelessness. Destinations toppled one after the other. First the calming churn of waves onto sand, the steady work of water for a billion years, and then Oregon, New Orleans, and Hawai'i. Beauty, challenge, and discovery at each stop, yet now a sense that she must step back inside the revolving doors, one more time.

Immovable and impervious solidity. There it was: the rock fingers reaching

5,057 feet skyward and aimed into the permanent bliss of it all. All along, through all the detours, the beacon had finally called her here, to the epicenter, where everything would play out, forty million years in the making: the mountain. Here she found both the opening to heaven and her own personal hell, too, where place and home merged into one and ended the search begun as a little girl.

A few weeks later, in May 2013, Karen had not heard anything and assumed the Oprah Winfrey Network producer had decided to pass. Then she got a phone call from Elrod. They wanted to interview and feature Karen and schedule interviews, at and around her home in Arizona, for the next month. And, while there, they wanted to hike to the top of the mountain with a full camera crew.

"Is it feasible to climb the mountain in June?" the director asked Karen.

"No, it isn't," she said, as a longtime Southwest resident who knew and respected the strength and danger of the desert sun. "Except the next thing I knew we were planning it."

Karen had started working full time again and, in June 2013, Gordon Barnard proposed, and he and Karen were engaged to be married. On June 23, Karen had been up all night working the Kona-LA route on Delta Air Lines. Then she took a commuter flight back to Phoenix and met the waiting film crew from the Oprah Winfrey Network.

The traveling entourage included Elrod, Ostrom and his fiancée Jenny Askew, who was the director of photography, producer Tobey Keller, and Brandon DeLany, supervising producer. Once in Arizona, they hired a full crew that included a production assistant, gaffer, audio technician, EMT, and two camera operators, including one who controlled a drone camera.

At Sky Harbor, they videotaped Karen in her Delta uniform coming down an escalator and into the terminal. Over the next two days, the crew assembled video of various interviews with Karen in and around her house. Like any movie or television production, it was slow, precise, repetitive work that required a lot of hours to get seconds and minutes of usable footage. One highlight was a surprise guest who turned up at Karen's door during taping. It was Ashley Davis Bush, the therapist from New Hampshire who had been helping Karen sort things emotionally. The producers had secretly arranged Bush to take a flight to

Phoenix to meet Karen for the first time and do some therapy work on camera. Bush, too, was amazed by the proximity of the mountain to Karen's house and the grand specter it imposed.

"We both got teary and held hands," said Bush. "We couldn't stop talking."

And then the moment had arrived: June 26, 2013, was the appointed day for Karen and her friends to lead the Oprah Winfrey Network production crew up almost one mile of elevation gain through a steep, rugged canyon. To do so safely, she had sought help from Paul Babeu, the sheriff of Pinal County and one of the men she had met on the night of the crash when he arrived at her house for the notification. He was happy to help and promised a pilot and PCSO helicopter to ferry everyone down from the top of the mountain, two by two, to avoid the extreme desert temperatures from noon until sunset. The predicted high for the day of the hike was 116 degrees. However, the day before the hike, the helicopter crashed near Casa Grande due to engine failure, with three staff aboard. There were no injuries, but it was an uncanny event for Karen and the crew alike.

"If the helicopter had lost its engine on the mountain the next day it likely would have been a fatal accident," she said. Although Karen warned that proceeding with the hike and now a descent could be dangerous, in the spirit of "The Show Must Go On" there was little consideration given to cancelling. The crew had scouted the trail by hiking up to Siphon Draw, and decided it would be a relatively easy trek even when laden with heavy packs, cameras, and bulky gear. That assessment was a bit misguided, similar to dipping a toe in the Pacific Ocean in Newport Beach and deciding the water was right for a swim to Catalina Island.

On June 26 at 7 a.m., a large group started up the trail. They were late by desert-heat standards, already behind the eight ball for beating the worst temperatures of the day. The group included Karen and Gordon Barnard; Eva Morgan, her son Bronson Morgan, and two of his friends; Robin Fochtman, a fellow flight attendant; and Beverly Perkins, a volunteer Pinal County Sheriff's Office search-and-rescue posse member who had befriended Karen. From the Oprah Winfrey Network there was the eleven-person crew. The goal was to get to the top by 10 a.m. and then get back down as quickly as possible to avoid the afternoon blaze. However, it was impossible to walk very far without encountering another beautiful scenic backdrop, so there were frequent stops to set up, shoot footage, break down the equipment, and start again.

By mid-morning the temperature had already passed 100°F, and the water supply was dwindling rapidly. Despite starting the hike with what they believed was more than enough water for everyone, they soon ran out.

When the large group arrived at the top, they worked for the next hour to get footage. The group started down the steep trail around 1 p.m. The classic Mount Everest truism applied: descending was actually more dangerous and more difficult, due to collective fatigue and the brutal toll on the legs, knees, and feet. Rather than life-threatening cold, here they faced potentially lethal heat pushing past 110°F. Minus any water, they were all in serious trouble.

Already kicking herself for knowing better and attempting the hike anyway, Karen soon started considering calling in a helicopter rescue. What a crazy repeat that would have been—the night of November 23, 2011, had started with the three hikers calling for help. Karen didn't want to wait too long to call for help, when rescuers would have to contend with the darkness, too.

Three-quarters of the way down the steep passage they encountered an older man, not part of their group, who was also struggling, alone, diabetic, and without water. Karen's husband-to-be Gordon Barnard lay down near him in a narrow patch of shade while Karen and Eva Morgan did the same just around a large outcropping of rock. They were all so exhausted that Karen couldn't even get up to walk ten yards around the rock to check on her fiancé. At age 60, Barnard was the oldest person in a group where even the youngest twenty-something men were struggling.

"I was dying," Karen said. "I physically couldn't move."

There was some panic in the air when people in their group fully realized the gravity of the situation: intense heat and no more water. The EMT started down to return with water for everyone, but became disoriented and did not make it back up. Some in the group simply abandoned backpacks and continued descending. Eventually Askew, Elrod, and Olstrom made it down, grabbed bottles of water, and started back up the trail to find Karen's group and avert tragedy. Askew especially, as the crew's only female member, had carried a heavy back-mounted camera all the way up and down the mountain and had hiked back up to bring water.

"We were on the mountain twelve hours that day," Karen said. "This could have turned deadly very easily and had a very different outcome."

The next day, June 27, the crew finished taping and wrapped the shoot. Editing, postproduction, and scheduling took almost two more years. The episode, part of a series called *In Deep Shift With Jonas Elrod*, aired March 2015 on the Oprah Winfrey Network as part of Super Soul Sunday.

ON December 3, 2013, local television anchor John Hook, of Fox 10 News, called Karen. The final NTSB report had been issued. Karen immediately called her lawyer Patrick McGroder, who read the following from the NTSB report:

Phoenix Sky Harbor (PHX) Class B Airspace Information. The Phoenix metropolitan area was designated and charted as Class B airspace, centered on PHX and the PHX VOR (PXR). The airspace elevation boundaries were defined by floor and ceiling altitudes, with lateral boundaries defined by distance and bearing from defined locations. Class B airspace is typically described as having the shape of an "upside-down wedding cake," where the airspace floor altitudes increase as the distance from the center increases. Aircraft operating under VFR are prohibited from entering Class B airspace without explicit permission from the responsible ATC facility. Mountainous terrain rises to 4,500 feet less than 1 nm east of the 5,000-foot Class B airspace, and the terrain rises to a maximum elevation of 5,057 feet about 3 1/2 miles east.

NTSB CONCLUSIONS: *Both engines and portions of their propellers were identified in the wreckage. Propeller, engine, and gearbox damage was consistent with high power rotation at impact. All three landing gear were identified in the wreckage, and damage patterns were consistent with the landing gear being retracted at impact. Some airplane skin segments exhibited significant accordion-like crush damage. Many cockpit-related items, including instruments, instrument panel sections, and pilots' seat fragments, were found on the terrain beyond the vertical rock formation; some were several hundred feet beyond the vertical rock formation.*

Damage patterns were consistent with the engines developing power at the time of impact. The majority of the first-stage compressor impeller blades were separated at the hubs. The second-stage compressor impeller blades were bent opposite the direction of rotation. There was rotational scoring on the aft side of the third-stage turbine blade platforms and metal spray deposits on the suction side of the third-stage turbine blades. No preimpact discrepancies that would have precluded normal engine operation were identified.

The blade damage to both propellers was severe, with leading-edge damage, multiple bends, twisting, concave bending of the blade chord at the tips, and tips that had fractured and separated. Two separate blade angle witness marks were each consistent with impact while at a normal (not in feather and not in reverse) operating position. No preimpact discrepancies that would have precluded normal propeller operation were identified.

The airplane was not equipped with a terrain awareness and warning system (TAWS). Six years earlier, the accident airplane seating configuration was changed to reduce passenger seat provisions from six to five by removing a seat belt from the aft divan, which was originally configured with seat belts for three people. This modification rendered the airplane exempt from the TAWS requirement; however, this modification was not approved by the FAA or documented via a supplemental type certificate or FAA Form 337 (Major Repair and Modification). Per the requirements of 14 Code of Federal Regulations 91.223, TAWS is not required for airplanes with fewer than six passenger seats. In this accident, onboard TAWS equipment could have provided a timely alert to help

*the pilot avoid the mountain. The National Transportation Safety
Board determines the probable cause(s) of this accident to be:*

*The pilot's failure to maintain a safe ground track and altitude
combination for the moonless night visual flight rules flight,
which resulted in controlled flight into terrain. Contributing to
the accident were the pilot's complacency and lack of situational
awareness and his failure to use air traffic control visual flight
rules flight following or minimum safe altitude warning services.
Also contributing to the accident was the airplane's lack of
onboard terrain awareness and warning system equipment.*

Legally, the case with Ponderosa Aviation was settled and in the books.
Even if they had waited for the final NTSB report, McGroder said it would not
have made much difference in their claim against the small aviation company.

"They (at Ponderosa Aviation) bought the airplane knowing that it wasn't
equipped with a terrain awareness warning system, yet they bought it and flew
it that way," he said. "What you're dealing with here all circles back to being 95
percent on Ponderosa Aviation, with the biggest link being pilot error."

Of course having TAWS on board might have avoided the crash, but only if
it was turned on and operational.

In the careful world of aviation safety and documentation, Karen was
disturbed to learn about the unapproved seat configuration that was not in
compliance. TAWS was required on every commercial aircraft with six or more
seats, but the unapproved modification six years earlier incorrectly negated the
TAWS requirement. These missteps seemed out of the norm for Ponderosa
Aviation, which until November 23, 2011, had had a stellar safety record.

"If the airplane had an operating TAWS on board, the crash never would have
happened," Karen said. "I wonder if the pilot ever had a sense in those last few
seconds of life that something wasn't right. Russel Hardy and Shawn Perry had
very good reputations," Karen said. "As aviators, we can never overlook safety
for convenience. That's called complacency."

Karen was finally getting some of the answers she had sought, which was that the crash on the night of November 23, 2011, was caused by a chain of avoidable events. With hindsight, correcting (removing) any one of those links in the chain would probably have meant her three children and the three adults would still be alive.

Before ever arriving at Mesa's Falcon Field Airport (FFZ) to pick up her children, based on the NTSB investigation, the aircraft was not in legal compliance. Investigators were able to determine that the required maintenance inspections, the 150-hour and the annual, which were legally required, had not been performed. Without those inspections the aircraft was not airworthy and *under no circumstances* should any passengers have been aboard.

Along with the seatbelt configuration, with one missing, and the absent Terrain Avoidance Warning System that should have been installed and operational, the aircraft should never have left Safford, let alone picked up passengers Morgan, Logan, and Luke Perry.

There was more evidence in the NTSB report that the airplane should have remained grounded, in Safford, after being purchased and flown there from Indiana:

> *The airplane's arrival at SAD terminated the ferry permit, and no inspections were accomplished to render the airplane airworthy after its relocation. Although other airworthy airplanes were available, Ponderosa Aviation, Inc.'s director of maintenance (DOM)(the accident pilot) and the director of operations (DO)... decided to use the nonairworthy airplane to conduct a personal flight from SAD to Falcon Field (FFZ), Mesa, Arizona, about 110 miles away. All available evidence indicates that the DOM was aware of the airplane's airworthiness status.*

In other words, the airplane was not legally airworthy and should never have been aloft in the dark skies on November 23, 2011. Another troubling find was that all the maintenance records were allegedly stored in the airplane and, therefore, destroyed in the crash. If nothing else, the maintenance records might have completed the picture of what occurred with the airplane the week leading up to the crash.

The next link in the chain was the delayed right turn after takeoff in Mesa, directed by the air traffic controller, which put the airplane on a direct course to the mountain. There had been inbound traffic that night, so the controller was maneuvering N690SM, *November six niner zero sierra mike*, around that traffic. With an air traffic controller issuing instructions to Russel Hardy on where and when to turn, the pilot may have been lured into a false sense that "big brother" was watching out for him.

Coupled with the airspace issue and having to stay below 5,000 feet, the Federal Aviation Administration and its air traffic controllers effectively boxed the pilot into a path to crash. Yes, the pilot could have requested VFR flight following, clearance to ascend beyond 5,000 feet, but with the ATC issuing the vectors, why would that be necessary? Hardy assumed he was being directed *around* the mountain, not straight toward it. Another link in the chain: the timing of the shift change that coincided exactly with the plane leaving air traffic control responsibility. The crash occurred less than a minute later.

The last links were simply natural occurrences: the time of day and the lunar cycle. Even with the heavy chain of tragedy being formed link by link, in the light of day pilot Russel Hardy would have simply seen the mountain and flown around it, or requested air traffic controller clearance to enter the "class bravo" airspace above 5,000 feet and fly over it. The same thing would have happened on almost any other night, too. But on the blackest of black moonless nights, there was no ambient light to highlight the rock fingers of Superstition Mountain. The oft-reported "Controlled Flight Into Terrain" had occurred again due to a loss of situational awareness.

"The biggest link was the pilot error," said the lawyer McGroder. "It was a perfect storm caused by hapless pilot error compounded by a number of other nominal legal causes. You just feel so bad that you're not able to make more of a difference."

Each link had its own powerful effect—including the FAA's culpability with the airspace design—and when fitted together formed the anatomy of a solidified chain of events that culminated in a catastrophic crash and the loss of six lives.

It had taken more than two years for the grieving mother to get these answers.

But, if anything, the unfortunate connecting of so many preventable variables only made her feel worse. A single, random cause—a bizarre and catastrophic mechanical failure—might have provided the finality of an unavoidable tragedy.

Instead, Karen Perry was left with a long list of human errors, procedural deficiencies, and federal aviation regulation (FAR) violations, all of which could have been corrected before or on the night of November 23, 2011. Nor would she get any accountability from the federal government in her case against the FAA.

"We were handcuffed because it was a discretionary function," McGroder said. That meant in appellate law, the government was immunized from any decision. The case officially settled in January 2014 under confidential terms. In the end, it was like aiming for the stars, asking Dad for a hundred bucks, and getting a handful of dimes and nickels. As with the first settlement: don't quit the day job.

Although the class B airspace issue was only an ancillary legal element, it was incomprehensible to Karen Perry and the wider aviation community that to this day, more than three years after the loss of six lives, the FAA had not redesigned the class B airspace near the mountain. As of 2015, restrictions remained in place down to 5,000 feet. Meanwhile, as it has for forty million years, the peak of Superstition Mountain rises into the skies, at 5,057 feet.

TWENTY-SIX

Ribbon of Life

WHEN AIRPLANES DIE THEY STOP OVER HERE, in a nondescript scrap yard in an industrial area west of downtown Phoenix with the distinct smell of roofing tar. At 3011 West Buckeye Road, the sign "Air Transport" is a gross misnomer for each craft relegated here to narrow numbered stalls, because none will ever again grace the skies. The fenced lot is densely packed with wrecked airplanes, rows and rows of them now motionless and silent, each a narrative of malfunction and error followed by adrenaline and immense relief, or by a chilling denouement of tragedy and death.

Almost three years after her children died, Karen Perry came here with her fiancé Gordon Barnard to pick through the wreckage, one last time, of the Rockwell Commander 690. Under a blazing summer sun that had already pushed the temperature past 100°F in the early morning, what was left of the once-gleaming, sophisticated piece of machinery no longer resembled an airplane. Now it was only obscene chunks and obliterated pieces of scorched, twisted metal and mangled wiring densely packed into huge white Tyvek transport bags. Almost three years prior, from atop the mountain, helicopters had airlifted the bagged wreckage down to flatter ground for transport here. The dozen or so stacked bags were in a numbered stall in a line of such stalls that held other aircraft similarly stowed in various states of disrepair.

This was a mortuary, of sorts, for inoperable and crumpled airplanes that sat in the scorching Arizona sun as state and federal examiners completed investigations and while civil aviation cases inched through courts. Once trials, final settlements, and dispositions had been rendered, the aircraft could be shipped off to salvage the metal and dispose of the rest. That there were so many wrecked airplanes here spoke to the danger inherent in aviation; despite the sophistication of modern machines, gravity remains the ultimate arbiter of fate.

A wide spectrum of lethality was on display within the chain-link confines. Many aircraft looked almost wholly intact, with only some sort of minor ding or dent that took the plane out of service and to this place; without question, those pilots and passengers had walked away. Further along the spectrum were airplanes clearly broken, wings clipped, noses crumpled; whether there had been loss of life was less certain. Then there were the obviously fatal wreckages. In the entire yard there was no other pileup as badly mangled as the airplane that had carried Karen Perry's three children and three adults on its last flight. But Karen didn't really notice the other airplanes or ponder the fate of those pilots and passengers. She had come here to undertake her own solemn tasks.

When her children died on the night of November 23, 2011, they departed this world leaving barely a trace behind. There were no small bodies in small caskets, with peaceful countenances, she could kiss one last time at a memorial service. There was no good-bye. There was no warning. They were simply gone, their final resting place at the top of a 5,000-foot mountain that was difficult to reach. In the almost three years since, this crumpled wreckage was the only tangible thing left behind from that horrible night, and so, Karen had wanted to hold on to it as the last connector to her children and their final moments. It wasn't much, but it was something she could touch, see, and hold. And until her two civil aviation cases had resolved, Karen had decided to keep the wreckage stowed, which was $200 a month for the open-air stall.

By January 2014, with both cases settled, there was no longer any legal reason to keep the wreckage. There were no more unanswered questions or hidden clues, at least legally, that might help a grieving mother or crash investigators draw yet more conclusions. The only attachment now was sentimental, which was one of the reasons she had come on this day, August 9, 2014, to say good-bye. Not to the pile of twisted detritus, but to what the airplane had represented as it safely cocooned her three children into the desert night, for just six minutes, and then took them to their graves.

And there was a second important reason for her trip here today, which fell firmly on the side of hope and remembrance.

LOUIS Longi, a Las Vegas native, knew from a young age that he wanted to be an artist. He entered the University of Nevada, Las Vegas in 1985, to study art on a full scholarship.

"When I poured bronze in art school I was hooked," he said.

Yes indeed—defying nature and manipulating molten metal would be his *How-cool-is-this?* anchor throughout a career casting in bronze. One of his first big breakthroughs was when Cirque du Soleil officials commissioned him, in the mid-1990s, to create nine different limited-edition bronze pieces to complement the abstract troupe's Las Vegas performances. Throughout his long career he has since created numerous pieces for private collectors as well as fifteen public art sculptures installed throughout Southern California and Nevada. Three of those public art pieces are in Laguna Beach, California, his home and studio space since 1996.

His combined living and studio workspace is adorned with sketches and paintings, sculptures in transitory poses, and the eclectic assortment of stuff of a working artist. Part of that collection, in metal, laid out in respectful repose, is the salvaged pieces from the Rockwell Commander 690 obliterated on the night of November 23, 2011. Several propeller blades, doors, and the frame of a seat with the seatbelt still attached. A piece of landing gear and a portion of a wing.

Longi, too, had been at the airplane salvage yard in August 2014 with Karen Perry and Gordon Barnard, carefully sifting through the mangled remains of an airplane with a very solemn purpose.

"All my art is about the strength of human will and overcoming obstacles," he said. "That was obviously a tough day for Karen as we went through the wreckage. And a tough day for me … Wow. It was pretty intense. We needed to find pieces that were recognizable. I believed that going through this process would be very cathartic for her. It would help her slowly get to a point of cleaning things up. Then she could get rid of all that other wreckage."

And with those few saved and recognizable pieces, Longi plans to help Karen fulfill a multipurpose mission by creating a bronze sculpture to honor her three children. The leadership at Superstition Mountain Museum had already donated a site with stunning views of the scenic mountain. More broadly, the sculpture will be a memorial to all the lives lost in the fabled and rugged mountain area.

Called "Ribbon of Life," Longi's vision is a fifteen-foot-long bronze standing twelve feet tall. The centerpiece is a waving bronze ribbon, or aviator's silk scarf, rippling in the wind, with various bronzed photographs of the children incorporated. At the base, woven and attached to the piece, will be the remains of the aircraft. Unfurled, tip-to-tip, the bronze ribbon will be fifty feet long. Once completed, the sculpture will weigh more than a ton, which will require deep concrete footings to anchor everything into the hill near the museum.

"The more simple it is, the more difficult it is to make," said Longi—that is, a structure that might appear relatively basic still requires careful engineering. The end result will be a public art piece representing the ebb and flow of life, with the tail end of the ribbon pointing skyward to the heavens and beyond. The mountain, the portal to heaven. Everything came back to the place.

Longi is donating all his time, so the "only" cost will be direct expenses for materials, transport (from his California art studio to Arizona), and installation. The bronze alone comprises the bulk of the cost at three to four dollars per pound. There is also the casting cost, at thirty-five dollars per pound of bronze. In total, the bronze memorial will cost around $70,000 to fabricate, transport, and install. Once the funds are in place, collected entirely through donations,

Longi will begin shaping the wax and fabricating the piece, and then install the finished sculpture six to nine months later.

"The beauty is my work in wax," he said. "There's fewer up-front costs."

That is, most sculptors working in bronze begin by molding a clay model of the sculpture-to-be. Then they construct a mold of the model from latex or rubber covered with plaster. Then they fill the hardened mold with wax to create a perfect scale replica of the envisioned sculpture. They dip the wax replica in ceramic slurry, which cures. Once heated, the wax inside melts away, leaving a vacant ceramic vessel to contain the molten bronze.

Longi skips those first two traditional steps—shaping clay and creating a mold—and begins by sculpting directly in wax. He started this technique early in his career, out of sheer necessity, because it eliminated two rounds of costs for the clay and the initial mold process.

Once complete, Longi takes his wax replicas to a foundry in Buena Park, California, for casting in bronze. Because he is sculpting directly in wax, his unusual technique incorporates many of the residual markings from the wax process into the final piece. These little striations and unintentional marks, cut by the hand trowel he uses to shape the wax, are the individual creative thumbprints forever etched in his work.

"The heritage of bronze stretches back two thousand years with its fundamental and timeless look," he said. "What makes it so beautiful is its longevity."

Because bronze oxidizes outward, rather than inward like other metals, Longi has no concerns about "Ribbon of Life" being exposed to the rigorous sun, heat, and cold of the Sonoran Desert.

"What you see today will be preserved for eternity," he said. "This sculpture is for generations. It will be a great documentation of history. I became so inspired by Karen. If I can help someone who inspires us that much, it's very meaningful. I'm really glad I can help."

Twenty-Seven

Arrivals

KAREN PERRY'S THREE CHILDREN OFTEN COME TO HER in her dreams. They leave gifts that make her smile. Morgan had a tiny little pig, about the size of a penny, that she loved and took everywhere. Amazingly, she never lost it. About a year after her death, Karen was going through boxes and found that little beloved pig. She found a note, under the dog's bed, written by Logan. And Luke, of course, left behind hundreds of photos.

The nightmares continue, too, about arriving home and finding yellow police tape wrapped around the house. Her heart pounding, Karen races to the door screaming *Oh my God, what happened?* In another vision an airplane crashes in her backyard. Then the nightmares give way to more benign dreams again: Logan asking for popcorn and a movie—*Mother, is it time for snack?*—or Morgan surrounded by hens of all different colors, her face beaming in a wondrous smile.

Luke reminds his mommy that, "Today is a beautiful day, Mommy!"

And then reality returns, and they are simply gone.

"In my mind Morgan was going to live with me for the rest of my life," Karen says. "It never dawned on me that she and my two sons would be taking care of me. It's totally not the way I expected it to be. It's like they've given me back this gift of calm and a sense of peace in life."

Calm. A sense of peace.

These are certainly the last things Karen might have imagined ever finding again. Much of her inner resolution derives from her work with the nonprofit she founded with Eva Morgan, 3 Wings of Life, and the kids they're committed to helping. They are transitioning away from classroom experiences to more outdoor activities and, eventually, equine-assisted therapy. To that end, in December 2014 Gordon Barnard surprised his wife-to-be with a horse, Dixon, that he bought her to incorporate equine therapy into her nonprofit vision. Additionally, in 2015 Karen bought a miniature horse named Clancy who will make therapy visits to hospitals, assisted living facilities, and schools.

From there the vision expands: multiple horses and other animals, a fully functioning ranch facility where kids come to heal and find hope for a better future. She and Gordon have not yet set a date for marriage, but that union is forthcoming.

"Karen is a different person than who she was before," says Eva Morgan. "She knows now that this life is our temporary home. The whole story hasn't been written. This is only the beginning. We all know what's most important, but do we live it? I pray that this book will bring encouragement to others and that it may turn a life around for someone reading it, that they will never give up on hope. We all need reminders of just how precious life is and all the blessings surrounding us."

The calm and sense of peace, however, are by no means permanent fixtures. They ebb and flow, and some days Karen only feels sadness and grief again. The hollow vacuum of despair can return in an instant and linger. *My children are gone.* On those days the sense of purpose fades, too, and she is left with the ongoing struggle of losing her original purpose: being a mother to Morgan, Logan, and

Luke. Those "grief bursts" are normal, natural, and healthy, according to Ashley Davis Bush, the therapist who helped Karen immensely and appeared with her on camera in the Oprah Winfrey Network special. But mere words—"normal, natural, and healthy"—do little to ease a mother's bottomless despair. She will never fully outpace the nightmare.

"We have a culture that likes quick fixes," says Bush. "Closure is not possible when it has to do with the human heart."

Closing the lid on grief might feel good short-term, but it would also mean closing the lid on her relationships with her children. That's the ongoing nature of grief. Rather than closure, Bush has helped Karen strive for synthesis, which is not avoidance but rather integrating and learning to live with loss.

"The price tag of loss is worth it because you had the love and got to experience that," says Bush. When she poses a hypothetical to clients, few take the bargain: *Suppose you could erase this intense pain you're feeling, but you would also have to erase the person you're grieving as though you'd never met her?* After November 23, 2011, Karen is learning to live at this crossroad: the road of bitter victim, or the road of transcendence and making meaning out of her loss.

"Karen Perry hasn't given up on life or shut down from it," says Bush. "She is very naturally resilient."

"She's one of the most amazing people I've ever met," says Nicole Hamming, the real estate agent who helped her through the foreclosure ordeal. "She's very giving and generous, and has taken a horrible tragedy and done something positive with it."

Says her fiancé Gordon Barnard: "She's still very fragile in a lot of ways. I think people expect her to get over it and move on. She's doing things day by day. It manifests itself sometimes unexpectedly. I cannot imagine the depths of grief ... it's so overwhelming."

FOR the first thirty-nine years of her life Karen had followed her passion for aviation, from the back of her father's Ducati to her own place in the pilot's seat that she gave up in 2002 when Morgan's seizures started. Although she could return to that original goal, to be a commercial pilot for a major airline, the idea is a lot more glamorous than the reality. Aviation has always been about having fun and freeing herself in weightlessness and wonderful romanticism. Flying an approach to minimums at night, with all the lights breaking out as the ground rushes closer, is an incredible rush unlike any other. But putting a paycheck to it changes everything. What she learned as a pilot at a regional airline is that the job becomes less a pleasurable pursuit and more grinding work. Now in her fifties, she really doesn't have the desire, energy, or stamina to start at the bottom of the pilot hierarchy again.

But one way she may very well climb back into the fun of flying is by getting her helicopter rating. She could be a flight instructor or just do it on her own for fun. She aims to keep her ratings current and envisions fun jaunts in small planes and seaplanes again with her pilot partner Gordon Barnard. The shocking impact of her children's departure from this earth has not diminished her passion for airplanes and flying. For her there's a much bigger picture to this collective human drama. That's why it's important to pay attention and keep the door open.

"There has to be a reason I'm still here," Karen says. "Every day I'm trying to discover new reasons why."

All of it—her musings, sadness, grief, joy, and happiness—continues to play out in the shadow of the majestic Superstition Mountain, which is always in full, glorious view where she lives. Within the timeline of eternity, the mountain's presence is an anchor stretching back before all of humanity and forward to well beyond. Whatever part the human race plays in the very big puzzle of the universe, the mountain is a steadfast and holy marker. Morgan Perry, who could not articulate very well, knew from an early age that she lived by the mountain. The same was true for Logan and Luke Perry. Now they have gone through the portal, a heartbreaking game of hide-and-seek: *Come find us, Mommy!*

For their mother to reach what she considers their gravesite, she has to hike steep slopes, narrow boulder slots, and slippery shale for hours and hours. Karen vows she will continue to hike there until she's physically unable to do so. Each time she traverses the steep rocks and shaded canyons, there is time and space to ponder.

Why were they all taken and I left behind? Do they see me now? Do they know I am near?

There must be a reason, a purpose—which she finds with each steady foothold into the difficult terrain. She has a new responsibility to use her remaining time here wisely, to do good work, to impart positivity for others. She strives to find meaning in what's left of her own remaining time that, she has learned, can end in one furious flash.

SWEAT beading on her forehead, quadriceps muscles burning, feet throbbing with each heavy step up the solidified formation, she is finally there, hours later, at the fifteen-foot rock wall near the top, which she has to traverse to meet her children just on the other side. She's been wedged in the rugged canyon for hours, and having to clear this vertical ledge is almost too much. It's all been almost too much. *Can she do it?* She has no choice. She must.

Thirteen years have passed since her daughter Morgan's birth. From almost the moment that beautiful little girl appeared, the seizures began. Then Logan and Luke, the autism, giving up a dream career, cancer, a near-death scare, two divorces, and financial calamity until the fierce whirlwind all exploded into a screen of static on that moonless November night before Thanksgiving. The thunder roar of silence will remain forever. On the mountain especially, there is time and space to pause, reflect, and process the tornado of joy and struggle that has been her life.

Karen reaches higher, her shoulder muscles straining, wedging a foot into a crevice and hoisting herself to the next foothold. Sweat stings her eyes; being plastered to this rock face gives her a disorienting feeling she doesn't like, but is forced to ignore.

Then it happens, the final push and steps, and she's over the intimidating wall of rock guarding her sacred plateau. She's looking up the steep slope now, directly at the spot where it happened. From there, the slope rises up sharply to meet the rock fingers of the hoodoos reaching straight into the sky. The portal. The signpost that called her home to this sacred place. She can relive the fine spritz of an Anaheim orange settling along an arm and raising the fine hairs; she can reach out and touch every sense impression through all the decades. She savors them all.

Just a couple hundred feet higher, and the airplane would have landed thirty minutes later in Safford, Arizona. Instead she is here. Karen again studies the rugged topography almost one mile above sea level. Off to her right is the large and imposing protrusion of Flat Iron, a massive slab across an open expanse of the dizzying canyon below. It's stunningly beautiful and emotionally wrenching to stand at the epicenter of her loss. Then a broad smile breaks open.

Her children wait just up ahead, secretly hidden away here to greet her with smiles, hugs, and laughter. She always gets a powerful rush of indistinguishable emotions, all emanating from the beautiful genetic pulse of a mother being pulled to her children, the mountain and this moment forty million years in the making. There can be no other way. Place and time cease to exist as she strains up the slope. Then each step, and her purpose, and all the questions and searching of a lifetime, meld together into brilliant sunlight.

EPILOGUE

Until We Meet Again

Image courtesy of Eva Morgan©2015.

My sweet little Morgan, every single night when I tucked you into bed I would ask if you were my little angel. You always told me, "Yes!" Now I know that you really are. No more seizures in heaven, sweet child. I can still hear you singing beautiful songs and, yes, you were amazing just the way you are. Morgan, you endured so much pain and displayed so much strength in your short time on this earth. I love you forever and will never forget the lessons you taught me. Bye bye, butterfly.

Image courtesy of Karen Perry family archives.

My dear son, Logi Bear, what an amazing eight years we had together! I would not have missed it for anything. You, little man, were the love of my life, and I will never forget you. I'll bet the movies, popcorn, and "snack" in heaven are pretty cool.

Image courtesy of Eva Morgan©2015.

Luke, you were my little man, a protective mama's boy who loved to grab my face and kiss me on the lips over and over again. My sweet little man, I blow a hundred kisses to you each day in the clouds that you loved so much. I will always remember your big brown eyes, your sweet smile, and your beautiful, pure, innocent heart of gold.

Image courtesy of Eva Morgan©2015.

To all of you, my Angels Three, looking back on all of it now I really appreciate how lucky I am to have experienced being your mother. You all had lessons to teach me. Loving you was so easy, difficult, beautiful, wonderful, crazy, and healing for me. I will always cherish and remember each of your precious souls, beautiful little human beings. Now and forever.

Until We Meet Again...

Acknowledgments

I, along with the author Landon J. Napoleon, would like to thank and acknowledge the staff and volunteers at the Pinal County Sheriff's Office (PCSO), and all first responders, who did everything possible to save my children and the other three passengers on the night of November 23, 2011. They also had the unimaginable task of cleaning up and investigating the crash: thank you all for your professionalism. Subsequently, their assistance with this book was invaluable.

For PCSO research support, big thanks to Garric Berry, Doug Brown, Scott Dill, Tim Gaffney, Blake King, Andrea Kipp, E. Scott Leonard, Susan May, Brandee Ralston, and Matthew Thomas. For taking the time to be interviewed and relive a difficult succession of days, the author and I tip our hats to law enforcement (all with PCSO except as noted): Scott Abernathy of Phoenix Police Department,

Paul Babeu, Russ Dodge of the Arizona Department of Public Safety, Jeff Love, Brian McGinnis, and Brian Messing.

In addition to the above people, I would like to thank everyone who took the time to be interviewed for this book: Gordon Barnard, Debbie Bunch, Ashley Davis Bush, Nicole Hamming, John Hook, Louis Longi, Vickie Longi, Patrick McGroder, Eva Morgan, and Pat O'Connell.

In the literary arena, thanks to agent John Willig for all his efforts. A special nod to publicist Carole Bartholomeaux whose volunteer efforts resulted in unprecedented local, national, and international media coverage. I also want to thank Brandon Stout for his stunning cover design and Amanda Fellows and Candice McManus, at Santy Integrated, for their beautiful interior page design. Also, a big round of applause for the excellent team of editors: Susan Campbell, Lisa Fontes, LeeAnn Kriegh, and Jim Moore.

3 Wings of Life

Born from tragedy, Karen Perry and Eva Morgan founded the nonprofit "3 Wings of Life" to honor the memory of Morgan, Logan, and Luke and improve the lives of all children.

To learn more, contribute, and volunteer please visit online.

www.3wingsoflife.org

LANDON J. NAPOLEON is the award-winning and critically acclaimed author of thirteen fiction and nonfiction books. He earned a bachelor's degree in journalism from Arizona State University, a master's degree from University of Glasgow in Scotland, and has been an author for more than two decades.

His debut novel *ZigZag* received starred reviews, was a Barnes & Noble "Discover Great New Writers" finalist (1999), and was translated into multiple foreign editions and adapted for a motion picture starring John Leguizamo, Oliver Platt, and Wesley Snipes (Franchise Pictures, 2002).

His nonfiction biography *Burning Shield: The Jason Schechterle Story*—an "inspiring true story" (*Kirkus Reviews*) that "celebrates the resilience of the human spirit" (*Publishers Weekly*)—was the March 2014 "Arizona Republic Recommends" selection. Interweaving narratives of human triumph, medical marvels, police procedure, and high-stakes legal showdowns, the book chronicles the triumph of a rare human being with an undeniable will to live.

Likewise, in *Angels Three: The Karen Perry Story*, the author takes readers inside personal tragedy and ultimately a hopeful journey of human perseverance through unimaginable loss.

www.landonjnapoleon.com

Made in the USA
Charleston, SC
19 January 2017